BREAKING BARRIERS IN COUNSELING MEN

Breaking Barriers in Counseling Men is a unique collection of personal and engaging contributions from nationally recognized scholars and clinicians with expertise in treating men. The editors have selected men's clinicians who address areas as diverse as sexual dysfunction, male bonding over sports, father–son relationships, and counseling men in the military. Featuring a mix of clinical tips, personal anecdotes, and theoretical reframing, this book takes clinicians invested in these issues to the next level, breaking down barriers to connecting with men and getting them the help that is so often needed.

Aaron B. Rochlen, PhD, is professor and training director of the counseling psychology program at the University of Texas at Austin. A licensed psychologist, he maintains a small private practice in Austin, Texas.

Fredric E. Rabinowitz, PhD, is professor of psychology and associate dean of the College of Arts and Sciences at the University of Redlands. He is the coauthor of several books, including *Deepening Psychotherapy with Men* and *Men and Depression.*

The Routledge Series on Counseling and Psychotherapy with Boys and Men

VOLUMES IN THIS SERIES

Volume 1: *Counseling Troubled Boys: A Guidebook for Professionals*
Mark S. Kiselica, Matt Englar-Carlson, and Arthur M. Horne, editors

Volume 2: *BAM! Boys Advocacy and Mentoring: A Leader's Guide to Facilitating Strengths-Based Groups for Boys – Helping Boys Make Better Contact by Making Better Contact with Them*
Peter Motorola, Howard Hiton, and Stephen Grant

Volume 3: *Counseling Fathers*
Chen Z. Oren and Dora Chase Oren, editors

Volume 4: *Counseling Boys and Men with ADHD*
George Kapalka

Volume 5: *Culturally Responsive Counseling with Asian American Men*
William M. Liu, Derek Kenji Iwamoto, and Mark H. Chae, editors

Volume 6: *Therapy with Young Men: 16-24 Year Olds in Treatment*
David A. Verhaagen

Volume 7: *An International Psychology of Men: Theoretical Advances, Case Studies, and Clinical Innovations*
Chris Blazina and David S. Shen Miller, editors

Volume 8: *Psychotherapy with Older Men*
Tammi Vacha-Haase, Stephen R. Wester, and Heidi Fowell Christianson

Volume 9: *Engaging Boys in Treatment: Creative Approaches to Formulating, Initiating, and Sustaining the Therapy Process*
Craig Haen, editor

Volume 10: *Dying to be Men: Psychological, Social, and Behavioral Directions in Promoting Men's Health*
William Courtenay

Volume 11: *Engaging Men in Couples Therapy*
David S. Shepard and Michelle Harway, editors

Volume 12: *Gender in the Therapy Hour: Voices of Female Clinicians Working with Men*
Holly Barlow Sweet, editor

Volume 13: *Tough Guys and True Believers: Managing Authoritarian Men in the Psychotherapy Room*
John M. Robertson

Volume 14: *Men, Addiction, and Intimacy: Strengthening Recovery by Fostering the Emotional Development of Boys and Men*
Mark S. Woodford

Volume 15: *Breaking Barriers in Counseling Men: Insights and Innovations*
Aaron B. Rochlen and Fredric E. Rabinowitz, editors

FORTHCOMING

Volume 16: *Resiliency, Achievement, and Manhood: Promoting the Healthy Development of African American Men*
Cyrus Marcellus Ellis and Jon Carlson, editors

Volume 17: *Project Gentlemen on the Move: Nurturing Excellence in African American Youth*
Deryl Bailey and Mary Bradbury-Bailey

Volume 18: *Counseling Widowers*
Jason Troyer

BREAKING BARRIERS IN COUNSELING MEN

Insights and Innovations

Edited by

Aaron B. Rochlen

and

Fredric E. Rabinowitz

NEW YORK AND LONDON

First published 2014
by Routledge
711 Third Avenue, New York, NY 10017

Simultaneously published in the UK
by Routledge
27 Church Road, Hove, East Sussex BN3 2FA

Routledge is an imprint of the Taylor & Francis Group, an informa business

Library of Congress Cataloging in Publication Data
Breaking barriers in counseling men: insights and innovations / edited by Aaron Rochlen and Fredric E. Rabinowitz.
pages cm. – (The Routledge series on counseling and psychotherapy with boys and men)
Includes bibliographical references and index.
1. Men – Counseling of. 2. Men – Mental health. 3. Counseling psychology. 4. Psychotherapy. I. Rochlen, Aaron B. II. Rabinowitz, Fredric Eldon, 1956–
RC451.4.M45B74 2013
616.890081–dc23 2013011255

ISBN: 978-0-415-83934-1 (hbk)
ISBN: 978-0-415-53289-1 (pbk)
ISBN: 978-0-203-11463-6 (ebk)

Typeset in Dante
by HWA Text and Data Management, London

Printed and bound in the United States of America by IBT Global

In memory of Drs. Kathy Zamostny and Bruce Wine,
two of the finest supervisors and people ever.
You left us too early,
but your impact and influence continues.

—Aaron B. Rochlen

To my late father Sam,
who always had my back,
and to my mother Barbara,
who continues to be a model of growth and renewal.

—Fredric E. Rabinowitz

Contents

Contributors

Jim Benson is a professional certified coach (PCC) and men's group leader in the San Francisco Bay area. He counsels men through sex, intimacy, and relationship issues. He may be contacted at www.jimbenson.net or www.awakenedmasculine.com. Together with his wife, Jessica, Jim co-facilitates shadow wedding rituals for engaged couples: www.shadowwedding.com.

Maneet Bhatia, MA, is a doctoral candidate in counseling psychology at McGill University in Montreal, Canada. His research specializations include psychotherapy research, emotions, and the psychology of men and masculinity. A practicing psychotherapist, Maneet has also appeared on sports radio discussing the intersection between sports and psychology.

Sam J. Buser, PhD, is the staff psychologist for the nation's fourth largest fire department. An Army veteran and former VA psychologist, Dr. Buser integrates wilderness experiences in his therapeutic work with men. His book, *The Guys-Only Guide to Getting Over Divorce,* offers practical advice to men on coping with divorce.

Therese Daniels, PhD, is a licensed clinical forensic psychologist working for the Correctional Service of Canada. For 14 years, she has worked with federally incarcerated men who have committed sexual offences and who are dealing with mental illness and/or significant cognitive deficits (i.e. brain injuries, mental retardation, Fetal Alcohol Spectrum Disorder (FASD), etc.).

Scott A. Edwards, PhD, has worked with men and boys in diverse settings for over 20 years. In 2009, he joined the National Guard where he currently serves as the officer in charge of behavioral health and aeromedical psychologist for

Indiana's 15,000 Air Force and Army Guardsmen. He is highly engaged in masculine issues in conservative Christian contexts.

Matt Englar-Carlson, PhD, is a professor of counseling and co-director of the Center for Boys and Men at California State University, Fullerton. He co-edited the books *In the Room With Men: A Casebook of Therapeutic Change*, *Counseling Troubled Boys: A Guidebook for Professionals*, and *Helping Beyond the 50-Minute Hour: Therapists Involved in Meaningful Social Action*.

Chris Kilmartin, PhD, is a professor, author, comedian, Fulbright scholar, actor, playwright, and consultant. He is author or coauthor of *The Masculine Self*, *Men's Violence Against Women*, *Overcoming Masculine Depression*, *Sexual Assault in Context*, and theatrical performances *Crimes Against Nature* and *Guy Fi: The Fictions that Rule Men's Lives*.

Ryon C. McDermott, PhD, is a post-doctoral fellow at the University of Michigan Counseling and Psychological Services where he is specializing in clinical services with college men and counseling outcome research. His research interests are in intimate relationships, attachment, and men and women's gender role ideology.

Ryan A. McKelley, PhD, is an associate professor of clinical/counseling psychology at the University of Wisconsin-La Crosse. In addition to his teaching role, he researches and publishes on men's issues related to therapy, help seeking, and health psychology. He is a licensed psychologist with a small private practice with individual and group therapy, and he conducts workshops on men's issues.

William Ming Liu, PhD, is professor in counseling psychology and program coordinator at the University of Iowa. His research focuses on men of color, social class and classism, and economic inequality and privilege. Dr. Liu is a licensed psychologist and provides psychological services at a homeless shelter.

Kevin L. Nadal, PhD, is an associate professor of psychology at John Jay College of Criminal Justice, City University of New York. A leading researcher on microaggressions, he has authored *Filipino American Psychology*, *Women and Mental Disorders*, and *That's So Gay: Microaggressions and the Lesbian, Gay, Bisexual, and Transgender Community*.

Jerry Novack, PhD, is a captain in the United States Air Force's Biomedical Science Corps. As a clinician and a researcher, he focuses on the psychology of men and masculinity, fatherhood, and military psychology. He can be contacted at gerald.novack@us.af.mil.

Mark E. Olver, PhD, is an associate professor in clinical psychology and clinical training director at the University of Saskatchewan. His research interests include sex offender treatment, evaluating offender change, psychopathy, treatment attrition, and young offenders. Dr. Olver is a registered psychologist and remains active in providing services, supervision, and training to youth and adult offenders.

Chen Z. Oren, PhD, is a licensed psychologist in private practice in Westlake Village, CA. He specializes in working with men, fathers, and athletes and co-facilitates a men's group. He co-edited the book *Counseling Fathers*, conducts research, and presents locally and nationally on counseling men and fathers from a strength-based perspective.

Dora Chase Oren, PhD, is a licensed psychologist in private practice in Westlake Village, CA. She works with men, women, and adolescents. She co-edited *Counseling Fathers*, a book designed to bridge the gap between therapists and fathers, and recently wrote a chapter for *Gender in the Therapy Hour*.

Ryan F. Pittsinger, MS, received a master's degree in sport psychology and is currently a doctoral student in the counseling psychology program at the University of Iowa. His research investigates the psychological impacts of engaging in physical activity, as well as the psychological aspects of coping among men.

Fredric E. Rabinowitz, PhD, is professor of psychology and associate dean of the College of Arts and Sciences at the University of Redlands. He is the coauthor of several books, including *Deepening Psychotherapy with Men* and *Men and Depression*.

David P. Rivera, PhD, is an assistant professor of psychology at William Paterson University. His research interests include microaggression theory and issues impacting the health of marginalized people. Dr. Rivera engages in clinical practice focusing on college student populations and conducts training workshops on a variety of multicultural issues.

Aaron B. Rochlen, PhD, is professor and training director of the counseling psychology program at the University of Texas at Austin. A licensed psychologist, he maintains a small private practice in Austin, Texas.

David E. Scheinfeld is a doctoral candidate in the counseling psychology program at the University of Texas at Austin. He is a lead instructor for the USA Outward Bound School and the principal research investigator for the Outward Bound for Veterans Outcomes Study. David has been developing and leading adventure therapy retreats for over 10 years.

Christopher R. Smith, PhD, is a licensed psychologist at the University of Missouri Counseling Center. He enjoys working with college age men regarding issues related to masculinity and identity. His other interests include sexual assault prevention and awareness, and diversity and multicultural competence in practice and in supervision.

Mark A. Stevens, PhD, is the director of University Counseling Services at California State University, Northridge. He is the co-editor of *In the Room With Men: A Casebook of Therapeutic Change* and a featured psychologist on a DVD on counseling men produced by APA. Dr. Stevens is the past president of APA Division 51.

Jack Y. Tsan, PhD, is a licensed psychologist at the Harlingen VA Outpatient Clinic as part of the VA Texas Valley Costal Bend Health Care System. His clinical and research interest is in the area of veterans' health care, help-seeking behavior, and health care services, with a particular focus on integrated care.

Dave Verhaagen, PhD, is the CEO of Southeast Psych in Charlotte, NC. He is the author or co-author of six books, including *Therapy with Young Men: 16-24 Year Olds in Treatment*. He is a frequent speaker at conferences around the country.

David B. Wexler, PhD, is a clinical psychologist in San Diego and the executive director of the non-profit Relationship Training Institute. He is the author of many books about men's issues, including *Men in Therapy* and *When Good Men Behave Badly*. He may be contacted through www.RTIprojects.org or dbwexler@gmail.com.

Series Editor's Foreword

I have devoted a great deal of my life to the fulfilling endeavor of mentoring boys and men. As a result, I always feel inspired whenever I see males mentoring males, which has certainly been the case as I have witnessed the mutual mentoring between Drs. Aaron B. Rochlen and Fredric E. Rabinowitz, the editors of *Breaking Barriers in Counseling Men: Insights and Innovations*, the latest volume in the *Routledge Series on Counseling and Psychotherapy with Boys and Men*. Their special friendship and how it led to the development of *Breaking Barriers* is a touching story illustrating the wonderful things that can happen when men mentor men, while demonstrating the growth and maturity of men's studies within the mental health professions.

This story begins with Dr. Rabinowitz, who completed his doctorate in counseling psychology at the University of Missouri – Columbia in 1984 and went on to become a founding member of the Society for the Psychological Study of Men and Masculinity (SPSMM), helped SPSMM become Division 51 of the American Psychological Association in the mid-1990s, and served as president of the division in 2005. In addition to the leadership he has provided to SPSMM, Dr. Rabinowitz, a professor of psychology and associate dean of the College of Arts and Sciences at the University of Redlands, has been an outstanding teacher and researcher whose important work has had a national impact on the practice of psychotherapy with men. With his co-author, Dr. Sam Cochran of the University of Iowa, Dr. Rabinowitz has written three outstanding texts that have advanced our understanding of men and how to help them: *Man Alive: A Primer on Men's Issues* (Rabinowitz & Cochran, 1994), *Men and Depression* (Cochran & Rabinowitz, 2000), and *Deepening Psychotherapy With*

Men (Rabinowitz & Cochran, 2002). In addition to these books, Dr. Rabinowitz has written numerous articles, book chapters, and conference papers on issues pertaining to men, including men's shame, masked depression in men, and men's groups.

One of Dr. Rabinowitz's many admirable and endearing qualities is his devotion to welcoming new members to SPSMM and his willingness to foster their development as professionals. One of those relative "newcomers" to the division was Dr. Rochlen, who first started attending meetings of Division 51 when he was a graduate student in counseling psychology at the University of Maryland during the late 1990s. Dr. Rabinowitz extended himself to Dr. Rochlen, helping him to feel at home in SPSMM, and encouraging him to exert his own influence on the division. To his credit, Dr. Rochlen accepted these invitations, and in no time at all, he, too, became a leader in the organization, absorbing the wisdom offered to him by SPSMM's more senior members, such as Dr. Rabinowitz, while making his own enduring mark on the division and the profession. For example, Dr. Rochlen, who is now a professor of counseling psychology at the University of Texas – Austin, served as division president in 2010, was chair of the Second National Conference on Psychotherapy with Men, and has been one of the most active researchers of his generation on the psychology of men and masculinity. As evidence of his scholarly productivity, a recent analysis regarding publications in *Psychology of Men and Masculinity* (PMM), a premier journal for research on men, revealed that Dr. Rochlen was the most productive *PMM* scholar from 2000–2008 (Wong, Steinfeldt, Speight & Hickman, 2010). Dr. Rochlen's scholarship has addressed a wide range of subjects related to men, including men's self-compassion and self-esteem, men's experience of sexual harassment, academic fathers pursuing tenure, adventure therapy with men, men's avoidance of intimacy, coaching men, and, like Dr. Rabinowitz, men and depression.

Not surprisingly, Dr. Rabinowitz quickly recognized that he had much to learn from the exciting contributions Dr. Rochlen was making to the field. So, a mutual mentoring relationship developed between the pair, fueled by their common interests, their devotion to men, and of course, their friendship. Through their extensive research on and clinical practice with men, Drs. Rochlen and Rabinowitz realized that there were numerous barriers that kept men from seeking professional help or from remaining in psychotherapy once they start. Specifically, they describe the journey from boyhood to manhood, the messages that males receive about "being a man" along that journey, and the reasons boys and men tend to avoid seeking help when they are in distress. They also were aware that the field needed a book explaining how mental health professionals can help men to move beyond these barriers and utilize psychotherapy to enhance their lives. Much to my joy, Drs. Rochlen and Rabinowitz have translated that awareness into this volume, which includes chapter contributions by an esteemed team of authorities, who have provided a wealth of practical ideas for helping men from many different backgrounds to explore their ideas about masculinity, and the tactics men can use to work through shame, accept help, and seek and experience intimacy with the important people in their lives.

I invite readers to discover the deep wisdom about understanding and helping boys and men that is contained in this book, and I thank Drs. Rochlen and Rabinowitz and their colleagues for adding this wonderful volume to this series.

Mark S. Kiselica, Series Editor
The Routledge Series on Counseling and Psychotherapy with Boys and Men
The College of New Jersey
February 1, 2013

REFERENCES

Cochran, S. V. & Rabinowitz, F. E. (2000). *Men and depression: Clinical and empirical perspectives.* San Diego, CA: Academic Press.

Rabinowitz, F. E. & Cochran, S. V. (1994). *Man alive: A primer of men's issues.* Monterey, CA: Brooks/Cole.

Rabinowitz, F. E. & Cochran, S. V. (2002). *Deepening psychotherapy with men.* Washington, DC: American Psychological Association.

Wong, Y. J., Steinfeldt, J. A., Speight, Q. L., & Hickman, S. J. (2010). Content analysis of *Psychology of Men and Masculinity* (2000–2008). *Psychology of Men and Masculinity, 11,* 170–181.

Acknowledgments

From our original conceptualization to crossing the finish line, editing this book has been a journey. *Most* of the journey has been a pleasure. Occasionally it's been a struggle. Through it all, we have learned plenty about ourselves as men, clinicians, fathers, and professionals. Importantly, this book and the path that got us there, would not have happened without the help and support of many.

We would first like to thank all of the male clients whose lives, challenges, and experiences in counseling helped provide the context for this book. Your experiences and being brave enough to ask for help has helped us understand what works and doesn't for other men.

Second, we want to acknowledge the efforts, creativity, and expertise of each of the chapter authors. This project was intended from the onset to be truly *different*, one where writers were asked to utilize their familiarity with the academic research, but keep the writing accessible, with clear guidelines and practical points. Each author met this challenge, with stories, insights, and applications that were personal and engaging. We are certain these efforts will help other clinicians, and of course the men they serve.

Third, we wanted to thank an organization that is near and dear to our hearts: *The Society for the Psychological Study of Men and Masculinity* (Division 51) of the American Psychological Association. As Past-Presidents, both of us are indebted to this group of individuals, particularly its founding members, who have made the study of male psychology an exciting clinical and research field. We have learned so much about men and masculinity, from a scholarly and personal perspective. Through our relationships and retreats, we have also seen how men can overcome their own internal barriers to become different, better types of men. Much of this experience helped us identify the need and form the structure for the current book.

We are also appreciative of the hard work and leadership of Dr. Mark Kiselica, our series editor, who wrote a moving foreword for this book (and many others). Almost 10 years ago, Mark had a vision for creating a top of the line book series on counseling boys and men. He has definitely pulled it off. We are proud to have this book be a part of this special series. Mark has inspired many of us to go from the "good idea" phase to a final product that makes a meaningful contribution to the literature. We admire his vision, leadership, and ability to turn dreams into reality.

We are also thankful to Anna Moore, our Editor at Routledge who fully supported us in this project. Anna jumped on board mid-way through and never missed a beat. Her faith in our vision and her feedback on the manuscript kept the book going through some occasionally rough water. We also appreciate her patience and advice in helping us find a title that worked!

Importantly, we would not have delivered this book on time without the dedication of Emily Rose Smith. Currently a doctoral student at the University of Texas at Austin, Emily went above and beyond her role as a research assistant to keep this project rolling. She was always available and ready to assist in any way possible. Her edits, comments, and attention to detail were key in making the book relevant and readable.

Finally, we are indebted to our families for supporting us in this project. Aaron's partner, Paula, and Fred's partner, Janet, gave us the space, time, and encouragement needed to brainstorm, write, edit, and complete the book. Thank you all.

INTRODUCTION

Jack, the Sun, and the Wind

Aaron B. Rochlen

There were *many* reasons we wanted to make this book happen. Yet perhaps the primary impetus and need can best be represented by sharing some details from a significant breakthrough with a recent client.

Jack, a 35-year-old divorced attorney and father of two, had been struggling for years. His most pressing stressors included a brutal custody battle with his ex-wife and an increasing number of high-stress, low-reward litigation cases. In many ways, his life could be characterized by a mix of professional successes and personal failures. A classic over-achiever, Jack had been successful at everything that came his way, *professionally.*

His relationships and family patterns were another story. His father, a high-functioning alcoholic, was largely absent in his childhood. His mother, a caring, yet self-centered and dramatic woman, often sent her son contradictory messages. Sadly, Jack's oldest sister was killed in a car accident at 15. The family never processed nor recovered from the loss. His relationship and marital history was absent of intimacy, unrewarding, and often hurtful.

In our work together, Jack had little insight and made minimal progress. Calling Jack "defensive" would be an understatement. Whatever I tried, he rejected. Any re-frame, interpretation, or intervention was met with a *"Yes, but..."* response.

And those were the better moments.

As I was driving to meet Jack for our fifth session, I felt a bit sick to my stomach. I was dreading the session, trying desperately to think of a way to switch gears, to get it going in a better direction. In doing so, I recalled the advice of one of my earliest supervisors, Dr. Bruce Wine. When working with resistant clients, men in particular, Bruce emphasized the importance of directly acknowledging struggles, being myself, and speaking from the heart.

I followed his advice. That session, I asked Jack if I could tell him a story. Relieved the focus of our session was going to be off him for a few minutes, he obliged. I shared my own twist on one of Aesop's Fables entitled, *"The North Wind and the Sun,"* a tale I first heard in a different format from my colleague and friend, Dr. Leslie Moore.

My version went something like this:

"The sun and the wind walk into the bar to get a drink. Well, being elements, they didn't exactly walk in… but you get the picture."

Jack chuckled. This was a good sign and a rare event.

I continued, *"There was a guy at the end of the bar wearing the ugliest jacket the sun or wind had ever seen. Being competitive types, the two made a bet on which one of them could get the jacket off first."*

A bit of a gambler himself, Jack seemed further intrigued.

I continued, *"The wind (of course) won the coin toss and elected to go first. And so he did. Yet the stronger the winds swirled around the bar, the more the man tightly clutched his jacket. Exhausted, the wind finally gave up. The man was more covered up than ever.*

"It was the sun's turn. Beaming beautiful warm rays, the sun heated up the bar to a perfect 85 degrees. Everyone, including the guy at the end of the bar, started shedding layers. He ended up taking off everything, leaving himself completely exposed and vulnerable.

"Knowing he was beat, the wind grabbed his credit card and started taking drink orders."

Then came the time for me to be vulnerable.

I concluded the story, *"Jack often in here, I feel like the wind. And I don't quite know how to be the sun. How does it feel for you?"*

The question changed that session and the nature of our further contact. He said he knew *exactly* what I meant and why the story mattered. We talked about what he needed to feel safe, less guarded. He shared why he found counseling threatening, why he needed to "cover up."

He further related to the story's theme of nature and warmth. This led to the idea of the two of us shifting *how and where* we talked to each other. We went on occasional walks instead of meeting in my office. This helped our relationship and deepened our contact. Changes in his life and mood, while slow, followed.

Sharing the story also led me to new insights. I realized I could do a better job of acknowledging my clients' strengths, shining on them a bit more, while still working on their problems. I also needed to occasionally share *my own* struggles—so he didn't feel so alone. Our paths and jackets differed. However, I also knew something about being a guy clutching to his defenses. I too resisted opening up to the pressures of those close to me.

In developing this book with my co-author, I further reflected on this story. In so many ways, this book is about the wind, the sun, and Jack. It's about finding different ways for men to open up in the presence of others, in particular their therapists helping men in a wide range of settings.

THE KNOWN AND UNKNOWN OF MEN AND COUNSELING

As mental health professionals, we remain largely in the dark when it comes to knowing how to help men, including what makes them tick or in many cases "ticked off." The emerging literature on the psychology of men has offered a helpful starting point for intervening therapeutically. But realistically, we remain in desperate need of clearly delineated approaches that can be effective for different types of men in diverse settings.

For those deeply invested in the topic and the solution, the scenario is further complicated by a classic "chicken or the egg" dilemma. We know there are men out there hurting and in need of help. We also know the outcome literature suggests few if any sex differences exist, meaning that *therapy can work for women and men*. But that's assuming men enter treatment. And we know most don't. Given this dilemma, as practitioners and researchers, should we focus on "changing men" to increase treatment usage? Or should we focus on adapting the ways we provide services for those who avoid more traditional approaches?

While we don't have all the answers, we do know there has been insufficient attention addressing the second part of this "chicken or the egg" scenario. We need more efforts and straightforward explanations for how to provide therapeutic interventions in *different ways*. This book is an important contribution to real world, practice-centered literature.

The importance of this issue and more broadly men's mental health concerns is clear. Among other problems, men continue to lead the way in substance abuse, domestic violence, heart failure, imprisonment, and violent crime (Wester & Vogel, 2012). Depression is an enormous concern (Courtenay, 2011; Kilmartin, 2005; Rabinowitz & Cochran, 2008; Swami, 2012). According to national surveys, there are six million depressed men in the US. Considering most avoid seeking help, this number is likely higher. Sadly, men take their own lives in alarming numbers, with an average of 83 men committing suicide daily, a rate four times that of women (American Foundation for Suicide Prevention, 2010).

COUNSELING AND MEN: A CULTURE CLASH

Clearly, men's help-seeking attitudes, preferences, and behaviors continue to be a major factor in men's health. Men's lower utilization rate for mental and physical help services remains one of the most robust and cross-culturally consistent findings in the help-seeking literature. To make a bad situation worse, we also know that the men arguably in greatest need of services are typically least interested in doing so. More than 15 years ago, Good and Wood (1995) called this help-seeking dilemma the "double bind," a phrase still very much relevant today.

The good news is that scholars have delineated some clear and consistent explanations that account for much of the problem. In essence, authors have suggested that the problem with men and traditional help-seeking comes down to "fit" or lack thereof (Wade & Good, 2010). This lack of fit pertains to men's socialization process and the counseling process. Stated differently, the "culture of masculinity" stands in contrast to the "culture of counseling."

How so? To begin, men are socialized to avoid intimate contact, restrain from expressing deep emotions, solve problems alone, and avoid vulnerability. Further, men often struggle with direct eye contact and ambiguous, often mysterious processes aimed at helping them solve problems. They like the clear, concrete approach (if they take or use instructions at all).

Yet counseling, as practiced in its most traditional formats, often embraces the opposite characteristics. Working in individual contexts is an intimate experience that values open expression of emotions. Further, counseling is a collaborative problem-solving process, where vulnerability is an essential part of the process. This is not easy for a lot of men.

OUR CENTRAL ASSUMPTIONS

A central assumption of this book builds on this point of the "culture clash" between men and therapy. In essence, we see the lack of fit between men's socialization patterns and the counseling process as a significant obstacle that we believe can be addressed effectively. To make therapy work, we need to lessen this discrepancy. Counseling men needs to be more consistent with the way in which men relate, connect, and open up. The process needs to feel less threatening, more problem-focused and, ultimately, more "male friendly."

We believe that if we lessen or eliminate the barriers that prevent men from benefiting from counseling, the impact on men and those who love them can be profound. Throughout this book, you will see clear and creative examples for exactly how to make this happen. *Breaking Barriers* brings these insights and innovations to the readers' attention. These chapters and the authors that wrote them do so in a user-friendly, yet research and theory-informed manner.

In approaching this project, we selected authors who have been resourceful and successful in connecting with men in creative ways, while maintaining ethical integrity. We also issued each author a challenge. The first was to describe and give clear examples of their argument and their therapeutic process. We also asked authors to outline how such creative interactions might improve men's willingness to seek help in other formats.

The purpose of this book is *not* to dismiss the potential utility of counseling in its more traditional one-on-one format, but rather to expand such options for helping men. Further, we hope to underscore how alternative approaches can be effective and encourage equally useful, but perhaps less "approachable," models of change.

BOOK STRUCTURE AND CHAPTERS

In developing this book, our aim was simple, yet its process complex. We sought authors who were able to describe their work, and articulate how to implement similar successful strategies. Further, we sought out authors who were willing to share some of their own paths, connections to clients, successes *and* failures.

We also aimed to provide a well-structured book. In doing so we wanted to offer readers an understanding of the various considerations involved in breaking down the typical barriers that prevent men from seeking and ultimately benefiting from therapy.

The first section of the book focuses on *approaches* that can be used within a wide range of counseling settings. These chapters highlight effective means to move productively with a man's resistance and encourage engagement in both traditional and non-traditional counseling. These creative, practice-oriented chapters include using metaphors (McKelley), humor and storytelling (Kilmartin), self-disclosure (Wexler), engaging men's hobbies and passions (Pittsinger and Liu), and using sports as starting points for rich therapeutic discussions (Bhatia).

The second section of the book focuses on delivering creative modes of counseling within unique therapeutic environments. These chapters focus on ways to connect with men outside of traditional verbal, individual, face-to-face therapy. These authors provide first-hand descriptions of how to implement activities and modalities that can be incorporated successfully into one's own practice. Included are practical and insightful tips on enhancing group counseling for men (Rabinowitz), utilizing the outdoors in adventure therapy (Scheinfeld and Buser), running weekend retreats (Englar-Carlson and Stevens), engaging men through technology (McDermott, Smith, and Tsan), and utilizing a coaching model (Benson).

The last third of our book addresses some of the unique needs and considerations of specific sub-groups of men. These chapters, while not intending to be an exhaustive list, show readers the benefits of understanding the sub-cultures of men with shared identities or experiences. These chapters look at diverse groups of men including military men (Novack and Edwards), incarcerated men (Olver and Daniels), teenagers (Verhaagen), gay and bisexual men of color (Nadal and Rivera), and fathers, (Oren and Oren). Finally, the book closes with an integrative chapter that brings the common elements of working creatively and effectively with men (Rabinowitz).

In closing, we hope you will find the chapters that follow both rewarding to read and helpful to your personal and professional interests in helping men. Like the sun's ability to remove the jacket, we hope that you will find the insights and interventions in the book energizing to breaking barriers in your work with men.

REFERENCES

American Foundation for Suicide Prevention. (2010). *Facts and figures: National statistics.* Retrieved from www.afsp.org.

Courtenay, W. H. (2011). Key determinants of the health and well-being of men and boys. In W. Courtenay (Ed.) *Dying to be men: Psychosocial, environmental, and biobehavioral directions in promoting the health of men and boys* (pp. 3–41). New York: Routledge.

Good, G. E., & Wood, P. K. (1995). Male gender role conflict, depression, and help-seeking: Do college men face double jeopardy? *Journal of Counseling and Development, 74*, 70–75.

Kilmartin, C. T. (2005). Depression in men: Communication, diagnosis and therapy. *Journal of Men's Health and Gender, 2*(1), 95–99.

Rabinowitz, F. E., & Cochran, S.V. (2008). Men and therapy: A case of masked male depression. *Clinical Case Studies, 7*, 575–591.

Swami, V. (2012). Mental health literacy of depression: Gender differences and attitudinal antecedents in a representative British sample. *PLoS ONE, 7*(11): e49779. doi:10.1371/journal.pone.0049779

Wade, J. C., & Good, G. E. (2010). Moving toward mainstream: Perspectives on enhancing therapy with men. *Psychotherapy Theory, Research, Practice, Training, 47*, 273–275.

Wester, S. R., & Vogel, D. L. (2012). The psychology of men: Historical developments, current research, and future directions. In N.A. Fouad, J. Carter, & L. Subich (Eds.), *Handbook of counseling psychology, Vol. 1*. Washington, DC: American Psychological Association.

PART I

Approaches

Working Therapeutically With Men in Ways that Connect Experience and Language

CHAPTER 1

Pushing Haystacks and Cracking Steel Balls

Using Metaphors With Men

Ryan A. McKelley

> When a contemporary man looks down into his psyche, he may, if conditions are right, find under the water of his soul, lying in an area no one has visited for a long time, an ancient hairy man.
>
> Robert Bly, *Iron John* (1990)

As a therapist, the above quote says more about how I think about working with men than any one clinical experience or theoretical perspective. For me, *water of the soul* conveys a sense of fluidity of feeling, and a crushing pressure and darkness in the depths of my own psyche. It also feels like a place that many are afraid to wander. Interpreting the powerful symbolic language embodied by Bly's quote can often be the key to uncovering meaning and self-understanding in ourselves and our male clients.

Before written language, humans sat in circles around fire and food, passing on wisdom through poems, fables, and songs (Parry & Doan, 1994). Over time these stories and symbols became metaphors, defined by psychotherapist Sheldon Kopp "as a way of speaking in which one thing is expressed in terms of another" (as cited in Gordon, 1978, p. 9).

In this chapter I'll argue that since the therapy room is one based on sharing through language, metaphors can be an important way for clients to talk about their concerns, problems, and goals. Metaphors have long been part of therapeutic approaches, from Freud's sexual symbolism for understanding dreams to Jung's archetypes to Perls' top dog and under dog (Gordon, 1978). They are useful tools for therapists to apply theory to practice and can be even more powerful when they come directly from clients themselves. Below, I will share examples from my own clinical practice while emphasizing why metaphors can be good for men, and how clinicians from various theoretical perspectives can use them effectively.

TEMPORARILY LOSING THE PATH

The idea of using metaphors with men in therapy is not new. In their book *Deepening Psychotherapy With Men*, Rabinowitz and Cochran (2002) stressed that, "the metaphor is a powerful way that men connect with their emotions" (p. 81). However, metaphor as a therapeutic tool wasn't discussed in my formal clinical training. In fact, I had the opposite experience. During my second year of practicum, my clinical supervisor and I were reviewing video clips of one of my sessions. She paused the clip and said, "Listen to how Darin is using metaphors to distance himself from his experience. He's intellectualizing, and he's pulling you into it. You need to break him out of that pattern and get him to speak *directly* about his feelings." Like a good supervisee I returned to my sessions with a new vigilance and commitment to call out my clients' metaphors.

I followed my supervisor's advice. I changed my behavior in session and expected my client to make progress and follow suit. It wasn't happening. With Darin, it was like that moment at a club when the record scratches (back when records were still played): the music stops and everyone looks at the DJ in confused silence. This was, in fact, the metaphor I used with him to describe the sudden shift in our therapeutic relationship. We both sensed it. I told Darin about my discussion in supervision, and how I was trying to help him use more direct language to describe his feelings. He patiently replied, "But that's what I know. That is the best way I can tell you how I'm feeling." From that moment on I swore I would honor the language that clients used in sessions and find ways to integrate metaphors in my work with men.

PUSHING HAYSTACKS

Before getting into recommended guidelines for using metaphors, I want to share a second critical lesson in my own training and interest in this area. Steve was in his late 30s and in therapy for the first time despite a lifetime of significant trauma. Some of his first words in session were, "I swear to you, if I saw my ex-wife's new husband outside that window right now there is nothing you could do to stop me from going outside and killing him." Not surprisingly, this comment scared me. I noticed myself tensing up. I found him abrasive, controlling, and unlikeable. Fast forward one year later, he ended up one of the most endearing, genuine, and likeable clients I've had. After giving Steve time and space to share his stories, I learned to relate to his material and experiences. Although our choice of words may have differed, I recognized similar fears (e.g., failure), disappointments (e.g., paths not taken), and joys (e.g., fatherhood) I held as well.

Learning about Steve's early years helped explain how he had become so angry and defensive. After his parents divorced when he was three, his father remarried an abusive woman. Steve's father was often away on business for months at a time. His stepmother beat him so severely that he would sometimes be out of school for up to several weeks. The bruises always healed before his father's return. At age nine he was forced to walk up and down the sidewalk wearing a sandwich board reading, "I am 9 years old and still wet the bed."

While there isn't room in this chapter to discuss the details of Steve's life, it was marked by drug addiction, abuse of his own first child, and several bankruptcies. Eventually, things turned around. By the time he came to therapy he had remarried, returned to college, and began raising another family. His presenting concern was his quickness to anger, and he wanted to learn how to deal with people without losing his temper. Although these were his initial explicit problems, I quickly learned there were many other concerns that could benefit from therapeutic work.

Six weeks into therapy Steve began a session in his typical fashion by retelling a story of a personal slight from the week. I noticed our sessions followed the same pattern of him working through frustration for 40 minutes, followed by 10 minutes of deeper material that could be captured by the infamous "doorknob comments." He left the most powerful material for me to struggle with as he was on his way out of the room.

He said therapy wasn't working, and that maybe it was a mistake. I felt the same. But I will never forget what Steve said next: "It feels like all we are doing each week is pushing haystacks. You know those giant ones you see spread out over fields? I feel like each week we take one and push it a few inches, and then move to another one the next session. I'm looking at the field and don't really see that anything has changed."

He was absolutely right. I had gotten caught up in his pattern of avoidance each week. He burned through the anger leaving a few minutes of vulnerability at the end. We explored the haystacks metaphor and immediately created a new, shared language for our work. Steve acknowledged that he had many concerns (haystacks of different sizes), all of which could be useful to work through in treatment. However, he wanted to "take one stack and push it all the way across the field" before beginning a new one.

This haystack metaphor became a playful way to "call him out" during times he might be avoiding working on issues. By pointing out that he changed haystacks he could make the conscious decision to change goals if needed. Alternatively, I could use his words to remind him that we switched issues again. We even learned over time that by moving one haystack, in his case breaking a 16-year fear and avoidance of crying, he could move several others forward more efficiently. When we became stuck in our communication, I became more intentional in my use of metaphors.

WHY METAPHORS CAN BE GOOD FOR MEN

It goes without saying that metaphors aren't for men only. It's not that women can't benefit from this approach. However, it's my perception that due to years of socialization, using direct language to describe their thoughts and feelings is often a struggle for men. Levant (1995) summarized several decades of research on gender-differentiated development of language for emotions with two key findings. First, parents were more likely to discourage sons from expressing vulnerable and caring emotions while encouraging it in their daughters. Second, mothers often use more emotion words when talking with daughters than sons. Over time it is easy to see how many men struggle to find the words to express what is going on inside, or that people assume men don't *feel* those vulnerable and caring emotions. Losing the ability to put feelings into words is called normative male alexithymia. Metaphors can help.

From its Greek roots, alexithymia translates to "without words for emotions." Levant (2001) argued that some men who experience this have greater difficulty in identifying and/or expressing emotion. I won't argue whether men are more alexithymic than women, or whether men cannot express their emotions. Countless therapy clients have shattered that stereotype. I will argue that many male clients struggle with putting their internal experiences into neat little terms and categories, and it doesn't make it easy for therapists to check off boxes of symptoms on a structured clinical interview form.

I find it comical to complete mood and affect lists on intake forms because many of the words are rarely expressed directly during initial sessions. When was the last time a client told you he felt *labile*? I've had a client describe his daily emotions "like one of those machines they hook you up to in the ER. One minute my line is climbing up steadily, the next minute I am coding and alarms are going off all around." I learned several things from that metaphor: (1) my client was aware that his emotions change, (2) there was some mystery about why they change, and (3) he experienced some distress during numbness. That one metaphor opened up several important lines of inquiry in his therapy.

MEANINGFUL METAPHORS IN THERAPY

If you take the time to carefully listen, I suspect you will begin to see this kind of symbolic language everywhere. Below are examples of how other metaphors unfolded in my own experiences with male clients. These are offered not to provide an exhaustive list. Rather, they illustrate different ways metaphors can become therapeutic tools and opportunities.

The Loose Grip

To relieve stress, "Haystacks Steve" liked to race motorcycles in the desert. Many times he came to session and told me about a particular race and the way he felt when the pavement would rush past his knees on a sharp turn. Although I didn't race motorcycles, I rode recreationally and loved to hear these stories.

At one point, we reached an impasse in therapy about how his need for control in his life was impacting his work and relationships. He made strong arguments about the value of maintaining control over his environment. He also noted how our culture often reinforces men's need for and benefits of control. In theory, he was able to grasp how his need for too much control was hurting him. I tried in vain to get him to put into practice ways of exerting less maximal effort while maintaining the comfort of optimal control.

And then came the powerful metaphor that furthered our work. I asked him, "When you are taking a sharp turn on your bike, what are your arms and hands like on your handlebar grip?" He said they were holding on "loosely but firmly." I then asked him what would happen if he muscled his arms and grip too tightly on a turn, and without pause he indicated he would tip the bike and end up with serious road rash. Almost immediately he realized where I was going. Steve's homework that week was to pay attention to interactions he was "muscling his way through" and to report on the experience the next session. By dissecting the process of something he knew extremely well (racing) he had a structured way to explore other areas of his life. The loose grip metaphor became common language in our work. It was used as a way to identify times he worked too hard for control. It further provided him a concrete way to loosen up his grip in social interactions.

Cracking the Steel Ball

I often use the title of this section for my clinician-focused workshops on using metaphors with men. The reference to steel balls gets a few chuckles. Obviously, colleagues begin to make their own assumptions about what that might mean for male clients. I will break the suspense first by assuring you that it has more to do with the upper than lower torso.

Ben was a client in his early 40s who was referred to therapy by his wife for "intimacy problems." Similar to "Haystacks Steve," Ben's early life included trauma and abuse, mostly in the form of hurtful comments from his mother. These were severe, including comments like, "I should have aborted you" and cracks from his father for being a "pussy" for crying. In late adolescence, he made a decision that he would never let anyone hurt him like that again. He described that moment almost as if he felt a sudden closing off in his body. I knew this was central, but it was about as much information as I could get about that turning point in his life.

By our third session I learned it was difficult to get any specific information about Ben's emotional state. If I asked directly how he felt about a story or memory, he returned with a blank stare. I was losing confidence in my ability to connect with him. I questioned whether he was ready for therapy. The next session I took a risk. I shared how little I felt I knew about him. Ben said he'd heard that line often, and was neither surprised nor troubled about my disclosure. I decided to ask one more time about that "sudden closing off in his body" from high school.

Ben told me to imagine a shiny steel ball the size of a baseball in his chest. There were no seams or cracks—it was an impenetrable ball in place of where his heart should have been. He added that the ball was "filled with all of these horrible feelings that I can't describe, and I have no idea how they got in there. I mean, there's no way in, you know? That means there's also no way out." He described an incredible internal pressure that was growing steadily each year. Hearing him describe this made me feel incredibly tender and concerned. It was the first time I began to understand how much Ben was struggling. I could now picture this steel ball, and it gave me something tangible to explore with him.

I assumed that Ben wanted therapy to be a place where he could get rid of the ball. He quickly disagreed as he emphasized how the ball (not uncommon from defenses) served a protective function. It held things together that were important to his past. We went back and forth about the building pressure inside. I expressed my concerns about what would happen if the pressure continued to build. He returned the concern and I caught a glimpse of the toll it was taking on him. I finally understood his confusion about how emotions ended up inside when there is no obvious way to get in. He wasn't interested in learning *how* they got there, but what he could do to ease the pressure.

I stopped trying to guess Ben's intentions and asked him what would be most helpful. He replied, "I want to make some small cracks in it to release a little bit of pressure without it exploding." In one session we moved from possible termination or referral to planning on cracking the metaphorical steel ball. Ben responded very well to behavioral assignments between sessions. He saw them as experiments in creating small cracks. By making the decision to leave the ball there it gave him a sense of comfort. He knew there would be some containment during therapy. Months later he ended up deciding he didn't need that containment anymore. He eventually learned ways to work through his past and present relationships in more adaptive ways.

A Wheelbarrow Full of Bricks

As in the examples of the haystacks, racing bikes, and steel ball, sometimes metaphors are easy to spot. Alternatively, they come in the form of stories or memories from clients' lives. David was a client in his late 40s referred for therapy after a short inpatient stay and seven weeks of an intensive outpatient program (IOP) at a local hospital. He was driving home to his wife and two kids after learning his second business had failed. Suddenly, he was overcome with an almost uncontrollable urge to drive off a bridge. Instead, he drove straight to the ER and was immediately deemed a threat to self and kept for observation.

Two months after the bridge incident, David came to my office in high spirits. He struck me as charismatic and self-assured. Although initially hesitant about therapy, he reported a positive experience with his IOP treatment. He had heard I did some executive coaching and wanted that approach instead of therapy. Although I worked at a community mental health center doing therapy, I agreed to use some language of coaching, if it made him more comfortable. David's memorable line during the intake session was, "I'm not here to talk about my past. I don't believe in those 'mommy and daddy issues.' I don't think we have to blame our parents for our problems. I'd rather focus on my goals for the future." I told him exploring the past could be helpful to understand current patterns, yet I agreed that we could take a solutions-focused approach, given this clear preference.

It only took a few weeks to notice that David consistently returned to the past, while discussing his present day concerns. By way of background, David described his parents as "traditional and stoic...with high expectations." I noticed he lived the same approach even though he struggled visibly in holding back negative emotions in our sessions. One day he recounted a very clear memory from his childhood that I will never forget.

David was 11 years old when his father asked him to lay a brick path in the backyard. As he had never done anything like it, the project terrified him. When he asked his father for guidance he said, "Figure it out." The specific memory was of him wheeling a heavy load of bricks across the yard in a downpour. He was in tears. At one point, he looked up at the sliding porch doors and saw his parents laughing at him. He proceeded to lay the bricks while crying in the rain, which had to be re-done professionally after his futile effort.

David cried while retelling the story. I found myself tearing up with him, as the image of this scared boy in the rain sank into our work. None of the previous sessions communicated his sense of shame and fear of failure as this wheelbarrow full of bricks. It was a critical moment that provided an anchor and metaphor to understand how therapy could be useful for him. I pointed out to him that he was still carrying these bricks currently, by refusing to acknowledge the wound they inflicted.

This big picture message took some time to sink in. Eventually, David realized that he'd lived much of his life seeking approval from people incapable of providing it to him. It was a hard way to live. As a way to frame his treatment, we used the brick metaphor consistently. He began to see interactions with people as bricks that he could now choose whether or not to add to his load.

Although not an original goal of therapy, by the end, he discussed the brick incident with his parents for the first time in his life. Subsequently, he began to repair relationships he thought were beyond fixing. I suspect therapy would have had a different ending had we seen the wheelbarrow full of bricks simply as a story rather than David's way of experiencing the world.

THE WORD ON THE (EMPIRICAL) STREET

There has been growing pressure in the mental health field to implement empirically supported and/or evidence-based treatments (Chambless & Hollon, 1998). Since symbolism is used to communicate meaning in and out of therapy, metaphors are a good starting place for creative and impactful interventions. A search of the literature on the use of metaphors returns hundreds of articles and book chapters, yet the number of randomized controlled outcome studies using metaphors is extremely limited (Powell, Newgent, & Lee, 2006). This appears to be an area wide open for creative outcome and process studies.

Most clinicians recognize the value in evidence-based approaches that come from trial and error with our clients. A growing body of evidence-based research using case studies and quasi-experimental designs shows that using metaphors helps in a wide variety of concerns and problems. Examples include treating autism spectrum disorders (McGuinty, Armstrong, Nelson, & Sheeler, 2012), improving the effectiveness of cognitive behavioral therapy with children and adolescents (Friedberg & Wilt, 2010), enhancing adventure therapy (Hartford, 2011), and increasing trust after an affair in couples therapy (Rider, 2011).

A handful of conceptual articles and case studies have explored the use of metaphor with men in particular. Examples include the usefulness of sports metaphors in treating secondary erectile dysfunction (Schweitzer, 1986), reducing inmate resistance to counseling (Romig & Gruenke, 1991), helping men express sorrow and anger during grief work (Schwartz-Borden, 1992), and translating metaphors from work to improve marital therapy (Miller, 1998). I suspect that there are many other examples out there from your own clinical work that could add to this list.

WHEN GOOD METAPHORS GO BAD

If you haven't reflected how you and your clients use metaphors in therapy, I encourage you to approach the topic with intentionality. There are several books published on useful therapeutic metaphors (Barker, 1996; Burns, 2001; 2007; Gordon, 1978; Starr, 2008). Many of these frameworks come from various sources including therapist-, client-, or joint-generated, or alternatively from existing myths and stories. Personally, I find the best metaphors to be the spontaneous ones that emerge in the consulting room.

From my own trial and error in using metaphors in therapy, below are some best practices that I'll offer for consideration. In reading these, think about your own successes and failures with metaphors in therapy and how you can make more effective use of them in future sessions.

Don't beat a dead horse: One common and useful metaphor to frame the therapy process is the toolbox, where clients gradually learn new tools to help solve specific problems. I've used it with success, as it is easy to understand and apply. However, there is a fine line between useful, well-placed metaphors and a stream of clichés that turn clients off. Use such metaphors strategically so you don't get caught speaking only in metaphors. Metaphors can be reinforcing when they work, yet clients can fall into the trap of intellectualization if you don't get beyond them. I have found added benefit in explaining why and how metaphors can be useful in therapy.

Swim close to the shore: As I mentioned earlier, I've found the most useful metaphors to be ones that speak directly to a client's experience. One of the reasons sports metaphors have been useful with male clients is that many of us have grown up with sports as an important part of our lives (as covered in Chapter 5). The same holds true for other traditionally male-oriented hobbies and pursuits like automobiles, the outdoors, and poker. Any topic is fair game *if you can talk about it with some degree of genuine understanding or shared experience.* Avoid those awkward moments where you overstep your area of expertise. Clients are good at sniffing out a fake, which brings me to my failed attempt.

I had a client who was an avid sailor. He grew up on a large lake and raced his Laser 2 on the weekends. My sailing experience was limited to a handful of rides with friends growing up. Yet I thought I knew enough to speak intelligently on the topic. I didn't. During the first session I explained that therapy doesn't always follow a straight line from A to B, and that it sometimes changes course based on the winds, so we would adjust along the way. He connected with the metaphor and I was soon stepping outside the bounds of my sailing knowledge. At one point I compared something to a bowline knot having seen the term before. I mispronounced the word and he said, "You really don't know much about sailing, do you?" We laughed it off and continued our work together. I recovered in the sea. But there may be cases where we can inadvertently turn clients off to therapy and would do well to stick to what we know.

Make sure you are on the same wavelength: This last piece of advice is perhaps the most important. It is very easy to assume shared understanding, particularly with metaphors commonly used in Western culture. It is humbling to have to explain a metaphor or idiom (e.g., "going under the knife" when referring to surgery) to someone not accustomed to a phrase due to language or cultural barriers.

One rule of thumb in competent cross-cultural healthcare is to ask patients to repeat—in their own words—your instructions rather than to ask if they understand (Gropper, 1996). I've found this guideline helpful when introducing a metaphor in therapy or to myself when a client generates his own. I've had experiences where a client introduces a metaphor and I say, "Do you mean XX?" and they reply, "No, I mean..." Being deliberate about understanding figurative language is an excellent way to deepen rapport and communicate using the client's terminology. Exploring a metaphor can generate inquiry leading to important diversions in therapy.

CONCLUSION

A primary theme of this book is how important it is to look for creative ways to engage your male clients. In doing so, remember that many men are natural storytellers. They have been communicating about their lives through myth and symbolism since the dawn of time. If a picture is worth a thousand words, metaphors have to be somewhere in that ballpark, and can be an effective therapeutic framework or intervention. Trust that when you hear possible metaphors in session, they are there for a reason: to carry you and your client to a shared experience in a more complex way. Therapy without metaphors would be like experiencing a symphony by reading the score instead of hearing the music performed.

REFERENCES

Barker, P. (1996). *Psychotherapeutic metaphors: A guide to theory and practice.* Philadelphia, PA: Brunner/Mazel.

Bly, R. (1990). *Iron John: A book about men.* New York, NY: Vintage Books.

Burns, G. W. (2001). *101 healing stories: Using metaphors in therapy.* Hoboken, NJ: John Wiley & Sons Inc.

Burns, G. W. (Ed.) (2007). *Healing with stories: Your casebook collection for using therapeutic metaphors.* Hoboken, NJ: John Wiley & Sons Inc.

Chambless, D., & Hollon, S. (1998). Defining empirically supportable therapies. *Journal of Consulting and Clinical Psychology, 66*(1), 7–18. doi:10.1037/0022-006X.66.1.7

Friedberg, R. D., & Wilt, L. H. (2010). Metaphors and stories in cognitive behavioral therapy with children. *Journal of Rational-Emotive & Cognitive Behavior Therapy, 28*(2), 100–113. doi:10.1007/s10942-009-0103-3

Gordon, D. (1978). *Therapeutic metaphors: Helping others through the looking glass.* Cupertino, CA: META Publications.

Gropper, R. C. (1996). *Culture and the clinical encounter: An intercultural sensitizer for the health professions.* Yarmouth, MN: Intercultural Press, Inc.

Hartford, G. (2011). Practical implications for the development of applied metaphor in adventure therapy. *Journal of Adventure Education and Outdoor Learning, 11*(2), 145–160. doi:10.1080/14729679.2011.633383

Levant, R. F. (1995). Toward the reconstruction of masculinity. In R. F. Levant & W. S. Pollack (Eds.), *A new psychology of men* (pp. 229–251). New York, NY: Basic Books.

Levant, R. F. (2001). Desperately seeking language: Understanding, assessing and treating normative male alexithymia. In G. R. Brooks and G. Good (Eds), *The new handbook of counseling and psychotherapy for men*. (Vol. 1, pp. 424–443). San Francisco, CA: Jossey-Bass.

McGuinty, E., Armstrong, D., Nelson, J., & Sheeler, S. (2012). Externalizing metaphors: Anxiety and high-functioning autism. *Journal of Child and Adolescent Psychiatric Nursing, 25*(1), 9–16. doi:10.1111/j.1744-6171.2011.00305.x

Miller, R. B. (1998). Metaphors for men in marital therapy. *Journal of Family Psychotherapy, 9*(3), 79–84. doi:10.1300/J085V09N03_08

Parry, A., & Doan, R. E. (1994). *Story re-visions: Narrative therapy in a postmodern world*. New York, NY: Guilford Press.

Powell, M., Newgent, R. A., & Lee, S. (2006). Group cinematherapy: Using metaphor to enhance adolescent self-esteem. *The Arts in Psychotherapy, 33*(3), 247–253. doi:10.1016/j.aip.2006.03.004

Rabinowitz, F. E., & Cochran, S. V. (2002). *Deepening psychotherapy with men*. Washington, DC: American Psychological Association.

Rider, K. V. (2011). Using a metaphor to help couples rebuild trust after an affair. *Journal of Family Psychotherapy, 22*(4), 344–348. doi:10.1080/08975353.2011.627804

Romig, C. A., & Gruenke, C. (1991). The use of metaphor to overcome inmate resistance to mental health counseling. *Journal of Counseling & Development, 69*(5), 414–418. doi:10.1002/j.1556-6676.1991.tb01536.x

Schwartz-Borden, G. (1992). Metaphor: Visual aid in grief work. *Omega: Journal of Death and Dying, 25*(3), 239–248. doi:10.2190/1QY6-38U7-XRHV-JE9X

Schweitzer, H. (1986). Ericksonian sport metaphors in the treatment of secondary erectile dysfunction. *Journal of Sex Education & Therapy, 12*(1), 65–68.

Starr, K. E. (2008). *Repair of the soul: Metaphors of transformation in Jewish mysticism and psychoanalysis*. New York, NY: Routledge.

CHAPTER 2

Using Humor and Storytelling in Men's Work

Chris Kilmartin

I hate that awkward feeling of being told a painfully long joke that ultimately isn't even funny. As a comedian, it's happened to me often, probably both as the recipient and teller of the joke. Listening to a poorly delivered joke with poor timing or punch can be brutal.

A lot of guys equate therapy with that same feeling. Wasted time—neither fun, nor funny. And when you think about it, part of that sentiment makes sense. True enough, what we ask men to do in therapy contrasts sharply with what the rest of society expects from us: express vulnerable emotions, introspect, pay attention to process rather than outcome, etc. In so many ways, we demand our male clients to "break free" from the pressures of masculine conformity. And that's not easy. As is emphasized in other chapters of this book, this work takes different, creative ways and strategies to get men to "go there."

So here is my twist: although therapy can feel like a bad joke to many men, I think using humor and storytelling more broadly can be a promising way for men to really benefit. Before understanding my approach and how you can consider this skill in your stand-up (or sit-down) act, it's critical to grasp how I conceptualize gender.

Ellis was a computer programmer who came into therapy with a number of typical masculine issues: he was struggling in his relationship with his wife, he frequently felt angry and did not know why, and he was having trouble sleeping and concentrating. As we focused on anger, Ellis told a story about how enraged he was when a coworker whom he considered less able was offered a promotion for a job that Ellis thought he deserved. I said, "That must have been very disappointing to you." He responded, "No! I was pissed off." I responded, "Could it be that you were disappointed as well?"

Ellis could not even handle the concept of disappointment; he only knew angry, so I said to him, "I think angry is your default option, as it is for many men. I wonder if you'd like to work on resetting your default. You can stay angry; I think I'd be angry too, but if we can expand how you process your feelings beyond the anger, I think you would benefit."

Now I was talking his language. He understood the default analogy and knew from his work that a computer could be more versatile and powerful if it were programmed well. But one cannot reset a default without exposing it first.

EXPOSING THE DEFAULT OPTIONS

The great developmental psychologist Sandra Bem (1993) referred to gender as the default options preprogrammed into the individual by the culture. Like default options in a computer, they are left in place by doing nothing. I took this analogy a step further by applying the idea to resisting conformity. If you boot up your computer, icons appear on the screen. The size of those icons is a default option; you can make them smaller or larger if you like (at this point, 25-year-old readers are saying, "Duhhhh." and 50 year olds are saying, "You can!!!?").

Changing the default requires three things: awareness, motivation, and skill. Awareness means knowing that something is a default; that it is possible to change. Then, you have to be motivated to change it. Maybe you are aware of the default, but those icons are fine the way they are. But maybe you don't see very well and need them to be bigger, or maybe you're such an incredible geek that you need to fit so many of them on your screen that you need them to be smaller, or maybe you just want your desktop to look different; it's a fashion choice. Then, you need to acquire the skill to change the default. Ellis and I worked on the idea that he needed to get to the point of executing the right sequence of keystrokes to manage his life better—a rough metaphor, for sure, but it was one to which Ellis could relate.

Gender education, whether in the classroom, theater, or therapy room, fulfills the first condition. It exposes the cultural pressure known as masculinity. My first mantra: it is very difficult to resist a pressure that one cannot name. Any feminist-identified woman will tell you that the first time she read an articulate piece of feminist literature, she was changed. Someone named her experience in a way that she had sensed, but had previously been unable to understand fully. We need to do the same for men.

Once the default can be named, we put men into a position to decide if they are motivated to resist the cultural pressure. My second mantra: a man is motivated to resist conforming to masculine demands when his gender conformity conflicts with an important life goal or value, or when it hurts another person. For me, this means that anyone who wants to be a better partner, father, friend, mentor, more relaxed person, or who would like to avoid mistreating people, is going to be motivated to reset the default. If he is, then he will have to invest the time and effort necessary to learn how to do so. My third mantra: a man needs to be shown alternatives and then be reinforced for acting independently of the cultural pressure to conform—to step outside of the box when the situation calls for it. I like to use humor and storytelling to help men navigate the journey of breaking free from gender defaults.

EXPLORING THE WORLD THROUGH LAUGHTER

In a strange way, psychotherapy is like stand-up comedy. In both cases, the audience (or client) comes wanting you to help them do what they want to do anyway (laugh, or change), but there is also resistance. Like a heckler in the room when I am doing my stand-up routine, there is a part of each male client that is actively countering my influence. I have found in the comedy club and in the office that engaging the "heckler" through humor can bring unexpected benefits.

E. B. White said, "Analyzing humor is like dissecting a frog. Few people are interested, and the frog dies of it." Nevertheless, it's critical to do a little analysis to understand the potential for using it to work with men in psychotherapeutic settings, and so, here goes.

Humor is hardwired in the brain. Babies smile when they experience pleasure; they don't have to be taught to do this. In every culture, people laugh when something strikes them as funny. And humor is emotional, so when we use it, we reach beyond the cerebral cortex (the thinking, analytical part of the brain) into the limbic system (the deeper emotional part). Both hemispheres are operating when you laugh and endorphins (the brain's painkillers) are being released.

Often one of the challenges to working with men is to bring them closer to their emotional experiences, since they have often been punished for expressing feelings. But socially, men are allowed to laugh and to make others laugh, and so humor can be an avenue for accessing some of the feelings they have been encouraged to bury in their masculine socialization.

LEARNING TO BE FUNNY

I know what you're thinking. "But Chris, how can I use humor if I'm not a funny person?" An excellent question, and I'm glad you brought it up. Well, I'm not a naturally funny person either (as you may have already surmised). But I am a person who thinks of funny things, writes them down, and memorizes them. Over time, I think I have become funnier. So think of humor as a set of skills that improve with practice. Like all skills, some people seem to be naturals, although most are not. But remember the first time you swung a golf club, played a chord on the guitar, sat with a client, gave a presentation, or wrote a paper? That seemed awkward at first too, but if you stuck with it, over time it became second nature.

The skill metaphor—trying to learn how to be funny or tell a good story—is a useful parallel with male clients, most of whom know a lot about skill development. So you can couch things that they think are "unmasculine," but that nevertheless are important, like understanding and expressing emotions or negotiating within a relationship, as skills that improve with practice. When do we invest time and energy in learning a skill? When we value the outcome. So we can ask our clients—do you want to improve your relationship and quality of life? If you are committed to it, you will do what it takes to make it happen. You can bring this to them without masculine shaming. I strongly recommend against beginning a sentence with something like "If you were any kind of man..."

The skill development metaphor is a way of instilling hope in men who think that some version of their masculinity is hard-wired in the brain. If I think that men—or think that I—can't cook, understand feelings, deal directly with my partner, why would I try? It's a kind of masculine hopelessness that reduces motivation to change. As I ask my students: if you thought that you were going to get the same grade on the next test no matter what you did, would you study or even come to class? Of course you wouldn't. So listen for the message of "I can't, because I'm a man" and try to transform it into "I haven't done this well, because I'm socialized to be masculine. I can learn new skills, as I have all my life."

WHAT ARE THE THERAPEUTIC USES OF HUMOR?

In my work with men, I am always looking for ways to get them to question the default options of masculinity, because we know that, in many cases, it's not healthy to blindly conform to the dominant version of what it means to be a man. So I use humor to:

Open an issue. I want to help them understand that masculine expectations are somewhat arbitrary. Jamie was a client whose partner often complained that he didn't do his share of household work. He considered himself incompetent at these tasks, but in our conversations, I discovered that he had gone to the hardware store and bought a gas grill, a power washer, and a shop vac. "So," I said to him, "that means you will cook, clean, and vacuum if you define it as masculine."

Facilitate an insight. Expectations change in different situations. You can pat your friend on the butt if he's on the same football team as you; don't try it on College Avenue.

Change a perspective. When I was in graduate school, my friend Liza was bemoaning the fact that she was going to get a B in a class. Another student who overheard her asked, "What do you call a grad student who gets all B's?" Answer: Doctor.

Build an alliance. We like people who make us laugh in respectful ways. Clients will gravitate toward you if you can laugh at yourself or at a situation. A lot of humor is observing absurdity. When we agree with our clients that something is a little bit silly, we join them.

Reduce tension and undermine resistance. Robert Brooks (1994) tells the story of his first meeting with a 14-year-old, very combative boy who was "dragged" into therapy by his parents. The boy began by telling him, "You are the ugliest looking shrink that I have ever seen." He reacted by saying, "Would it help if I went into the closet so that you wouldn't have to look at me?" (pp. 53–54). The therapist stayed in the closet for most of the first few sessions (and imagined his colleagues asking if his malpractice insurance was paid up) but eventually the boy began to see him as an ally rather than an authority and began to open up to him.

Imagine possibilities. Bette Kisner (1994) specializes in treating cancer patients. One of her clients said, "Why bother making plans when I might die next year?" She responded: "Wouldn't it be a let-down then if you actually lived another 40 years? Then what would you do?" (p. 142).

Playfulness-regression in the service of the ego. A therapist was treating a man who was very intellectualized. During a session, he said, "There is a feeling..." and the therapist jumped up, looked out the window, and said "Where?! Is it over there at the ice cream shop?!"

Corrective emotional experience. A client of mine related a story about his girlfriend. When he would express displeasure at her behavior, she often told him that he was a "pussy" and that he should "grow a pair." Sometimes, she threw things at him. I responded in a matter-of-fact way: "Well—just speaking for myself—I would not stay in a relationship with someone who shamed me and threw things at me." A smile came across his face as he said, somewhat sardonically, "Yeah, it IS kind of a deal-breaker, isn't it?" In that moment, he realized that he is entitled to feelings and to disagree with his girlfriend, and that he could decide which of her behaviors were and were not acceptable to him.

Taking the power out of the narcissistic fantasy. Grandiose fantasies have a lot of power, and narcissists take themselves way too seriously. These fantasies of unlimited success, power, and brilliance are painful reminders that one feels pretty empty and ashamed. It's like the harsh, untutored superego beating up on us. But if we acknowledge and have a laugh about the fantasies, they become less hurtful.

Armand was a client who was nearly obsessed with being highly attractive to women. I said to him, "You want to be 'the Most Interesting Man in the World,'" as in the Dos Equis beer commercials. "His blood smells like cologne. His legend precedes him the way lightning precedes thunder. He once had an awkward moment, just to see how it feels. He lives vicariously...through himself. He is the most interesting man in the world. I don't always drink beer," excuse me... I looked at her and she had an orgasm... (okay—I added that part), "but when I do, I prefer Dos Equis. Stay thirsty my friends." Because "the Most Interesting

Man in the World" is so over-the-top, we could laugh at the absurdity of the narcissistic fantasy, and Armand had a new perspective. He even began to be aware of times when the fantasy arose and called it a "MIMITW" moment.

I know I'm not the most interesting man in the world (although, to paraphrase Woody Allen, eighth place is not bad) and so I can be disappointed or even angry if others don't hang on my every word and revel in my brilliance and "cool." Humor allows us to take pleasure in the fantasy and protects us from hurt when it is not fulfilled, which is inevitable. In the course of developing a sense of humor, we also develop the ability to soothe ourselves when we experience negative emotions, which is also inevitable.

Paul and his partner Susan were in couples therapy and making good progress. During one session, he related a story of going to an open mike night with her and bringing his keyboard. When he got up to play and sing his three songs, he expected her to pay close attention to every note and admire his skill and passion as a performer. Unfortunately for Paul, she spent the time chatting with friends, as she had not seen them in a while. When Paul got off the stage, he sat down and waited for fawning compliments, which were not forthcoming. Finally he became desperate and asked her, "So, what did you think?" She responded, "Oh, I'm sorry, I wasn't listening." And he responded in a self-effacing and sardonic, "Well, I'm going to be pouting here for a little while. I'll be with you in a few minutes."

This was real progress. Before he began in counseling, he really would have pouted a long time, but he had learned enough about himself to understand that he had a tendency to pout when she (his narcissistic extension) failed to hold up the mirror to him (committed an empathic failure, resulting in a narcissistic injury). His humor allowed him to reduce the frequency, intensity, and duration of his pouting and helped him to avoid making unreasonable demands of her, and in the process he began to develop a greater ability to understand her perspective and thus empathize with her.

The ability to soothe the self is critical to mental health. No matter how doting a partner is, he or she will always get tired, fail to pay attention, get absorbed in his or her own needs, or otherwise exhibit empathic failures. When you first meet someone and begin to fall in love, empathy is everywhere, all your stories are fascinating and you emphasize your commonalities ("You drink water?!! I drink water too!!!!). But after you get to know a person, they start to lose a little of their magic, and if you can't manage the minor disappointments of everyday life, the relationship will not mature. Having a laugh at these fantasies of unlimited brilliance and desirability is critical to doing so.

Humor is the highest and most mature of all defenses when it is philosophical (as opposed to mean-spirited). It is "thoughtful spontaneity" and can be used when the benefits outweigh the risk. The therapist who jumped up and looked out the window when her client said, "There is a feeling" would not have done so until she had established a relationship that allowed this kind of playfulness. I always think of psychological interventions in terms of three considerations: tack (What is my strategy?), timing (When am I going to deliver the intervention?), and dosage (How much intensity am I going to use?). Never be funny in a disrespectful way if you're trying to teach something, and consider whether the audience is ready. They might get defensive and shut down or become combative, thus damaging your relationship with them.

Humor is also useful for therapists to manage their (countertransference) feelings outside of the session. One of my supervisees described a passive–aggressive client who showed her a story she had written. The therapist praised her by saying, "Wow. That's really creative." And the client responded, "Well, I don't think it's very good; I've written a lot better." (This was the therapy equivalent of a heckler.) After she related the story, the trainee drove a fist into her hand forcefully and said "Die, therapist, die!" Provocative clients can hurt us; we're human. If we are going to give them the best treatment, we have to manage our negative reactions to them, and humor is a great tool for doing so.

A CAUTION: SOMETIMES FUNNY ISN'T FUNNY

If you are going to use humor in any setting where you are trying to do more than merely entertain, it is important to know the difference between being funny and being a clown. When I first arrived on my campus more than 20 years ago, several people seemed to think that because I was a comedian, I didn't take anything seriously. I have come to this insight (which I think is profound and brilliant; see "narcissistic fantasy" from earlier in the chapter): the words *funny* and *serious* are not opposites. You can be funny *and* serious at the same time; that's what good satire is. The comedians I most appreciate are the ones who want to use their humor to make a statement: Robert Klein, Godfrey Cambridge, Woody Allen, George Carlin, Patton Oswalt, Maria Bamford, and Richard Pryor. My "profound" insight is that the opposite of *funny* is *humorless*, and the opposite of *serious* is *indifferent*. I may be funny from time to time, but I am a serious person, and I am anything but indifferent. Humor is a joy that our brains give to us; use it for good, not for evil.

STORYTELLING

I have lots of different career identities. I'm a professor, consultant, therapist, comedian, actor, and playwright. I "suffer" from a condition called *hypernarria*. Don't look it up; I made up the word. It is the compulsion to tell stories. Along with my background in studying and writing about men and masculinity, I tell stories, often funny ones, to educate people about gender and to help therapy clients manage their lives more effectively.

Like humor, storytelling is hardwired in the brain. As soon as we enter REM sleep, our prefrontal cortexes take random neural signals coming up from the brain stem and weave them into a dream story. Narrative is one of the main ways we make sense of our lives, and people are hungry for new stories, as evidenced by the multibillion-dollar movie and television industry. We're so hungry for stories that we'll even watch a film about the process of producing a feature film (e.g. the Making of *Titanic*)—a story about the making of a story.

My solo theatre performance, *Crimes Against Nature*, was a synthesis of my experiences as a comedian, writer, scholar, and a person who grew up as a male in mainstream United States culture. When I first began to write, I was inspired by performance artist Holly Hughes (1996). Holly wrote about her question and answer sessions following performances, saying that she often got questions about a lot of different topics:

> There's often a question beneath the questions I'm being asked, and often it's this: *tell me a story* [emphasis original]... They want a map, a set of directions saying "This way out." Of course, they have to make their own maps. But something in my story might help them with theirs. They might begin to think of their own life as a story, might realize they can write this story, that they can be the heroine, that they can write their own plot rather than go on living inside the standard narrative. Of course, maybe the stories I give them won't work for them in the way I hoped, but I'm sure they can find some use for them. As far as I can tell, everyone can always use a story.
>
> (pp. 8–9)

My other major inspiration was my director, Gregg Stull, who helped me to understand the distinction between theatre and mere entertainment. Entertainment provides pleasure but no learning; theatre simultaneously entertains and informs. As Gregg put it, "I go to the theatre to change," and he later added, "the story is about the character who changes the most."

Therapy is a lot about storytelling. In a first interview, when we ask, "What brings you to the Center?" we are really saying, "Tell me a story." Telling the story to an interested listener is healing in and of itself. In most cases, I can tell from the client's statements and body language that he or she is beginning to feel better by the end of the first session.

Men are socialized to be storytellers, but in a masculine mode in which the story is used for entertainment and competition. My solo theatre performance, *Crimes Against Nature* (Kilmartin, 2000), includes a sketch with "Mr. Construction Worker" where he explains his conception of storytelling and male camaraderie:

> Usually, a guy will start telling a story about how he shot a deer but it didn't die right away so he had to take his belt off and strangle it and he got all bloody and the deer kicked him in the leg but he got the job done anyway. While the other guy's telling the story, I try to *appear* to be listening attentively, when really I'm

planning what I'm going to say next, so that when *he's* done, I can jump in with *my* story, and hopefully it'll top his. The whole idea is to create the *illusion* of an interactive conversation, when in actuality, you're just taking turns talking.

That's the masculine mode: tell a wildly entertaining story that's better than the one the other guy just told. Many of us learned how to do it early in life. But this part of masculine socialization can be a real advantage. Many men know how to tell a story. Our job as therapists and educators is to help them tell it in a different and deeper way.

One of the most memorable stories my father told me was about being a star minor league baseball player. He was leading the league in hitting and happened to meet the opposing pitcher in a bar the night before the game. The pitcher, who was a decade older than my dad, told him, "You're not going to get a hit off of me, young fellow." My father took this as a warning that the pitcher was going to try to intimidate him by throwing at him instead of home plate, and my father resolved to hang in the batter's box, believing that the pitch would be a curve and break off at the end. Importantly, this was in the era before batting helmets had been invented, and a pitched ball had actually killed a major league player. The pitcher threw at his head and my Dad hung in there. It didn't break and the pitcher yelled, whereupon my father collapsed on to the ground, the ball barely missing his head. The punch line ending of the story was "and I didn't get a hit that day."

It was an entertaining story, but if he had been a therapy client, I would want to have known about what was missing in the story—the fear and vulnerability of being within inches of becoming seriously hurt. In psychotherapy, we want our clients to relive and process these kinds of experiences. In many other parts of their lives, they may believe that nobody wants to hear about it and/or may fear that others will shame them for revealing this side of themselves. In therapy, we can move beyond the stereotypical masculine mode of storytelling by highlighting emotional and relational themes contained in the stories. And in this way, we help men to tell their stories in different and deeper ways.

One of my clients, a male college student, came into treatment because his girlfriend had broken up with him following a number of weeks in which her behavior towards him became increasingly provocative and passive–aggressive. In the third session, I asked him to tell me the story about the whole process of the breakup. I wanted to know everything from the time in which she started doing things like telling him she would meet him at a party and then show up hours late, to the time when she told him she no longer cared to be his girlfriend.

He told the story with a great focus on her behavior and talked very little about his reactions, and so I interjected edits into his story. When he said she was acting crazy, I added, "and you were confused and uncomfortable" and when he said that she showed up hours late, I added, "and you were hurt…she hurt your feelings." And he said, "Yes, I was, and she did." As we were finishing, I said to him, "I get the feeling that you had not gone through the whole breakup story with anyone before today." He acknowledged that he had not; that his girlfriend was the only person to whom he felt he could disclose his feelings, and now that she was gone, he had no one. I came back to my skill building analogy—that perhaps he could develop the kinds of emotionally disclosing relationships with others that he had had with his girlfriend. His storytelling increasingly became a corrective emotional experience as it increasingly became emotion-focused and introspective.

SUMMARY

Men can be moved by humor and storytelling. As a therapist, teacher, and actor, I bring these tools into all of the work I do with men. In the process, they learn how to question the masculine assumptions that shape their lives and break out into new possibilities of thinking, feeling, and behaving. In therapeutic and psychoeducational work with men, we can tap into masculine modes of laughter and storytelling and use them as a "foot in the door" to healthy awareness and change through facilitation of insights, catharses, and accessing the support of therapists as well as others around them.

One of my favorite quotes about men is from Fred Rabinowitz (2011), one of the editors of this volume: "Men are deep, but they need a space to explore that depth and time to do it." If we are able to get men to tell their stories and laugh in different ways, we help to create that space and motivate them to invest their time to explore the complexity that the culture tells them they do not possess, even though in their heart of hearts, they know that they do.

REFERENCES

Bem, S. L. (1993). *The lenses of gender: Transforming the debate on sexual inequality*. New Haven, CT: Yale University Press.

Brooks, R. B. (1994). Humor in psychotherapy: An invaluable technique with adolescents. In E. S. Buckman (Ed.), *The handbook of humor: Clinical applications in psychotherapy*. Malabar, FL: Krieger.

Hughes, H. (1996). *Clit notes: A Sapphic sampler*. New York: Grove.

Kilmartin, C. (2000). *Crimes Against Nature* (solo theatre performance DVD). Fredericksburg, VA: author.

Kisner, B. (1994). The use of humor in the treatment of people with cancer. In E. S. Buckman (Ed.), *The handbook of humor: Clinical applications in psychotherapy*. Malabar, FL: Krieger.

Rabinowitz, F. E. (2011, August). *Outside of the box: Alternative group therapy approaches for men* at the American Psychological Association Annual Convention, Washington, DC.

White, E. B. (n.d.). BrainyQuote.com. Retrieved April 26, 2013, from http://www.brainyquote.com/quotes/quotes/e/ebwhite100291.html.

CHAPTER 3

Approaching the Unapproachable

Therapist Self-Disclosure to De-Shame Clients

David B. Wexler

If you are a clinician, you know that men are very sensitive to shame and feelings of incompetence. As a result, we have to do whatever we can to de-shame the therapeutic experience. Otherwise, men won't show up. And if they do show up, they won't stay. And if they do stay, they won't be as real as they need to be in order to get something out of the experience.

There are a thousand ways to do this which I and others (Englar-Carlson & Stevens, 2006; Good & Wood, 1995; Levant & Pollack, 1995; O'Neil, 2008; Pollack & Levant, 1998; Rabinowitz, 2006; Real, 1997; Wexler, 2004, 2006, 2009) have written about extensively over the past 20 years or so.

One way to disarm typical male shame (and its behavioral cousins: denial, minimization, defensiveness, and avoidance) is by the appropriate use of therapist self-disclosure. I have found this to be invaluable in my work with men.

Therapist self-disclosure, carefully calibrated, can be extremely effective in fostering the therapeutic alliance and helping bring men out of their shell. We can create an atmosphere of increased trust and intimacy by acknowledging that the same struggles and conflicts have taken place in our own lives and in our own relationships. This helps men normalize their experiences.

As clinicians, shame is our enemy here—and therapist self-disclosure often defuses shame. Sometimes this means getting creative and going "out of the box" with what we reveal about ourselves and how we do it.

THE VALUE OF SELF-DISCLOSURE

A recent review of published studies (Henretty & Levitt, 2010) exploring verbal therapist self-disclosure found that it almost always had a positive effect on clients; that clients had a stronger liking for, or attraction to, therapists that self-disclosed; that clients perceived therapists who self-disclosed as warmer; and—most importantly, for our purposes here—that clients self-disclosed more to therapists that self-disclosed.

Men often say they remember the personal stories that I have revealed in individual and group sessions—more than anything else.

I recently told what I call my "Bicycle Shame" story to Jack, a mid-30s male client who was still living off and on with his parents, had never really developed a career, and had never had a real girlfriend. He was feeling humiliated about trying to change any of these things because he felt like this all should have happened long ago. Here's what I told him:

Like most of my friends, I tried learning how to ride a bicycle at about age five. They all got the hang of it, but I could never quite pull it off. After a while I gave up because I felt so stupid. When my friends would ride their bikes, I acted like bike-riding was kind of lame—my way of defending myself from shame. I felt more ashamed of this with each passing year.

Finally, when I was about 11, I decided I HAD to learn how to ride a bike. I went off by myself one afternoon and just kept trying it until I finally got it. I caught up quickly, and the history never mattered after that.

Jack nodded and mumbled some polite noncommittal response. I thought I had missed the boat, but at least there was no harm done. Then, a few months later, when he was leaving therapy, he told me, with tears in his eyes: *You know that story you told me about you and the bicycle? That is such a perfect example of what I was feeling. That helped me so much, and I'll never forget it.*

In the books that I have written I reveal a number of personal examples to illustrate male dilemmas and sometimes resolutions. I often have men quoting one of my stories to me in the middle of a therapy session: those nuggets resonate with them more than my brilliant theories and therapeutic prescriptions. Here's what has finally dawned on me after many years of trying hard to strike just the right tone, use just the right intervention, and implement just the right technique: sharing more of myself might be the most important work I can do for someone else, and especially for a guy.

The same is true when I teach professional workshops: I can literally feel the crowd awakening when I tell something about myself or my marriage or my family to make my point. The more vulnerable I am, the more their receptors seem to wake up.

When done right, this evens the playing field. Men who are highly sensitized to the hierarchical structure of the therapeutic relationship (with the male client in the vulnerable underdog position) tend to relax the more "real" the therapist gets. When I have done this, I have often seen some of the most defensive men quickly engage and open the door to the insight and interventions that our therapy sessions can offer. It's not that they forget that I'm the professional in the room and they're not—it just seems like they don't care about that difference any more, because the relationship of "man-to-man" (or "parent-to-parent" or simply "human-to-human") has become more prominent.

I recently told what I call my "Paris Purse" story to my client, Andrew, who was struggling with feeling like a "pussy" when he tried to tell his wife about the panic attacks he was having. I wanted to get the point across that we guys are totally capable of ascribing manhood tests to practically anything—and that, once we did this, we were screwed because we felt like we had to stay in this confining box of male gender role expectations. Here's what I told Andrew:

Several years ago, I was on a family trip, sitting on a bench with my wife in a plaza in Paris. Loaded down with shopping bags, she asked me to grab her purse and carry it over to a new spot across the plaza. That's all. Yet, even though I knew I was being stupid, I couldn't do it. The 15 seconds being seen carrying a purse were beyond my capacities as a card-carrying male. My wife looked at me like I was nuts and shook her head in disgust.

The background to this was that I had recently undergone back surgery and was instructed not to lift heavy bags on this trip. So my wife was doing a lot of the heavy lifting—which contributed to my de-masculinization, of course.

So what was my problem? All I could envision were people smirking as they saw me publicly toting that damn purse, all of my hard-earned Guy Points accumulated from my half-century of being male suddenly vanishing without a trace.

Andrew (and his wife) laughed at the absurdity of my purse-phobia. He told me: *I guess you get it.* I nodded. And I reminded him that a secure man can temporarily carry a purse and can have a real and honest conversation with the woman he loves about his inner world.

Keep in mind that the therapeutic alliance, according to volumes of therapeutic outcome research, is vastly more significant in determining positive treatment outcome than any specific intervention or technique. Measures of therapeutic relationship variables consistently correlate higher with client outcomes than specialized therapy techniques (Lambert et al., 2002). This comes as no surprise to students of treatment outcome research in many settings with many different populations over many years.

Often this alliance is generated naturally, if the clinician has an intuitive sense of how to foster alliance and if the male client is receptive. Most therapists are already skilled at this—but it helps all of us to recognize particular strategies that often enhance the therapeutic alliance, thus potentiating the positive effects of treatment.

Enriching this alliance with male clients is the central rationale for my self-disclosures. Below I'll illustrate a few key points about disclosing with male clients, with specific examples from my experience and suggestions to consider in your own work.

TYPES OF SELF-DISCLOSURE

There are two main types of therapist self-disclosure (Henretty & Levitt, 2010). The first is *Self-Involving Communication (Here and now)*, which requires the therapist to express immediate feelings or reactions to the client. For example, when my client Josh told me about how he apologized to his son (for the first time in his life), I said to him, *I am so moved by what you are facing here and the courage it takes to do so*. When my client Daniel slipped into his old familiar pattern of minimizing how his drinking was affecting his family, I stopped and said, *When you talk like this, I feel really worried about you and it's so hard to connect with you.*

This is always a crapshoot: most men are deeply touched by this more "intimate" response. Others are turned off or downright overwhelmed by the intensity of emotion. There is no specific formula—but keep in mind that the research literature strongly indicates that clients in general (both genders) respond very positively to this level of therapist personal involvement.

The second type, more commonly identified, is *Extra-Therapeutic* self-disclosure, as in bringing information about yourself into the consulting room that has actually taken place elsewhere: *I got stuck in traffic today* or *I was raised Catholic, too* or *I went skiing with my family last week* or *I have been diagnosed with colon cancer*. All of these, ranging from the banal to the extremely serious, reflect a counselor's decision to reveal something about himself or herself that is otherwise not readily apparent to the client.

THE "TWINSHIP" FACTOR AND PASSING TESTS

The rationale for therapist self-disclosure is best understood by the self psychology construct of the *twinship* (or *kinship*) selfobject function (Basch, 1990; Shapiro, 1995). According to this model, an individual experiences increased self-cohesion through an identification with others. The more that someone feels kindred or has the sense of a shared human experience, the more emotionally integrated and centered he feels. This self-cohesion experience is the essential component of human experience that self psychology focuses on, and the *twinship* selfobject is (like the *mirroring* selfobject and *idealizing* selfobject and others) one of the pathways that facilitates it.

Another important rationale for the judicious use of therapist self-disclosure requires us to understand how important it is for us to pass the male client's tests of us. Control-Mastery theory (Engel & Ferguson, 1990; Weiss & Sampson, 1986) is based on extensive research involving detailed observations of psychotherapy sessions. One of the most valuable findings from these studies is that clients often enter counseling (or all relationships, for that matter) with preconceived pathogenic beliefs about themselves, about others, or about how the world works.

According to this model, the client uses the therapy relationship and other intimate relationships to conduct a series of tests. Think of this as an unconscious scientific inquiry in which the client wishes to confirm or disconfirm certain beliefs. In this study, he enters into the investigation expecting to have his original and longstanding pathogenic beliefs confirmed—but he secretly hopes that maybe, this time, they will be disconfirmed.

The old beliefs can change or at least become more flexible. How? By the repeated discovery that, this time, things are different. Or, in some cases, that this time he can handle the situations effectively.

Here's an example. My client, Curt, was relating an incident when he had screamed at his 12-year-old son in front of his friends when the boy just refused to listen to him. Curt told me this story tentatively—I knew he was (consciously or unconsciously) testing me to see how I would handle hearing this, particularly if I would reprimand or shame him like he was so used to. He was sending up a trial balloon to see how safe it was to reveal so much about himself in our therapy world.

I went for self-disclosure. I told him my "Throwing Joe's Pog Over The Back Fence" story:

My seven year-old-son Joe was not cooperating with me. We had a deal that he would stop playing when I gave him the time warning, clean up his stuff, and get dressed and ready to go wherever it was that we were going. He had plenty of warning. So the time comes around, I let him know it's time, and he just looks at me and keeps playing. I give him a minute, and then gently tell him again, no response. We go through this a few times.

Then, as parents tend to do, I started to feel frustrated and powerless and angry. I started the threats. I knew that his most precious possession during that period of his young life was one of his treasured "pogs" (if you don't remember pogs, it doesn't matter—it could have been anything): "If you don't start getting ready in the next 30 seconds, I am going to take away your special pog for the rest of the afternoon." No response. Then it was for 24 hours. Then for the weekend. Then for the whole week.

Finally, in one last desperate attempt to gain control, I pulled out the big one: "If you don't get ready now, I'm going to take your pog and throw it over the back fence into the bushes and you'll never find it again!" When even this didn't move him, I did it. I hurled the pog over the fence. And of course he burst into tears.

I don't know exactly what I should have done. But nothing justified what I did. Especially after seeing the look of total betrayal on his face. I am sure that all he took away from this was that his father did a horrible thing.

Curt relaxed. He started telling me even more. I had passed the "equality" test, and he was freer now to own and genuinely examine this part of himself that was capable of destructive behavior.

The HBO show *In Treatment* portrayed a vivid example of struggling to pass the client's test involving therapist self-disclosure. Sunil, a 50-ish man recently arriving in America from his home country of India, is depressed. His wife of many years has recently died, prompting his son and daughter-in-law to insist that he fly to New York and live with them rather than sink into debilitating depression. They convince him to come to a therapy session to get help with his moods and increasingly erratic behavior.

In the first few sessions, Sunil remains almost mute. He occasionally speaks (in his native language only) to his son, who translates. Then he reluctantly attends a couple of individual sessions, not revealing much.

In his next session, his analytically-trained therapist (Paul) invites him to talk more about his grief and depression. Sunil says to Paul, *Where I'm from, when we want to talk, we meet a friend for tea, and then one person speaks and then the other. This is very strange to be expected to do all the talking continuously...I am expected to disclose the details of my life, to speak about my wife, about my pain...* Paul is taken aback. He takes a deep breath, then says, *I did have a wife, but we're divorced now.* (Sunil: How long were you married?) *Twenty-one years...* (Sunil: Do you miss her?) *Sometimes...yes, I do.* Like magic, Sunil starts opening up about his feelings, filling in many details about his history with his wife and his culture and what her loss has meant to him. He goes on, uncharacteristically, for several minutes.

The therapy has started. Why? Because Paul stepped "out of the box" (especially his psychoanalytically trained box) and self-revealed more than he would with almost anyone else. He knew that Sunil needed this reciprocity, this level playing field, to open himself up. While Sunil's story comes from a fictional HBO series, this particular scenario is quite realistic and provides all of us with a powerful illustration of the power of getting real (or what Latinos refer to as *personalismo*), particularly for men scared and resistant to the counseling process.

With Sunil, Paul had passed the test. He responded differently than Sunil expected, and genuine therapist self-disclosure was the key.

SELF-DISCLOSURE GUIDELINES

The fundamental caveat of appropriate self-disclosure is this: only do it when you are pretty damn confident that sharing this information is genuinely in the client's best interest. The potential advantage with male clients is that they are more likely to relax their defenses if they experience a sense of affiliation and kinship rather than distance and inequality. I often tell male clients stories about horrendous blunders I have made with my kids or stupid things I have done or struggled with in my marriage. Sometimes these are humorous, sometimes deadly serious.

I have found these self-disclosures to be absolutely critical in my work with men. Of course, I'm aware of inappropriate self-disclosure or going overboard. And I've definitely erred in this direction at times in my career. But my successes with this far outweigh the mistakes. I've repeatedly found that when I self-disclose it helps de-stigmatize what my client has done or how he feels. It opens up more possibility for them to self-reveal, without the excessive shame that tends to shut them down.

But you can only reveal what you feel comfortable revealing. And if you are not reasonably sure that it will serve a therapeutic purpose (even talking about traffic), then don't do it.

Here are the typical types of self-disclosure that counselors sometimes choose to offer:

- Demographic info (education, theoretical orientation, marital status)
- Feelings and thoughts about the client and/or the therapeutic relationship
- Therapy mistakes
- Relevant past struggles that have been successfully resolved
- Similarities between the client and counselor

The main reasons that any of us would even consider self-disclosure include the following:

- To foster the therapeutic relationship/alliance and promote client disclosure
- To validate the client's reality
- To normalize/promote universality (twinship)
- To offer alternative ways to think or act based on the therapist's experience
- To provide clients with authentic, human-to-human communication

INAPPROPRIATE SELF-DISCLOSURE

Although it is difficult to establish an absolute set of rules of when to self-disclose and when not to, you may assume that therapist self-disclosure is contraindicated if, in any way, the conscious or unconscious purpose of the self-disclosure is to serve the needs *of the therapist!*

Here are some other specific pitfalls of excessive or inappropriate self-disclosure:

Revealing the "too personal": Be careful about revealing information that may place a burden on the client to take care of you, or may lead to a loss of your professional credibility if others in your field found out this same information. You may be tempted to reveal that you too were sexually abused as a child. However, this information may end up getting revealed to others—and it also may lead to the client actually refraining from revealing more, because he doesn't want to re-traumatize you!

Needing a friend: The reason to self-disclose is to offer something to help the man who is sitting across from you. If you find yourself talking about your recent divorce because you need to talk to someone about it and your client is very interested, you are making a mistake: *I've been going through the same problems with my wife lately, let me tell you about it...* This also can take the form of gossiping: *Yeah, I've heard some real dirt on that other therapist.*

Needing admiration: Sometimes people in the counseling field, if they are not careful, use their clients to feel admired for personal accomplishments (famous people you know, a book you have published, an important position you have been chosen for): *I had an interesting experience when I was in Milan speaking at the international conference.* Admiring the therapist is not the job of the client.

Losing credibility: If you think that revealing personal information may actually lead you to lose credibility with your client, then don't do it. I know of a female therapist who was once in an abusive relationship. She almost revealed this to her men's domestic violence group, hoping this self-disclosure would let them know that she really understood a lot about this area. But she decided not to—because she suspected (correctly, I believe) that these men would suspect that she could not see them clearly because of her bad experience. Sometimes I choose to reveal that I have been happily married for almost thirty years, to give men some confidence that I know something about making a relationship work—but with some men this signals that I don't know enough about their tormented relationships.

Over-reacting to trauma/abreaction: When the client is showing a strong emotional reaction to trauma, you cannot allow your own traumatic experiences to emerge. These personal experiences might have been useful in the early stages of the therapy to help you "get a foot in the door" with the client, but now, the focus must be on attunement: bearing the client's traumatic experience together. It is counter-therapeutic for the client to recognize that your emotional state is a result of the emergence of your own trauma; the client will be vulnerable to feeling unsafe and ashamed (Carr, 2011).

You may look at these examples and these needs and scoff, certain that you would never make these mistakes. Be careful. No self-respecting, well-trained, non-psychopathic therapist would ever *consciously* use his or her clients to meet these needs or misread his client in these ways. But we all have this potential in us. I know that I have sometimes caught myself slipping some reference into a therapeutic conversation about the success of one of my kids—and then later thought to myself: *How did that ever get into this conversation and what was I getting out of it?* I trust therapists who know that they are capable of this—and who are on watch for it—more than those who say they are unsusceptible.

Often clients won't tell us when we're self-disclosing too much. They want to be polite, plus they often idealize us and are thus very interested in our lives: even if it has nothing to do with their treatment and is wasting their time by taking care of our needs. For many clients, this may represent an unconscious and unwanted repetition of some very old dysfunctional family patterns.

SELF-DISCLOSURE STORIES THAT HELP MEN IN THERAPY

Here are a few more stories I tell male clients, in groups or individual sessions. Some of these stories are just at the limit of revealing information about myself that I am not at all proud of—but I have decided I can handle the self-exposure. The ones that are past that limit never see the light of day.

These are my stories, and they work for me because they are my stories—you'll have to find your own. They have to be real (although a little dramatic embellishment is no crime) and they need to reveal some vulnerability on your part. They can be either humorous or deadly serious.

My "Santa Cruz Boardwalk" story is used to illustrate the power and dangerousness of perceived narcissistic injury or what I call "broken mirrors":

It happens to the best of us. One time my 15-year-old daughter sat through a lecture I gave in San Jose, California. I showed a film clip from the movie Affliction *where the main character cops an attitude with his daughter because she is not having a good time at a party he planned for her. Right after this presentation, my family headed off on a drive to the Santa Cruz boardwalk and amusement park. I had been planning this for a long time as a special treat for my kids, and I knew they would like it. My daughter, however, copped her own attitude and complained that this was really kind of boring. I became defensive, and I said to her, "I planned this for you, and it's like nothing's going to make you happy!" She looked at me and calmly said, "Dad, you sound just like that dad in* Affliction.*" I was busted, and she was right.*

I have another story that I call "Calling Off the Wedding," to illustrate the power of messages from fathers to sons—especially messages that positively reframe masculinity:

When I was in my late 20s, I became engaged to a woman whom I had been dating for several years. To make a long story short, we experienced a major crisis several weeks before the wedding and decided to call it off three weeks before the set date. We canceled caterers, bands, and photographers. Family scheduled to fly in from out of town canceled their trips. We returned some presents that had already arrived.

My most intense anxiety, barely second to the pain of this crashing relationship, involved informing my parents, and particularly my father, of this "failure." With the help of a couples therapist who was guiding us, I managed to handle this with some dignity and success. And, although both my parents behaved themselves with grace and came through, I always worried that my father was secretly disappointed in me.

Actually, I didn't even realize that I was still carrying around this worry and shame. But several months later, out of nowhere in the middle of another conversation, my father (not known for being particularly emotionally articulate) turned to me and said, "You know, I don't think I would have had the courage to do what you did when you called off your wedding."

I said thanks. And I remember that moment now, more than 30 years later, like it was yesterday. My father had given me his blessing. He had reframed the decision I had made as one requiring courage rather than one worthy of shame and indicating failure. I probably shouldn't have needed him to tell me that, but we are all human.

Another one that comes in very handy for a male client is my "Surprise Party" story, when I am trying to make the point that he needs to love his partner (or his kids) based on who they really are and what they genuinely need:

My (now) wife and I had been dating for a year and a half. She had told me early on and very emphatically that she was NOT the type of girl who likes surprises: no blindfold dinners, no weekend getaways that she didn't help plan, no surprise parties.

And of course I didn't take her seriously. Her birthday was coming up and I started planning a surprise party. What girl doesn't love a surprise party? And wouldn't I be a great boyfriend if I planned one?

I pulled it off beautifully. All of our friends showed up and she was totally surprised and (apparently) delighted. Until after everyone finally left, when she totally lit into me: "How dare you throw this party when I told you I HATE surprise parties? What do I have to do to get through to you?" And we didn't speak for a couple of days afterwards.

It all worked out, because we have now been married 29 years (I add that piece of information very strategically. The meta-message is this: "Good men can behave badly and learn from their mistakes, and good relationships can suffer a serious rupture and still recover."). But I learned an important lesson: the most truly loving thing I can do for my wife is to offer her what she really wants and needs. Not what I think she needs, not what I would need, not what I would want her to need. I have to pay attention to who she is and what means the most to her. That's genuine love. What I did was, ultimately, selfish, more for me than for her.

CONCLUSION

As therapists, we always need to think pragmatically. In the end, it does not matter (or should not matter) what theoretical orientation we subscribe to or what techniques we employ. The only relevant question is this: Does it work?

With men in therapy, many of our approaches have not always worked, or at least not always worked as well as we would have liked them to. So—when we try to think "out of the box"—we have to keep pursuing approaches that are most likely to attract men, engage men, reassure men, and open the window to helping men access the best qualities in themselves.

If I thought that standing on my head would facilitate this, I would do it (if I could do it). Instead, I have found that the judicious use of self-disclosure (when it is carefully calibrated and quite likely to be in the best interest of the male client) paves the way for reaching men and helping them change.

REFERENCES

Basch, M. F. (1990). *Understanding psychotherapy: The science behind the art*. New York: Basic Books.

Carr, R. B. (2011). Combat and human existence: Toward an intersubjective approach to combat-related PTSD. *Psychoanalytic Psychology, 28*(4), 471–496.

Engel, L. B., & Ferguson, T. (1990). *Imaginary crimes: Why we punish ourselves and how to stop*. New York: Houghton Miflin.

Englar-Carlson, M., & Stevens, M. A. (2006). *In the room with men: A casebook of therapeutic change*. Washington DC: American Psychological Association.

Good, G. E., & Wood, P. K. (1995). Male gender role conflict, depression, and help-seeking: Do college men face double jeopardy? *Journal of Counseling and Development, 74*, 70–75.

Henretty, J. R., & Levitt, H. M. (2010). The role of therapist self-disclosure in psychotherapy: A qualitative review. *Clinical Psychology Review, 30*(1), 63–77.

Lambert, M. J., Barley, D. E., & Norcross, J. C. (2002). Research summary on the therapeutic relationship and psychotherapy outcome. In Anonymous (Ed.), *Psychotherapy relationships that work: Therapist contributions and responsiveness to patients* (pp. 17–32). New York: Oxford University Press.

Levant, R. F., & Pollack, W. S. (Eds.) (1995). *A new psychology of men*. New York: Basic Books.

O'Neil, J. M. (2008). Summarizing 25 years of research on men's gender role conflict using the Gender Role Conflict scale: New research paradigms and clinical implications. *The Counseling Psychologist, 36*(3), 358–445.

Pollack, W. S., & Levant, R. F. (1998). *New psychotherapy for men*. New York: John Wiley & Sons.

Rabinowitz, F. E. (2006). Crossing the no cry zone: Doing psychotherapy with men. Retrieved from http://www.continuingedcourses.net/active/courses/course026.php

Real, T. (1997). *I don't want to talk about it: Overcoming the secret legacy of male depression*. New York: Scribner.

Shapiro, S. (1995). *Talking with patients: A self psychological view of creative intuition and analytic discipline*. Lanham, MD: Jason Aronson.

Weiss, J., & Sampson, H. (1986). *The psychoanalytic process: Theory, clinical observations, and empirical research*. New York: Guilford Press.

Wexler, D. B. (2004). *When good men behave badly: Change your behavior, change your relationship*. Oakland, CA: New Harbinger.

Wexler, D. B. (2006). *Is he depressed or what: What to do when the man you love is irritable, moody, and withdrawn*. Oakland, CA: New Harbinger.

Wexler, D. B. (2009). *Men in therapy: New approaches for effective treatment*. New York: W.W. Norton.

CHAPTER 4

Moving With Men and Their Passions

Lessons From Surfing

Ryan F. Pittsinger and William Ming Liu[1]

> You can't stop the waves, but you can learn to surf.
>
> John Kabat-Zinn, *Wherever You Go, There You Are: Mindfulness Meditation in Everyday Life*, p. 30

I (Ryan) was ten years old and scared out of my mind. To make matters worse, my "high-tech" wetsuit, intended to keep me warm, fit more like an oversized wool coat. Regardless of the chill in my bones, I will never forget the feeling of riding that first wave off the Southern California Coast. Launching up on my board, I was immediately hit by a feeling of sheer joy and excitement. I felt accomplished, proud, and hungry for more. Looking back now, I recognize that experience forever changed my life and initiated my life-long infatuation with the sport.

For seventeen years, I have been an avid surfer, driven by the sea. Surfing is more than a passion; it's part of my identity. This passion has influenced my personal and professional paths. On a personal level, I've challenged my physical limits, made good friends, and expanded my self-awareness. As a therapist, through experiences I've had in the sea, I have become more attuned to my male clients' self-revelations. Like waiting for a wave in the distance, I have learned to time my interventions. This timing has helped my clients ride the emotional intensity of our work, rather than fight it or fear it. Finally, surfing has given me the language and framework for how to think about my own life and work with clients.

Surfing, ocean language and metaphors translate well to my life and how to work with male clients, as they describe their life journeys. I've had turbulent times in my life and have frequently said to men (and students) I've counseled, "Sometimes you have to just go with it." The surfer perspective is that life's challenges are like big and daunting waves, but not insurmountable—that there's always a way, that it's your choice, and that there are benefits and consequences no matter the choice.

In this chapter, we will be exploring how integrating men's passions into the therapeutic process can aid in creating useful therapeutic discussions. The focus will be on the therapeutic benefits of surfing and how surfing can allow male clients to gain perspective, increase self-efficacy, and aid therapists in developing meaningful relationships with their clients. While we will use surfing as our emphasis, other passions like golfing, painting, poker, or tennis all have rich potential for facilitating therapeutic progress with men.

BENEFITS OF ENGAGING IN PHYSICAL ACTIVITY

A first step in this chapter is to briefly document the benefits of surfing that align with physical activity more broadly. Engaging in physical activity has been shown to have numerous physical health benefits. Some of these include lowering blood pressure and significantly reducing the risk of coronary heart disease (CHD) in men (Sesso, Paffenbarger, & Lee, 2000). Further, numerous psychological benefits have been well documented. In a study on surfing in particular, Pittsinger, Kress, and Crussemeyer (2010) concluded that 107 surfers experienced significant increases in positive affect / tranquility and significant decreases in negative affect after surfing for thirty minutes. Thus, the physicality related to emotional expression is important to recognize as a therapist. Encouraging men to engage in their passions, including surfing, comes with tangible, empirically supported benefits.

Yet, there is another important benefit. Along with the physical health benefits, through surfing men can gain a sense of support, acceptance, and permission to express themselves in a variety of ways. A number of years ago a friend and prominent member of the Southern California surfing community passed away due to a mental illness. This triggered a wave of sadness that swept over the community, including over me. Upon hearing the news, I immediately grabbed my board and headed to the surf. It just seemed natural. I look back now and think that, like a lot of men, this was my way of dealing with the sadness. Surfing was my outlet for allowing myself to express the sadness I felt.

As I paddled through the lineup with a heavy heart and tears in my eyes, I was met unexpectedly by numerous other surfers experiencing similar emotions. In some ways, we were each using the ocean and surfing for the same purposes—as a way to feel a sense of comfort, support, and connection with a lost friend. Considering the importance of social support and male friendships in general, the surf can be a powerful asset to men's need for connections and camaraderie, particularly during difficult life events.

RIDING THE WAVES: METAPHORS FOR THERAPY AND LIFE

At a basic level, surfing is an activity that allows for creativity, solace, social engagement, and fun. The core tenets and skills of surfing, including confidence, trust, devotion, and courage, are central to success in the sport. Yet these skills are of course useful when maneuvering the trials and tribulations of daily life as well. Helping clients (those who surf or are familiar with the sport) understand this connection and the life / sea parallels can be incredibly powerful.

Interestingly, when people first think of surfing, what often comes to mind are thoughts of sunny beaches, warm water, and people successfully riding massive waves. Although partly accurate, the sport is not always that glamorous, and it is far more complicated. Surfing consists of elements such as paddling out through the turbulent surf, waiting patiently, precise decision making skills, risk management, and constant cost / benefit analysis.

Further, there is an awareness component that is ever-present in the sport. When out in the ocean, you must constantly be aware of your surroundings. This includes the surfers close by, incoming waves, and the ever-changing ocean conditions (i.e., tides, currents, wind direction). This increased sense of awareness enhances and allows correct placement to catch the best possible waves. Along with increased physical awareness, it is important to pay specific attention to your emotional responses (e.g., fear, excitement, and alertness).

Similarly, in everyday life, increased awareness in everyday settings yields many of the same benefits. Getting men to see this connection, through talking about surfing or another favorite sport is key. I was once talking to a friend about this very connection. In the surf, this guy was a master, yet, on land, he was amazingly unaware of what was going on around him. He appeared disconnected and aloof, due to his lack of emotional awareness.

Another concept that translates well from the sea to our daily life is balance. Physically, balance is about the person's relationship to the surfboard, finding the "sweet spot" for the best ride. Working with a surfer who understands this concept can lead to promising discussions of balance in one's non-sea life. I once had this type of conversation with a client who also surfed. The conversation allowed him to realize he could utilize skills he already applies while surfing. This led to him developing powerful new insights, which allowed him to feel more centered and satisfied in his life.

Similarly, another psychological aspect of surfing is the immediacy of the event and need for focus. These activities require men to be "present." Losing focus or not being present almost always leads to "wiping out." By using a surfing experience as an example, a clinician can help recalibrate a man's attention and focus. This change in perspective, even for a few minutes, may provide a welcome relief from ruminating about a problem or situation in life. Redirecting attention allows the clinician to potentially have access to feelings, thoughts, and memories that may be inaccessible via direct talking and exploration in therapy.

The fourth element that comes with surfing is acceptance. For the sake of giving life and personality to an inanimate entity like water, the wave is alive. It has a beginning, a middle, and an end. Of course, the end in surfing only marks the retreat of the wave back into the ocean, to start the cycle again. Surfing teaches you quickly that a wave has its own process and it will go where it wants.

A surfer must decide to "catch" the wave or let it go. Letting it go sometimes comes with its own perils and decisions of getting past "this" wave. Once a surfer decides to catch the wave, the decision requires full commitment. Being on the wave, the surfer must accept that "he is along for the ride." Even young surfers know they cannot make the wave do something different or be something it is not; the only decision is "how you choose to ride the wave."

As a doctoral trainee, learning to accept the fact that conducting therapy cannot always be a well-calculated endeavor is key. A few years back, I remember discussing a challenging client during supervision. I was having a difficult time working with a client who was extremely anxious and worrisome. As my supervisor and I talked through the case, he asked me, "When you are surfing, what happens when you fall or get clocked by a wave?" I thought a minute and responded, "Well, I try to stay calm and find my way to the surface." He said, "Exactly! If you panic and try to fight the waves, you will only become tired and ultimately be unsuccessful." His point was that I needed to remain calm, trust my clinical abilities, and "ride the wave." I needed to master the concept of acceptance, that I couldn't take responsibility for all of my client's problems. It was a lesson learned more slowly than in surfing, but has continued in its significance as a professional.

THE THERAPEUTIC EFFECTS OF SURFING

The therapeutic effects of surfing are starting to be well documented. In a novel program, wounded Marines newly returned from Iraq and Afghanistan participated in an adaptive therapeutic surfing program called Ocean Therapy. This innovative intervention was facilitated by the Jimmy Miller Memorial Foundation. The men reported that surfing allowed them to successfully cope with the physical and mental pain they suffered as a result of their injuries (Pittsinger & Liu, 2010).

One of the more central lessons these Marines gained from the program was that they weren't always in control. Surfers can try and fight the ocean but in most instances they will ultimately "lose." Mother Nature will always be victorious. These Marines learned how to gracefully adapt to the conditions the ocean presented in order to ride waves. Just like in life, it is helpful for a man to learn how to accept his feelings and emotions for what they are rather than fear them and expect to be overwhelmed and powerless. I remember a great quote from one of these men who noted, "When I am in the ocean surfing, all of my worries and concerns are washed away!"

In many ways, the mind–body connection inherent in surfing also simulates the therapeutic process. A man in counseling who disengages the intellectual from his body will only get minimal benefit. On the other hand, like a surfer who must be in tune with his body as he takes the ocean conditions into account, a male client will deepen his self-understanding when he is in touch with his memories, emotions, and sensations. I find it important to make sure that the body is brought into my psychological work with my male clients.

Of course, we know that men are often much less likely to openly express their emotions through productive and adaptive avenues. As has been emphasized by many scholars, men grow up being told a number of messages that are linked to this struggle with emotional expression. Some include the need to be "the man of the house," be tough, and/or strong. Many men come to believe that being vulnerable, emotional, and expressive are attributes of "weakness." The inability to express emotion because of shame can leave men feeling isolated and lonely, particularly after experiencing traumatic events.

On a recent trip back home to Manhattan Beach, California, I was approached by the wife of a good friend who quickly asked, "Can you please get my husband out surfing? He hasn't been in a while and is going nuts!" The following morning we set out to surf. As we normally do, we began chatting when the waves were sparse. He noted that he'd felt extremely stressed out recently and unable to surf due to the demands of his job. As we walked up the beach after our surfing session, he muttered, "That's just what I needed, a few fun waves!" Although he vaguely verbally acknowledged the benefits he gained from our time surfing, it was blatantly observable. Surfing is not only physical and expressive, but also an important reminder that there are important and enjoyable aspects to one's life even in times of perceived disarray.

IMMERSION IN MOTHER NATURE

One of the unique components of surfing is being immersed in the ocean and Mother Nature as a whole. Whether surfing, swimming, or simply standing at the water's edge, many find that they are consumed with an overwhelming sense of calm and tranquility that is difficult to describe to someone who has not experienced the ocean. Surfers often mutter the words, *"Only a surfer knows the feeling."*

This immersion experience of being in the water translates successfully into how to encourage clients to think about therapy (and how to benefit). That is, to really engage in the therapeutic process clients must first immerse themselves fully in the therapeutic process. This is not easy to do, but can happen—and metaphors for allowing men to see how this connects with other activities that people "dive into" helps.

As an example, I once worked with an extremely emotionally guarded man. Due to his traumatic past, he was unwilling to allow himself to be vulnerable.

It wasn't until he expressed himself emotionally that he felt trusting enough to divulge his fears to me. I conceptualized his resistance as being very similar to someone afraid to take that first surfing ride. Just like being in the ocean, you aren't able to enjoy all the beauty it has to offer until you allow yourself to feel vulnerable and uncomfortable.

For most, the ocean is a sort of mythical and magical space where little is predictable. This can often allow one to feel a sense of powerlessness, understanding that the ocean is something that cannot be controlled but instead needs to be respected. With this perceived lack of controllability often comes fear, an emotion that must be constantly regulated.

The fear associated with surfing is analogous to many of the fears men experience throughout their life. Frequently, in one form or another, this fear is present in the context of being vulnerable with other men. As a therapist, I often emphasize the power of choice when discussing a client's reaction to a fearful or anxiety-provoking situation. While surfing we have the ability to feel empowered and choose the waves we paddle into or the tricks we perform. Similarly, it is important to remind our clients they often have the ability to choose the way they respond to the various events that occur in their daily life.

The ability to feel comfortable in an environment that is beyond one's control is a skill surfers must develop to be successful. This may mean relinquishing control completely or taking calculated risks that may not pay off. Similarly, when navigating difficult and uncomfortable situations in life, the development and maintenance of these very same skills is necessary. Best yet, it's a framework that seems to be convincing and makes sense to male clients—those who surf or who are passionate about the sea in general.

A SAFE AND COMFORTABLE ENVIRONMENT

As clinicians, the importance of creating a safe and comfortable environment for our clients has been well documented. One way surfing can be used therapeutically is by using the environment of the beach and the ocean (often considered a "safe place") in the therapeutic process. This may mean taking a couple of long boards and paddling out to sea or watching and listening to the waves crash while sitting on the shore of an uncrowded beach. Allowing the men you are working with to feel comfortable in their "own" space, that is non-threatening and familiar, can be very useful.

One afternoon while I was working with one of the Marines during an Ocean Therapy session, he began to reflect upon his experiences. As we floated out to sea, waiting for another set of waves to roll in, he turned to me and said: "It's just so peaceful out here, I don't have to worry about anything!" The ability to find peace in being in or nearby the sea can prove to be extremely therapeutic for a man whose life is otherwise filled with chaos. Similarly, engaging in your client's passion of choice, such as taking a hike or playfully shooting a few hoops, may allow him to feel calm enough to express himself emotionally. Being comfortable, relaxed, and engaged in one's passion allows for many men to open themselves to the often threatening (and yet still central) feeling of truly being vulnerable.

Will and I recently conducted a study addressing how surfing can be an effective coping strategy for dealing with traumatic life events such as a death of a loved one, occupational difficulties, and relationship concerns (Pittsinger, Rasmussen, & Liu, 2011). The results were striking. One participant explained how surfing was the only way he effectively copes with the difficulties he experiences in his life. Others noted that when in the ocean they felt free from all of the burdens and stressors that were overwhelming them in their daily lives. From these descriptions and the results, we concluded that surfing and men's presence in the ocean translates into a "safe haven," allowing many to think, reflect, and even connect emotionally with themselves and others.

This finding also connects with other experiences I have had. I once worked with a client who used to surf as a young man. He was struggling with his shift in identity and his role as a man after recently getting married. He explained his fears of losing control and his independence, which he saw was connected to this transition. I asked him to remember what it felt like when he used to paddle for a wave but unsuccessfully caught it. He answered, "Uh, I just turned around, paddled back out and caught another one." I responded, "Even though you lost out on the first wave, you knew that you would ultimately be successful in the near future." I was using surfing, something he identified with, as a way to convey the message that he didn't always need to be in control or do everything he wanted in his relationship in order to feel "like a man."

Allowing the men you are working with to feel a sense of control and autonomy can decrease feelings of defensiveness as well as minimize the stigma that is often prescribed to seeking mental health services. It may be that men do not appreciate counseling because therapists may expect them to immediately become emotionally vulnerable and open to talking about intimate details. Yet some men may feel conflicted that not only are they expected to be something they are not, but, as a man, they cannot fulfill their masculine ideal of meeting and exceeding another person's expectations. Surfing, as a physical activity, reminds therapists that understanding and recognizing the abilities and limitations of a man—meeting a man where he is physically—is as important as meeting the man where he is emotionally.

LOOKING THROUGH THE BARREL: GAINING PERSPECTIVE IN AND OUT OF THE OCEAN

Most surfing is an individual activity. There is only one surfer on the surfboard. In that way, surfing is often understood by non-surfers to be an individual activity. New surfers quickly learn they are part of a larger community. Often, there is great camaraderie among men who are strangers to each other on shore. Discussions about weather, surf conditions, and water temperature can be invitations to more personal discussions.

In this way, surfing is a sport that is fun, but also allows for perspective to be gained both internally (i.e., intrapsychically) and externally (i.e., physically and interpersonally). Surfing focuses the individual's attention to use multiple senses to read and understand the ocean. Seeing the ocean swell up to build a wave is only one way to understand the ocean. The man on his surfboard is also feeling how the water moves around him and listening to the various sounds. Only using one sense (e.g., sight) often causes the person to misread the ocean and can result in a failure to catch the wave or to wipe out. Surfing teaches the person to trust all the senses.

For example, I recently worked with a client who was extremely "stressed" and did not know why he was experiencing panic attacks. After much discussion and perspective taking, he came to the conclusion that he wasn't actually stressed but rather feared failure. It was important for him to objectively evaluate what his feelings were and gain perspective into his emotions. Through this, he was better able to express himself and increase his sense of emotional awareness.

Perspective is also gained in the way surfers approach the actual act of surfing. Instead of thinking of surfing as a means to an end, it is rather viewed as a process that is to be enjoyed and valued in its entirety. There is value in the little things, such as waking up and imagining how much fun you are about to have while checking the waves before running down the sand to the water's edge. There is an anticipation and visualization of pleasurable feelings that begins prior to entering the ocean. Of course there is value in riding waves, but also in laughing with friends while telling a story about how epic your last ride was and in feeling rejuvenated after enjoying a quick surf session. The ability to view and engage in experiences as an entire process rather than as merely a sequence of events can be extremely beneficial therapeutically.

ENHANCING SELF-EFFICACY

If you watch someone being taught to surf, often the instructor goes through some basic steps that feel stilted and rudimentary. "Pretend to do a pushup," "pop-up," and "get into your stance with your knees bent." Beginner surfers learn each of the steps and then attempt to connect them all in one fluid motion, while using a surfboard on the beach. What does the instructor say when the person is sent out into the surf? Generally, it's something like, "Have fun, you'll figure it out." At that point, in the water, the person is left on his own, with basic instructions, to learn to surf. The feeling of accomplishment when all of these pieces come together is nearly always expressed through a smile, a high-five, and/or a boisterous hoot. The man may only stand on the board for a second, but even for that second, he feels accomplished, prideful, and an overwhelming sense of joy. Learning micro-competencies through continued practice eventually leads to longer wave rides and an opportunity for the man to experience continued achievement.

This process can be very similar to how a therapist can approach a client's goals or therapy progress more broadly. As a volunteer for the Ocean Therapy program, I routinely have the pleasure of introducing deserving men and women to the sport of surfing. Recently, while volunteering, I was paired up with a young boy who was extremely scared about stepping foot in the ocean, let alone trusting a stranger to take him surfing. After much coaxing and gradually easing him into the ocean, he was finally willing to trust both himself and me enough to lay on the surfboard and give surfing a shot. Once he began to scream and grasp the board, I gently pushed him into a wave. I then supportively coached him as he stood up and rode his very first wave. In mere seconds all of his hesitation and fears were wiped clean and he couldn't wait to surf again after only one successful ride. Throughout the rest of the day he continually noted how many waves he had ridden and through his increased sense of confidence came an increase in self-efficacy.

This is a good example of how useful a purposeful, supportive, and encouraging statement can be in increasing a client's sense of self. It may sometimes be beneficial to support your client when he is navigating uncharted waters, as you can provide him with the added encouragement that is necessary. This can allow for a genuine trusting relationship to form between you and the client.

RIDING THE MASCULINITY WAVE AND KNOWING WHEN TO ASK FOR HELP

Interestingly, the process of learning how to surf can cause men to reflect (consciously or unconsciously) on core aspects of their masculinity or what it means to be a man. As discussed earlier, there are the positive themes of mastery, camaraderie, and increased perspective.

Yet, men also have to recognize that you need to reach out for help. Lessons of admitting one's vulnerability and even incompetence are core to the learning process. During my teenage years as a surf instructor, I routinely encountered men who were too "manly" for a lesson. Often, these were the same men who would sheepishly ask for instruction once they encountered struggles along the way. Even then, I knew it was important to offer them assistance in a way that was not humiliating. Importantly, this also parallels life and allows opportunities for insight and reflection regarding seeking assistance that can be therapeutic.

Along with riding waves, one major component of surfing is falling! With every wave ridden to completion, there are numerous waves that are only surfed for mere moments before you fall off your board. When surfing you must make the ever-important decision to get back on the board and paddle out to the line-up or swim to the comforts of the shoreline.

The ability to bounce back from setbacks or less than desirable situations is something that every surfer learns very quickly to one capacity or another when first beginning. A colleague of mine recently reminisced about his first time surfing. In doing so, he framed the initial experience as emasculating due to disappointing himself and his instructor, as he needed to be paddled back to shore by his far more competent male instructor who was barking instructions of how he "missed his wave." Therapists should welcome discussions of successes and failures, as they may allow for rich discussions, symbolic of other important areas in their life.

Of course, in the sea, my life, and my office, I have had my share of crashes and missed waves. As a therapist, I remember when one man who needed more time to process some deep emotional material began to cry when I pushed him to express his emotions. Rather than feel a release, he verbalized his shame for having cried. In this case, I pushed too hard, leading to a wipeout, rather than a smooth, positive, insight-generating ride.

Due to the individualistic nature of surfing, surfers are often forced to rely upon themselves to learn from their mistakes while in the ocean. Having the confidence to engage in the process of learning from past experiences in order to bounce back from setbacks and continue to try and be successful is a skill that is highly adaptable to nearly every facet of daily life. In addition to surfing, this ever-important skill can also be acquired through participation in a variety of other activities.

CONCLUSION

Surfing is a passion that has provided me with an overwhelming amount of joy, challenge, and appreciation for life. More importantly, I have had the opportunity to learn many valuable lessons through my time in the water that I continually apply personally and professionally. Just like learning to tailor my surfing style to each particular wave, I have learned the importance of working with the unique set of challenges each client presents in order to fluidly "ride the waves" in the therapy room.

As was illustrated throughout this chapter, breaking barriers with men by utilizing many of the therapeutic aspects inherent in the sport of surfing can be extremely beneficial. Although we focused our discussion on utilizing the numerous components of surfing in a therapeutic fashion, many of these same ideas can be applied to nearly any hobby or passion your client values.

As therapists, it is important to hear the stories of clients and incorporate specific elements of their passions into your work together. Offering parallels and/or relating their emotional experiences in the therapy room to their physical experiences while engaging in hobbies of choice can prove to be invaluable.

Next time you're feeling like taking a risk, remember to paddle confidently, trust your intuition, and "ride the wave!"

NOTE

1 Personal stories shared in this chapter were written from the experiences of both authors. The pronoun "I" was selected for clarity and to reinforce the primary messages and implications.

REFERENCES

Pittsinger, R., & Liu, W. M. (2010, August). Surfing Intervention for Men with Combat-Related Post-Traumatic Stress Disorder. Poster presented at the 118th Annual Convention of the American Psychological Association, San Diego, CA.

Pittsinger, R., Kress, J., & Crussemeyer, J. (2010, August). Effects of a Single Bout of Surfing Upon Exercise-Induced Affect. Poster presented at the 118th Annual Convention of the American Psychological Association, San Diego, CA.

Pittsinger, R., Rasmussen, W., & Liu, W. M. (2011, September). The Impact of Surfing on an Individual's Ability to Cope With Traumatic Life Events. Poster presented at the 26th Annual Conference of the Association of Applied Sport Psychology, Honolulu, HI.

Sesso, H., Paffenbarger, R., & Lee, I. (2000). Physical activity and coronary heart disease in men: The Harvard alumni health study. *Circulation, 102*, 975–980.

CHAPTER 5

Going Deep

Using Sports to Engage Men Therapeutically

Maneet Bhatia

Author confession: I have been obsessed with sports since I was a little boy. At the age of seven, I remember sitting in my living room watching the 1992 World Series. Suddenly, something went wrong with the television. I responded like any rational seven year old: I became enraged. I spiked the remote control, smashing it into pieces; it didn't stand a chance, and neither did my mom's effort to calm me down.

My passion for sports and this type of enraged response continued into my adolescence. I would never miss a big contest featuring my favorite teams. If it took feigning an illness to see a game, I switched from ESPN to WebMD to figure out the symptoms. When I had no other choice, I would record the game, making sure I did not answer calls to hear score updates from friends or family. I lived the life of a crazed sports fan that displayed the features of dedication, obsession, rage, insomnia, and timely illnesses.

As I became a teenager, I started looking around, seeing how I measured up with others. I realized my obsession was not particularly unique. Most guys I knew were just like me: we all loved sports. Privately, I mused about the psychological impact of sports on my life. Maybe it was our way to escape from life's pressures or allow us to fantasize about being the next great superstar.

Any way I looked at it, it was as clear as day that sports did "something" for me—and I wasn't alone. Unfortunately, these moments of inner reflection didn't last long. I instead focused my energies towards my love for the game and being a fan.

It wasn't until I started graduate school in psychology, working with men in therapy, that my perspective on sports changed. As I developed personally and professionally, I began to think deeply about the role of sports in men's lives.

New questions emerged: What functions do sports serve beyond entertainment? Why are men so drawn to sports? Why is it that men become so emotionally and socially invested in a game? Why is it that men are much more affectionate and intimate with each other when engaging (watching or playing) in sports?

In this chapter, I'll be utilizing my sports background and professional experiences to provide some insights into these questions. In doing so, I'll offer up suggestions for how you also might be able to engage men in your practice through their interest and observations from the sports world. I strongly believe that sports provide men opportunities for psychological growth, insight, and change.

IT'S NOT JUST A GAME: THE PSYCHOLOGY OF WATCHING SPORTS

I Want To Be Like Mike

If you are a sports fan, you might remember Charles Barkley infamously stating that "I am not a role model" in the mid 1990s. Well, Mr. Barkley, you may not have intended on being a role model, but the powerful influence athletes have on society is undeniable. Whether athletes like it or not, they are definitely role models and influence young people's attitudes and behaviors.

I was no exception. While growing up, all I wanted was to "be like Mike" just as much as any other teenage boy. I wore Air Jordan's, my number 23 Chicago Bulls jersey, and spent countless hours on my driveway trying to master the "fade-away" jumper (unsuccessfully). MJ was my role model.

How did this affect me? When he scored, I felt good. When the Chicago Bulls won, I won. And when he talked, I listened, secretly wishing they were my own words. I couldn't articulate the feeling then, but now realize that watching sports made me feel like a part of something greater than me. It was a significant psychological truth that underpinned my male identity. We identify with the winners, the champions. Conversely, we distance ourselves from the losers, the "bad guys" in sports.

And when we can't distance ourselves from the teams we love—it hurts. Rarely do we see men more vulnerable or emotional than when their favorite teams suffer a devastating loss. When our teams are champions—we feel like we scored the winning goal.

It is no surprise then that for many men, sports are religion: they eat, sleep, and breathe sports—much to the chagrin of their loved ones, who do not always share the same passion for sports. Entire books have been written on this topic (see *Not Now, Honey, I'm Watching the Game*).

However, if we look deeper into men's association with sports, *I believe that watching sports with other men can allow for short, but meaningful moments of psychological growth, insight, and positive change.* Next, I describe how.

Warm-Ups: The Perfect Icebreaker

For starters, sports provide a unique opportunity for men to connect with each other. When men meet other men for the first time, whether it is at a social event or another type of event, one of the first common points of conversation is sports. "So, who's your team?" or "Did you see the Lebron James dunk last night?" Sports bring men together with a *socially acceptable* topic of conversation. Talking sports is the ultimate "ice breaker" for men to talk with each other, which for many is not easy.

THERE IS NO "I" IN TEAM: SOCIAL SUPPORT

Watching sports provides men with an opportunity to create, enhance, and maintain social networks. Many scholars have commented that men, more than women, struggle with support systems in various capacities (Courtenay, 2011). When they do not seek out social support, there are immediate psychological consequences. Bonding through sports can provide that important sense of support and connection that is needed. Also, when difficulties do arise in their lives, watching sports with friends can act as a way to ameliorate challenges and facilitate healthy coping.

Halftime: Bonding and Shared Moments of Conversation

Watching sports with friends can also provide men with rare opportunities to discuss issues *outside* of sports. During commercial breaks and intermissions, post-game drinking and eating, opportunities surface for men to have conversations. Discussions about relationships, children, work, among other topics, enter into the narratives.

I was once watching a game with a friend who was in the middle of a nasty divorce. It wasn't until halftime that we finally heard the details, and heard his fragile emotional state. Interestingly, having a clear beginning, middle, and end of the time for this talk might have been the key variable that allowed him to finally open up.

As such, these moments may seem small or limited, but for some men they may be their *only* opportunity to share intimate details of their lives with friends. Since men find sports to be supportive and comforting, these conversations become easier because they are anchored on sports.

Father–Son Moments

My father died when I was nine years old. When I reminisce about memories we shared together, I recognize now that many revolved around sports. I'm proud of that point. I remember eating dinner in the kitchen while watching the hockey game on a 13-inch television screen. My father was in the family room watching on the "big" 27-inch television screen. Every time the Toronto Maple Leafs would score, I'd run into the family room and give him a big hug. If they won the game, we'd be all smiles. If they lost, we were sad together. Hockey connected us. It brought us close. We always had a loving relationship, but watching hockey was part of that loving relationship.

Now, 20 years after his death, I still like to think he watches the games with me. I miss you dad.

For many fathers and sons, this story is not unique. Of course the ways fathers and their children connect over watching or playing sports differ. But its consequences and impact often share a common theme. For kids, watching sports with their fathers allows for a small window into their emotional lives. We get to see them laugh, scream, cheer, yell, even cry. And, once in a while, we can be champions together.

THE POWER OF SPORTS TO CHANGE US

Interestingly, sports embody many of the norms and restrictive aspects commonly associated with traditional notions of masculinity. Conventional masculinity is shaped heavily by gender role socialization, which is covered in various sections of this book and others (Nutt & Brooks, 2008). Competition, aggression, violence, and the sexualization of women feature prominently in traditional masculinity *and* in the world of sports. Men are taught to value these characteristics and are often rewarded for following these norms and punished for deviating from that path.

While I grasped these concepts academically, I didn't understand what they were in my teenage years. Playing basketball, I would do anything to win: trash talk, hard fouls, or selfish play. "Just win" was the motto. These competitive, aggressive, and even violent characteristics are transferred onto professional athletes when we watch them play. That is why, in part, we yell and scream and cheer with such passion. It is because we see ourselves in these athletes. The players we admire can be the vehicle through which we get to live out these impulses, drives, and fantasies.

However, this process of men's socialization can lead to many negative consequences, including gender role conflict (GRC). GRC occurs when rigid, masculine gender roles that men have learned through patriarchal socialization lead to behavioral, emotional, and cognitive difficulties for men (Englar-Carlson, 2006; O'Neil, 2008; Wester, 2008).

As I advanced in my graduate studies, I began to notice the ways in which athletes were reinforcing traditional masculinity. This included my awareness that some athletes seemed to be suffering from GRC. But, I also noticed the ways some men were rejecting traditional masculinity and breaking down the barriers that cause so many men to be constrained by the way they were socialized. I believe that examining these violations of traditional masculinity in sports can *go a long way* to help men overcome overly rigid connections to traditional masculine role norms.

In essence, while the game remains the same, the means by which men enact masculinity on and off the court have evolved. These positive trends enable men to reflect on their role models of masculinity.

Let's look at a few examples.

Restricted Emotionality

Most men, in one way or another grew up hearing the mantras *"big boys don't cry"* or *"suck it up and be strong."* I know I did. Research and theory continue to point to the significant challenges men face in identifying and expressing their emotions (for a review see Courtenay, 2011). These messages and the related behaviors impact athletes as well during sporting events.

For example, in the summer of 2011, I watched as Dirk Nowitzki of the Dallas Mavericks ran to the locker room just before the final whistle with his team winning the NBA Championship. He later noted that he was overwhelmed with emotions. He did not feel comfortable crying on the court in front of others.

I wrote an article in a popular men's magazine about this incident. I emphasized how far professional athletes would go to restrict the expression of their feelings because of the perceived negative consequences. True enough, some athletes and coaches are ridiculed for crying. In that same NBA season, there were a slew of jokes about how Miami Heat players cried after a string of unexpected losses.

Less Expression, More Psychological Problems

Importantly, expressing overly joyous emotions, grief, or sadness, and exhibiting those emotions in the form of touching or crying, do not fit the script for most men. Sometimes, violating these scripts leads to punishment in the form of shame, embarrassment, and social disapproval. These experiences play a key role in shaping men's attitudes and beliefs about emotions. The stronger the enforcement of these messages, the more we internalize them.

Dirk's response not only made him miss out on an important celebration and positive experience with his teammates, it also shed light on the struggles men have with emotions and the potential health risks that can ensue. Emotional restriction is linked to many health issues, including major depression, anxiety, stress, and interpersonal difficulties. For some men, their difficulty expressing emotions is so severe that they are diagnosed with a psychological disorder termed alexithymia (Berger, Levant, McMillan, Kelleher, & Sellers, 2005; Taylor,

Bagby, & Parker, 1997). When we restrict ourselves emotionally and keep our emotions bottled up, there can be significant physical consequences as well.

Athletes are Imperfect Humans Too

The reality is that men are human. Being human means that they are prone to the same mistakes and ailments that affect us all. If you are reading this chapter, you are well aware of the stories of sports figures that fell from grace over the past few years. Tiger Woods, and his infamous fall from grace, when his marriage crumbled due to his chronic infidelity. Joe Paterno, the former Penn State coach with the most wins in college football history, and a great reputation in his community, had his wins erased from the record books, his statue torn down outside the stadium he coached at for 60 years, and his image forever tarnished due to his reported silence during the Jerry Sandusky child molestation scandal. Lance Armstrong, the former seven time Tour de France champion, the most dominant cyclist ever, a cancer survivor, the champion for cancer awareness and overall inspiration, had his entire reputation and career achievements erased after he was exposed for putting together the biggest and most sophisticated doping ring ever seen in sports.

Like the rest of us, these men are not immune to errors in judgment and making bad decisions. But when tragedies befall athletes, shock is a common response. It makes sense. We consider these people to be our heroes. We put them on pedestals (or erect statues of them outside arenas).

From hero to zero.

Just like that.

While sad, these incidences provide opportunities for men to explore several key psychological themes. First, it allows them to recognize that good people who can be heroes and outstanding contributors to culture and society in one dimension can make enormous errors in other areas.

Secondly, such examples can lead to rich discussions of errors, missteps, and misjudgments in our own lives. This can then lead to follow up discussions on how to guard against such dramatic falls as well as how to recover once they do happen. In the end, these examples reinforce what we all know: everybody is human and most things are not black and white.

Changing the Message

In general, times are changing. We are seeing some examples of athletes being more expressive, and comfortable showing their emotions. We have seen how sports can exert its powerful influence on men in terms of valuing and reinforcing traditional gender roles. Yet sports can have the same power to promote values, causes, and beliefs that run counter to these pre-conceived notions.

Some recent examples: Mark Ingram cried openly after winning the Heisman Trophy in 2009. Zach Thomas had a moving, tear-flowing locker room speech after playing his last NFL game. Such examples show models for healthy emotional expression.

Therefore, if viewing sports is one way men learn about masculinity, changes in athletes' behaviors and attitudes might reflect changes in masculine norms. In recent years, there has been a marked shift by professional athletes and teams towards a more encompassing and inclusive stance when it comes to real life issues.

If you work with men who might be traditional or restrictive in their subscription and enactment of men's gender roles, sharing examples from such incidences in the news can lead to healthy, insight-generating discussions. Further, there is a growing list of men in sports using their influence to help society overcome negative stigmas toward seeking help. And this is also changing men's views in real and positive ways.

Mental Health Stigma

It was the 2010 NBA Finals; the Los Angeles Lakers had just beaten the Boston Celtics in another legendary battle of two iconic franchises. I was watching the celebrations with friends. Some of us were happy that the Lakers won; others miserable.

Suddenly, something caught our attention. Ron Artest (now Metta World Peace) thanked his psychiatrist for helping him overcome his mental health difficulties. We all looked at each other in surprise. Psychiatrist? Mental health issues? This was a rare moment in sports: a male athlete, a champion no less, admitting on the world stage that he had suffered from mental health difficulties. (Later, Metta World Peace auctioned his NBA title ring for $500,000 with the proceeds going to his charity, which works with high-risk youth on mental health issues.)

While a controversial figure, this was still significant. These types of confessions can encourage other men to seek help. Other athletes who have been vocal about their struggles with mental health issues include: former NFL Hall of Famer Terry Bradshaw, NFL player Brandon Marshall, former NHL star Stephane Richer, NBA player Delonte West, former MLB star Darryl Strawberry, and current MLB stars Joey Votto and Zack Grienke. The importance of such confessions in impacting other men's views toward mental health and seeking out help cannot be understated.

Conversely, a lot of times, athletes suffer in silence, unable to share their pain with others or get the help they need. Recently, Junior Seau, a former NFL superstar and sure to be first ballot Hall of Famer, committed suicide. In the NHL, two players, Rick Rypien and Wade Belak, committed suicide in 2011. Both suffered from depression. These tragic stories strike a chord with fans that follow them. They can also lead to discussion of how we all—even our heroes—are prone to mental health issues; that there does not need to be shame in it and that even the "toughest" men out there need help.

Homophobia in Sports

Clearly, one of the most long-standing norms of traditional masculinity that flourishes in sports is homophobia. Particularly in the realm of North American professional team sports, there have not been any active openly gay male athletes. Until now. On April 29, 2013, Jason Collins, a hard-nosed and tough NBA center who has played professionally for the past 12 years, took the very brave and courageous step out, and let the world into his personal life by becoming the first active openly gay male professional athlete in the 4 major US sports (football, baseball, basketball, and hockey). His courage was met with congratulations from fellow athletes, the LGBT community, and even the President of the United States Barack Obama. A true watershed moment. Jason's coming out and the overwhelming support his decision has received indicate an increased acceptance and tolerance of the LGBT community by athletes. This is a great start and hopefully the beginning of more athletes being able to take this brave step.

Along the same lines, late in 2009, Brendan Burke, son of Brian Burke, former President of the Toronto Maple Leafs, came out, disclosing he was gay. Shortly after this, he died in a tragic car accident. Since then, Brian Burke has walked in the Gay Pride Parade every summer. As a sports fan, this event led to many discussions about what it meant that one of the toughest, no-nonsense executives in hockey, openly and passionately supported his son's homosexuality.

In the NFL, Minnesota Vikings punter Chris Kluwe and Baltimore Ravens linebacker Brendon Ayanbadejo garnered headlines when they openly advocated for same-sex marriage in Maryland. Kluwe—who has posed for a gay magazine to increase awareness for the gay community—wrote an open letter to Maryland state delegate Emmett C. Burns Jr. after Burns Jr. contacted the Baltimore Ravens owner voicing his displeasure with Ayanbadejo's support for same-sex marriage. Kluwe's letter to the editor was hailed for its compassion and passion for the gay community.

Further, a number of professional sports leagues have endorsed anti-bullying campaigns, with a particular emphasis on having a positive impact for gay adolescents and the gay community. This includes MLB's "It Gets Better" campaign which is supported by nine MLB teams including the San Francisco Giants and Boston Red Sox. As well, the NHL has adopted the "You Can Play" movement, which sends the clear message that men of any sexual orientation are accepted in hockey.

Fatherhood

Another great example in sports is men pushing the boundaries of what it means to be a father. Drew Brees, the New Orleans Super Bowl champion quarterback, is a sponsor for Pampers. Drew Brees' involvement with Pampers communicates a key message: it is okay for men to be actively involved in childrearing. Not surprisingly, his kids were on the field when he was proudly carrying the Lombardi Trophy.

Additionally, NBA superstar Dwayne Wade recently wrote a book on fathering. This serves as another important example of a young, flashy, superstar NBA player espousing the value of being a father.

Embracing a More Balanced Perspective of Masculinity

Notably, there is a key thread that ties these stories together. Whether you are Drew Brees, Ron Artest or Brian Burke—a professional athlete or a sports executive—you can be a "tough guy" and still have compassion, tolerance, and acceptance for parts of the human experience that are stereotypically not masculine. This is a critical point that can provide opportunities for discussions for men who closely follow sports.

Further, these athletes are embodying the same messages that therapists try to impart: *what it means to be a man is much greater and multifaceted than the previous, less functional models suggest*. The message for men is to embrace a mature and authentic masculinity, one that is more nuanced, caring, genuine, vulnerable, and brave.

Sharing Affectionate Feelings with Other Men

In many ways, watching sports provides men with rare opportunities to *express affectionate behavior with other men*. And it is this reciprocal benefit that for many can lead to a greater sense of connection and closeness (Rime, 2007). In general, men avoid physical contact, including hugging and touching, in any way with other men.

However, it is amazing to observe how this social norm deteriorates among men during sporting events. How common is it to see grown men hugging and "going crazy" at the local bar after their team won the big game? Emotional bonding like this has many health benefits, yet sport is one of only a few venues that allows for this.

I remember watching the gold medal hockey game between Canada and the USA during the 2010 Winter Olympics. As the game went into overtime, anxiety filled the room. That changed suddenly when Sidney Crosby scored the "golden goal" to seal the victory for Canada. I remember jumping out of the couch and joining a big group hug with my friends. We were able to experience and express our feelings with *each other*. These feelings were honored and enhanced through this shared moment. There was no censor. Sports gave us permission to freely express our emotions.

THERAPEUTIC MOMENTS: ADDING SPORTS INTO THE THERAPIST'S "PLAY BOOK"

In many ways, men who view sports will share similar values and messages that sports promote. As has been emphasized in this chapter, too often sports reinforce aspects of traditional masculinity. For therapists working with men, we need to listen to the gender role narratives men hold and be attentive to these scripts. In doing so, we need to ask questions about the sources of those influences, and find ways to engage men in dialogues around gender role expectations.

To get there, sports can be a powerful place of entry. As many men attest, via their own personal and professional experiences, gender role messages that are intended to define men serve to restrict their progress. This central paradox can often be understood through discussions of favorite athletes and defining sports moments.

Building Therapeutic Rapport

As therapists, we can sometimes be afraid to discuss issues that may seem overly casual or superficial. Such conversations can be placed in "small talk" category. There can be strong messages to avoid this talk instead remaining focused on "therapeutic content." I would challenge this assumption. I believe this attitude can rob therapists and clients of wonderfully enriching therapeutic moments, particularly when sports is part of that conversation. We know how difficult it can be for men to engage in the process. Using sports as a vehicle for establishing rapport and facilitating dialogue can be quite important.

Those of us who work regularly with men know just how difficult it can be for many to engage in therapy. Conversations around sports can help demystify therapy and the therapeutic process. Such talks can also serve to identify problematic patterns of male socialization that may be at conflict or the source of issues they are facing in relationships and/or work.

A colleague of mine, Jonathan, recently shared a story about a particularly challenging and apprehensive male client, Tim. Jonathan was having a difficult time connecting with his client, in particular finding a promising entry point for therapeutic work. At one point during a session, Tim mentioned in passing that he was from Argentina.

Jonathan—a fellow soccer enthusiast—asked him if he was a River or Boca fan (both famous clubs in Argentina). Tim, smiling, responded, *"Boca of course. It has been a long time since I've been asked about those teams."* Jonathan later remarked how that exchange helped break the ice.

Jonathan's story is not unique. I've had similar experiences of sports allowing me to join with otherwise challenging clients. Jonathan's story demonstrates that when therapists share parts of themselves, including their love for sports, this can lead to valuable moments and a deeper, genuine connection. In these moments, clients get a sense of who we are and what they might learn from us. If done appropriately, this serves to model closeness and intimacy.

Sports as a Tool for Emotional Expression

Having dialogues with men about their experiences and observations watching sports can help facilitate the therapeutic relationship. One specific area is in the arena of emotional expression. Therapists can ask men who have restricted emotionality or negative beliefs about emotional expression to describe how they feel or think when they see emotions in sports. For example, therapists can ask clients, "What is it like to see a male professional athlete cry? What does this bring up for you?"

The idea with this type of question is to bring into awareness the reality that men can be "manly" while still in touch with their emotions. This wording may not work for everyone—but can be promising for those holding on to problematic, rigid, and restrictive ideas of gender. Athletic expressions of emotions can be highlighted in such a way that it provides our clients with the permission to feel; something many men do not think they have the right to do. With our male clients, we can work towards having them face those very emotions in the room with us.

Perspective Taking

Earlier in this chapter, I highlighted examples of athletes who have promoted social causes and enacted positive messages of masculinity. Some of our clients who watch sports may not share those beliefs and values. As therapists, being able to share stories about men who are able to overcome problematic masculinity can be powerful for our clients. In essence, such material can provide promising material for challenging men's beliefs in these areas (e.g., if Michael Irvin, a hero of yours, is supporting his openly gay brother, why not be more open to having gay friends yourself?)

These stories and examples can serve to provide a different perspective. Doing so can challenge clients to step outside of their comfort zone. Through these examinations, male clients may find that they are being irrational, self-critical, or hypocritical. These realizations may motivate them to want to view themselves and others differently.

A Fear of Failure: "If first you do not succeed..."

> I can accept failure, everyone fails at something.
> But I can't accept not trying.
>
> Michael Jordan

Many men enter therapy with a fear of failure. This fear can manifest itself in many forms, including fear of failure at work, relationships, or other life goals. Men often carry self-critical and perfectionistic ideals. When men bring this attitude into therapy, I have found that sharing parallels in sports can have a significant cognitive impact. For instance, I'll reference sports statistics to drive home the point that perfection is myth. Failure is inevitable in life and sports. For example, a "great hitter" in baseball will fail at the plate seven out of ten times (i.e., .300 batting average); a "great" shooter in basketball will hit only half of his shots; in football, quarterbacks will throw a lot of interceptions. Tournament poker players are doing fantastic if they cash in 20% of their tournaments (i.e., lose only 80% of the time).

Particularly with male clients who are sports fans, consider using these statistics. Ask about what sports athletes your clients admire and why. Show them that they too are human and imperfect. Consider discussing their off-the-field problems (that may be well documented). Doing so can help normalize "failure" and allow for conversations around your client's insecurities and vulnerabilities.

As an example, I recall working with a client who was perfectionistic about everything. He was a decent golfer, with aspirations of being a pro. I could tell that golfing was linked to his sense of self. During a session of expressing frustrations with his game, I stopped him mid-sentence, *"Has Tiger Woods ever missed a golf shot or had a bad day on the course?"* The obvious answer was yes; he's had bad games. I then asked the client, *"If Tiger Woods can have bad games and play well, why do you hold yourself to a standard the number one golfer in the world [at the time] cannot maintain himself?"* This elucidated the unrealistic nature of my client's perfectionism and self-criticism. It also led to a powerful insight: if one of the best players in the world isn't perfect, why do I have to be?

CONCLUSIONS

As has been emphasized by a range of different authors in this book, by participating in therapy with men we are asking *them* to step "outside the box." Perhaps, if we as therapists can challenge ourselves to do the same we'd have more powerful, authentic therapeutic moments.

By sharing parts of my own sports journey through a psychological lens, I hope I've shown how you can use both the positive and the potentially damaging side of sports to help men reflect on their lives. The imagery, lessons, and vocabulary of sports resonate with many men, making them more open to self-exploration. Sports for both therapists and clients can be a particularly promising (and fun) area to increase these opportunities.

Game on.

REFERENCES

Berger, J. M., Levant, R., McMillan, K. K., Kelleher, W., & Sellers, A. (2005). Impact of gender role conflict, traditional masculinity ideology, alexithymia, and age on men's attitudes toward psychological help seeking. *Psychology of Men & Masculinity, 6*, 73–78.

Courtenay, W. H. (2011). Key determinants of the health and well-being of men and boys. In W. Courtenay (Ed.), *Dying to be men: Psychosocial, environmental, and biobehavioral directions in promoting the health of men and boys* (pp. 3–41). New York: Routledge.

Englar-Carlson, M. (2006). Masculine norms and the therapy process. In M. Englar-Carlson, & M. Stevens (Eds.), *In the room with men: A casebook of therapeutic change* (pp. 13–48). Washington, DC: American Psychological Association Press.

Nutt, R. L., & Brooks, G. R. (2008). Psychology of gender. In S. D. Brown, & R. W. Lent (Eds.), *Handbook of counseling psychology* (4th ed., pp. 176–193). Hoboken, NJ: John Wiley & Sons.

O'Neil, J. M. (2008). Summarizing 25 years of research on men's gender role conflict using the Gender Role Conflict scale: New research paradigms and clinical implications. *The Counseling Psychologist, 36*(3), 358–445.

Quirk, K. (1997). *Not now, honey, I'm watching the game*. New York: Fireside.

Rime, B. (2007). Interpersonal emotion regulation. In J. J. Cross (Ed.), *The handbook of emotion regulation* (pp. 466–487). New York: The Guilford Press.

Taylor, G. J., Bagby, R. M., & Parker, J. D. A. (1997). *Disorders of affect regulation: Alexithymia in medical and psychiatric illness*. Cambridge: Cambridge University Press.

Wester, S. R. (2008). Male gender role conflict and multiculturalism: Implications for counseling psychology. *The Counseling Psychologist, 36*, 294–324.

PART II

Modalities

Working With Men Utilizing Unique Therapeutic Environments and Activities

CHAPTER 6

Innovative Group Therapy With Men

Fredric E. Rabinowitz

For over thirty years, I have been leading and writing about therapeutic men's groups (see Rabinowitz, 2005; Rabinowitz & Cochran, 2002). Having personally witnessed hundreds of men benefit from this approach, it still frustrates me to think of those who *might* have been helped but never made it to a group.

But then again, I get it. For the average guy, getting together to talk about emotions, conflicts, and struggles isn't high on the priority list. I've been there myself. There have been times in my life where I have flipped on the television, surfed the Internet, or had a few brews to avoid confronting my own issues. Being vulnerable in the presence of other men is not easy.

Most men grow up being told that a real man is tough, strong, and in control. These messages are then often confirmed in what they see in the real world, the "cool guys" who *seem* to meet these criteria. But these messages and perceptions are often an illusion. When men take the time to look inward, they often see confusion, indecision, and unmet potential.

My sense is that most men avoid introspection because it stirs up insecurities. We feel out of control, flawed, and ultimately less of a man. And here's the key point: participating in a group allows other men to realize they are not alone. They can get support in challenging how to deal with inner doubt and what it means to be a man.

Of course, in considering the above barriers, it is no wonder that men don't just appear for group therapy. It often takes something really significant to get them to choose this help-seeking option. Typically it is the loss of a long-term job, the break up or threatened break up of a primary relationship, the death of a close family member, the cascading consequences of an addiction (alcohol, drugs, gambling, sex), or the extreme discomfort of anxiety or depression (Rabinowitz & Cochran, 2002).

In these destabilizing situations, men often feel at a loss as to what to do. Questions abound and often include: *What is happening to me? Why can't I fall asleep? What happened to my optimism? Does anyone really care if I'm around? Who are my real friends? What can I do to make this sense of dread stop?* This period of self-doubt can be the opening for a man's receptivity to some kind of new strategy.

In these situations, the door is open for meaningful therapeutic interventions. But having men give access to these opportunities is challenging. Too much help too fast can push a man away. For me, the big challenge is how to introduce group as a reality for men who are hurting. And then, even if a man chooses this venue, what are the ingredients that would make him give up a night during the week to work communally on his personal issues? In this chapter, I will address these challenges.

OLD SCHOOL RECRUITING

The first men's group I did was in 1981. Given the prevailing cultural denial that men had "issues" like women, it was radical at the time. Our initial group was an outgrowth of our public showing of the documentary *Men's Lives* (Hanig & Roberts, 1974). The film was provocative in its blatant exposure of the detrimental consequences of the rigid male roles of always appearing strong, avoiding femininity, and not talking about deeper concerns. After a discussion of the film, eight men committed to meeting regularly. Our goal was to talk about how they might personally challenge the "masculine mystique" in their own lives. My co-leader and I considered this a major victory. These days, when group plans get finalized, that same appreciation and sense of accomplishment remains. It's not easy—and the foot in the door philosophy is often the hardest part.

For later groups in the pre-Internet era, my co-therapist and I wrote letters to counselors, therapists, social workers, psychologists, and psychiatrists describing the group and explicitly saying we were open to referrals for men they thought could benefit. We were willing to give any man who showed interest in sharing and interacting in the context of an all male group a "tryout." Of course, we relied on our clinical training to assess who were good fits, mainly men without serious psychopathology, who tended to be verbal, open to new experiences, and who had some familiarity with the benefits of counseling.

RECRUITING IN THE INTERNET ERA

Now, things are much different. In this time of online communication, we have successfully expanded our reach to men we would have never found in any other way. The privacy afforded a man on the Internet fits perfectly with the traditional masculine message of "finding your own solutions." By highlighting "men's issues" as the primary focus of my practice, anonymous web surfing has led to clicks on my web page, emails, and subsequent personal response to their inquiries. This has been key for our group and might be a productive way for you to get your groups off the ground.

In your own approach, consider how you might use the web to increase traffic. Tim, a recent recruit to the group told us in his interview, *"I was looking for a men's group after moving from out of state. When I Googled it, I saw the description and had a gut sense it was what I was looking for."*

ONCE HOOKED, REEL HIM IN

Once a man has contacted me either by phone or email, his next hurdle is coming in for an interview. The interview is to ensure that the group is mutually a good fit and to rule out severe pathology that might hinder the other members in the group from benefitting. We know a man is going to feel anxious in this type of meeting, so we reframe it as a "getting to know you" interaction. I usually praise him for making it in with a comment like, *"I appreciate your bravery and willingness to give up Wednesday night! Most men don't have the guts to be here."*

I typically start by asking the prospective group member to tell me his story to hear how he describes his life journey. In our interaction, I reinforce his unique experiences as a personal narrative. Rarely does a man get to hear his own story and have it framed as what Campbell (2008) calls the "hero's journey." Often I disclose relevant pieces of my own journey as a man. For example, I've briefly touched on difficult times in my own life such as my divorce, struggles being a father, issues with my dad, or how challenges I've faced connect to my emotions. I've found these self-disclosures critical. For one, they help normalize the vulnerability a potential participant may be feeling. Doing so also connects him to me as a fellow man, resulting in a felt sense of camaraderie even before the group has begun.

"MAN CAVE GROUP ROOM"

When considering your group space, be cognizant of what it communicates to a potential group member. It is an important feature of what can make the men's group intriguing. It is a masculine environment that foreshadows the experience.

Our group room is a large, cavernous space located in the basement of our office. It has two river rock walls, giving it the feel of a "man cave." On the walls are primitive art photographs and masks. There are worn African drums on the floor. In one corner of the room is a punching bag with a pile of boxing gloves nearby. On a shelf there are old tennis racquets and pieces of hose. There are no chairs, just an odd collection of large pillows used for sitting on the floor. The potential group member often eyes the room and it either speaks to him or not. Men in the group have acknowledged in retrospect that the room held some fascination, even before they had actually come to the first session.

When thinking about your own space, try to make it feel both safe and challenging. To me, it is important that the physical space reflects a male reality that does not say, "check your masculine self at the door," but rather "bring your whole being into this room."

RESISTING RESISTANCE

After making it through the gauntlet to be a group member, there is still a risk that a man may back out. In fact, we warn men in the interview that it is almost guaranteed that sometime in the first six sessions he might find a more compelling Wednesday night basketball game on TV. This means he is actually being impacted by the experience. Resistance to changing long-standing patterns is normal. Often, initial relief gives way to a feeling of incredible vulnerability.

Over the years, I have noticed that the challenging of the patterns, habits, and emotional reactions produces a "rebound" effect. The rebound is a desire to return to what is familiar. One man described his resistance as "feeling naked and not wanting anyone to see him." In your own group, anticipate the resistance after particularly deep sharing. If you know it is coming you can take steps to talk about the concept of change being difficult and scary. We tell men that when this urge to avoid group comes, show up that night and talk about what is going on inside. It is important to share the resistance, understand what it is about, and get support from the other members who have all been through equally challenging circumstances.

ANTE UP EARLY

Early group sessions are all about building trust and giving permission to step outside the normal confines of social behavior. Even though the world teaches us that we have to keep our guard up, each man needs to be able to share a piece of himself so that he can be trusted. As a leader, I give explicit permission to raise one's voice, curse, and even express anger in a physical way (e.g. striking a pillow, fist in hand, etc.). This kind of permission to be expressive often leads to a deeper level of sharing.

I expect interpersonal discomfort in early sessions. Conventional group therapy guidelines might suggest initially keeping the conversation light and non-threatening. I disagree. Rather than have the men go around the room and say something superficial, I have found it important to have each guy "ante up" a part of themselves they have rarely shared to other men. Consider this point in your work. Like teammates or soldiers, men need to have some common shared experience of emotional intensity to facilitate bonding.

A core value of coming to group is to not have the same dialogue one can have in a social setting, but rather one that is more authentic. For example, one year at the beginning of group, my co-leader and I asked each guy to talk about something he admired and disliked about his father. Another time, we asked the members to share a significant dream they had recently. We have also begun our groups by asking a man to describe an emotional state that was uncomfortable or talk about an unfulfilled goal. By taking this initial risk to delve deeper, men find more acceptance from the rest of the group than they expected. This reduces shame and increases bonding.

MALE-FRIENDLY BODY-ORIENTED INTERVENTIONS

It is important to think about what kinds of interventions will work best with men. As noted, I want to push them into uncomfortable, but not overwhelming situations. My ultimate goal is to produce a memorable and transformative experience. Including the body as a part of therapy is a great way to help a man deepen his self-understanding (Rabinowitz & Cochran, 2002).

I often introduce physical exercises early in our group sessions. Doing so allows men to become more aware of their breathing and connection between thoughts and body states. Being physical is familiar to men from childhood, but often it has been discouraged as adults. Men know it is fine to rough house with one's kids, play basketball, or lift weights, but they must contain their physical expression in most interpersonal and work settings. Men often report bottling up emotions. This can manifest as chronic muscular tension. By giving permission to be physical in the group, men can have a connective flow of thoughts, emotions, and body expression. I've seen such work to be transformational.

Len, struggling with the death of his wife in a car accident a year ago, was encouraged to hit the punching bag. After initial hesitation, he landed steady and increasingly powerful blows, pummeling the bag for more than ten minutes. His anger soon turned to tears, and by the end of the exercise, he collapsed into the arms of one of the other group members and sobbed. *"I knew I had this in me, but I couldn't get to it."* His grief needed a physical jumpstart to be accessed and worked through.

It is important to be creative in helping men express emotion. In our group, we encourage hitting the punching bag when angry, pushing against another man when frustrated, drumming to express creativity, and screaming to let out pain, anger, or deep loss. We also do relaxation exercises that involve yoga stretches to heighten awareness of the body. Mindfulness becomes a natural part of being in the group when a member stays aware of how his body is reacting to others in the group and his own internal process. This often translates to heightened awareness in everyday life encounters outside of the group.

Psychodrama and gestalt empty chair techniques are other powerful ways to encourage men to revisit past trauma, experience catharsis, and gain some insight into unfinished situations in their lives.

Roger, who came to group under the threat of divorce from his wife, gained deep insight into the origins of his sexual addiction issues from replaying disturbing scenes from his childhood. With the support of other group members, he confronted his absent father and sexually manipulative mother in ways he couldn't as an adolescent. In one scene, he expressed both his fear and rage at his mother. With the support of group members, he stood up assertively to her in the empty chair to let her know he would no longer be under her control. He later reported less anger at women and especially his partner. Roger has since left his job as an accountant and become a successful sculptor, utilizing themes from his childhood as his artistic inspiration. He now channels much of his deeper conflict into his art, and is more genuine and straightforward in how he communicates.

A RETREAT TO FACILITATE BONDING

Extended time together can be an excellent way to increase intimacy and commitment in the group. I've found it to be critical. In our own group, we have added a weekend retreat to our bonding process. Once in the fall and once in the spring, the group camps out in a rugged, national park. While the co-leaders manage aspects of the trip, the retreat is really a group project. Members divide up the duties in terms of carpooling, bringing food and camping equipment, and being responsible for some of the activities we engage in on site. For example, one group member Frank, a nurse, has always wanted to do his own eco-tourism business. As a part of the retreat, he has given us tours on native plants and geological formations. For Frank, his leadership provides an outlet for his passion. It also gives the rest of the men a more expanded view from the Frank they typically see in just the group setting.

The retreat often serves as a way to deepen the connection between members, especially those who are new to the group. It provides an extended period of time to relate on varying levels of intimacy from pitching a tent together to hiking to cooking food. While sitting around the campfire in the evening we often play drums and eventually get into deeper discussions about our relationships, fears, dreams, and goals.

THE GROUP LIST-SERVE

Given the hesitancy for men to connect interpersonally, it is important to find as many expressive outlets as possible. A few years ago, one of the tech savvy group members created a list-serve exclusively for their usage. This allowed us to communicate between group sessions and during the summer when we don't meet. Some traditional group theorists would argue that this drains from the group process. In contrast, I have found it to enhance the relevance of the live group. Often men will post significant happenings in their lives, including relationship situations and internal thoughts and feelings.

For many men, posting on their digital devices is often less threatening than saying it out loud and less labor intensive than a handwritten journal. Larry, a 40-year-old man who works in the construction business, shared a poem online about feeling lonely and misunderstood. When he came to group the following week, he initially stayed quiet until one of the members directed a comment to him about how moved he was by Larry's prose. Larry, who never went to college, was taken aback by the compliment.

The poem led to a deep discussion about male loneliness and how unacceptable it is to talk about. It also allowed Larry to talk about his regrets about not going to college. Several men resonated with Larry's difficult dilemma, which at the time was to become independent and get away from a controlling father. They also encouraged Larry not to give up on pursuing academics.

I feel that the list-serve not only serves as a good communication tool, but also provides another expressive outlet for men who often have no one to talk to in the outside world. Looking back, I think this has been so successful because it has created continuity between meetings for members that didn't exist before.

USING MEDIA TO STIMULATE MALE THEMES

I love using films and shows that depict male themes. Men resonate with the hero's journey that typically involves emotional challenge, coping with loss, aging, male friendship, and finding meaning in life. I remember crying in the movie theatre while watching *Field of Dreams*, when Ray, the main character, is able to play catch with his father, who in real life never had time for him.

We have watched movies and TV shows like *Glengary Glen Ross, Braveheart, Sideways, Shawshank Redemption, 40 Year old Virgin, A Few Good Men, About Schmidt, 12 Angry Men, Fight Club, Stand by Me, The Hangover, Men of a Certain Age,* and *Mad Men*. Using media does stimulate deeper discussion, especially when all members of the group have made the choice together.

Harold, a 38-year-old man recently divorced, identified with the dueling aspects of the main character in *Fight Club*. A part of him felt very emasculated by the demands of his ex-wife, but he also was aware that he had let that happen to him. *"I created the situation where she told me what to do. I did it and resented it, but didn't have the balls to confront her or myself directly. Instead, I found solace in bourbon and weed. I am realizing that I need to not betray myself in relationships."* I recommend that men's group leaders experiment with the use of media in the form of short clips to show in the group or assign a film for later discussion.

PRE-GROUP PREPARATION

I've learned that it is critical to "check in" with my co-leader prior to each session. We have a long-standing ritual in the hour before group. We order takeout food and discuss our own lives, each member of the group, and the group process. This often leads to an exercise, a theme, or several ideas about which way we might guide and facilitate the group that night. Over the years, several of the men have emulated the process by meeting the hour before group at a local sports bar. They have dinner, tell stories, and loosen up their defenses before coming to group. What is significant about this is that the men deepen their connections beyond the group room. Rather than compartmentalize their growth to two hours a week, they are extending and generalizing their interpersonal and communication skills.

The men who start talking at dinner often act as facilitators when they arrive and seem to be more in touch with those issues they would like to work on in the group. One man who can't attend the pre-group gathering said, "*I am jealous. You guys get an extra hour of time together. I wish I got off from work earlier so I could join you.*" The dinner group still appreciates the privacy of the group room to talk about more intimate topics. Jay, a pre-group regular, noted, "*The restaurant is fine for catching up and joking around, but really it is just a warm-up for the deeper stuff that comes out in the group, where we have the privacy to yell, cry, or hit something if we need to.*"

THE FINAL GROUP

Before we break for a three-month hiatus in the summer, we have a final potluck dinner at one of the leader's homes. Usually the first part of the dinner is very social with lots of storytelling and discussions about external events. The second half is always a deeper group reflection about how the year has gone and what each member is going to work on in the summer.

Frequently, we sit around the swimming pool, legs dangling in the water and talk about what each man has learned. It has also been a tradition to get feedback from each of the other participants on how they see the individual who is speaking. The feedback entails perceptions of progress and includes suggestions on what one might continue to work on over the summer. Greg, a third-year member, spoke about his tendency to hold back his reactions and how this year he had become more assertive in his work relationships.

The feedback he received from several of the men was that he had become one of the "initiators" in our weekly group sessions. In contrast to his passivity when he first came to group, Greg often took the lead, bringing up unfinished conversations from the previous weeks and significant events that had come up in his life during the week. When Greg asked what he might work on, another member remarked, "*You definitely are more assertive, but you still seem like you want approval from us.*" Greg smiled, "*You are so right. It has helped to have your support, but sometimes I don't fully trust myself. This is definitely something I still need to work on.*"

In initiating your own men's group think about how you might be able to create the intimacy described. It might take a different form, but really it is about a space and process that encourages the men to reflect and, importantly, be themselves.

CURATIVE FACTORS

Above, I've described many different ways of doing group with men that work. Of course, it's also critical to respect and work within pre-existing findings in the group literature. I've been particularly influenced by self-report data we've collected from our group over time that confirms the power of the interventions we use.

Our collected data suggests the following themes and exercises to be the most impactful: *shame* (i.e. a man sharing past trauma that had happened to him); *anger release* (i.e. being able to hit pillows with a tennis racquet to work on release of frustration, rage); *grief especially around father* (i.e. using guided imagery to encounter father in fantasy); *trust and interpersonal doubts* (i.e. creating a sociogram of how close and trusting a man feels to those in the group); *masculine and feminine differences* (i.e. exercises to explore what has been typically considered masculine and feminine ways of being in the world); *dark side of the personality* (i.e. feeling one's more aggressive and sinister self through towel twisting, speaking to one's shadow); *sharing honest feelings* (i.e. interpersonal confrontation) (Rabinowitz, 1998).

Based on his research about group process, Yalom (1995) has documented the key curative factors in mixed gender group therapy. These factors also seem particularly relevant to what we do in the men's group. Our research found these elements to be most important:

Catharsis (e.g. taking the therapists on in confrontation; not holding back on negative feelings I was having within session; breaking through to real emotion and letting go of control; projection and working through of my authority issues toward leader; growling and releasing my aggression; towel twisting; forced self-expression).

Interpersonal learning input (e.g. the group's feedback that I am a decent person worthy of being loved; finding out that another member would be willing to socialize with me outside of group; getting feedback about how others really see me).

Interpersonal learning output (e.g. standing my ground when confronted; trusting myself to stand firm with my feelings more often; confronting the group about "reporting"; asking for and receiving acknowledgment in the group from the other guys).

Family reenactment (e.g. realizing my current baggage is due to childhood wounding; confronting my father first in the group and then in real life; symbolically killing my mother in a psychodrama, knowing the group was a safe place to work).

Existential issues (e.g. knowing I can't take responsibility for everyone else's actions; no one can fix my life except me; realizing life is worth living fully, not half-assed; I need to make tough choices, knowing there are consequences for not choosing also).

Universality/group cohesion (e.g. realizing I'm not alone in my struggles; how similar we all feel; a willingness for us all to explore the dark side; relating and identifying with the stories of other group members; being able to help another man in the group with my sharing) (Rabinowitz, 1998).

FINAL WORDS

I hope you got a sense of the process, environment, and strategies we use in our men's group. Our model for the current men's group has shifted in innovative ways over its 25-year history. Initially, it was enough to bring the few men interested together to talk about their lives. Now, we have expanded the way we recruit men and talk to them about the group. By being accessible and genuine in our leadership, we have made the whole counseling process less threatening and more inviting. Many of our interventions are based on "doing" as a form of expression in a space that encourages men to dig deep, take emotional risks, and feel a sense of camaraderie. Over the years it has been a rewarding and refreshing process to create new ways to help men connect with themselves and each other, such as the list-serve or camping. I encourage you to experiment with your leadership style and stay open to expanding the boundaries of doing your group work with men.

REFERENCES

Campbell, J. (2008). *The hero with a thousand faces* (3rd edition). New York: Pantheon.

Hanig, J., & Roberts, W. (1974). *Men's lives.* Antioch Documentary Films.

Rabinowitz, F. E. (1998). Process analysis of a long term psychotherapy group for men. In F. E. Rabinowitz (Chair), *Researching psychotherapy with men: Findings and prospects.* Symposium conducted at the American Psychological Association, San Francisco, CA.

Rabinowitz, F. E. (2005). Group therapy with men. In G. Brooks, & G. Good (Eds.), *The new handbook of psychotherapy and counseling with men* (pp. 603–621). San Francisco, CA: Jossey-Bass.

Rabinowitz, F. E., & Cochran, S. V. (2002). *Deepening psychotherapy with men.* Washington, DC: American Psychological Association.

Yalom, I. D. (1995). *Theory and practice of group psychotherapy.* New York: Basic Books.

CHAPTER 7

Adventure Therapy With Men

David E. Scheinfeld and Sam J. Buser

Years ago, I (Sam Buser) spent a long, cold night near the ledge of a sheer precipice in Big Bend National Park. A friend and I had set up a cramped two-person tent. As the wind howled outside, we did our best to stay warm in our sleeping bags. To pass the time, we decided to reflect on our lives by recounting the events we experienced in a particular year. We shared stories of parallels in our experiences, differences in the courses of our lives, losses that we encountered, and crises we had faced. Somehow, my reticence of sharing such intimate details with another man wasn't operating at that moment, nor was his. He told me about his childhood of feeling unloved. I talked about the rejection I experienced from my mother when I chose to marry.

Later, I reflected on why it had been so much easier to talk about such personal matters in the midst of the wilderness than in my living room or therapy office. Although I had a special interest in providing psychotherapy to men, I knew that guys were more than a little reluctant to share of themselves. I wondered if other men might also be more willing to be open if we engaged as a group outside of the therapy office. This was the kernel of the idea that led me to try adventure therapy (AT) with men. Over the years I learned that other therapists, including my colleague and co-author, David Scheinfeld, were employing adventure-based activities with clients, especially men.

WHAT IS ADVENTURE THERAPY?

Adventure therapy goes beyond talk therapy by getting the client out of the chair or office. The heart of the approach engages clients through experiential activities integrated with structured or unstructured psychotherapy. Adventure therapy can be conducted in an office, but often takes place in natural settings. Any psychotherapeutic approach can be incorporated in AT. However, our own approach has been influenced by gestalt and psychodynamic theory and techniques. We will expand on this definition throughout the chapter, but for the most recent comprehensive review of AT theory, research, and practice see Gass, Gillis, and Russell (2012). In this chapter we will share our personal insights, suggestions, and short case examples to exemplify the power of AT with men's groups.

Although AT is useful for men and women, we will focus on the unique factors that make this approach effective and appealing for men. Men who are ambivalent about engaging in therapy often respond better to "out-of-office" therapeutic approaches (Brooks, 2010). We have found that AT's physicality and focus on teamwork aligns well with men's affinity toward coming together through shared physical activity. As many men can attest, guys feel a greater sense of confidence and motivation when they come together to accomplish tasks. For men, AT is often akin to the kinds of positive experiences they may have felt on camping trips, sports teams, bands, or within the military. The gestalt of AT provides an invigorating and adventurous experience, while also creating space for intrapersonal and interpersonal insight.

For many men wilderness or adventure experiences have unintentionally ended up being quite therapeutic. For example, as a former soldier, I (Sam Buser) remember the sense of camaraderie I felt as my unit faced a challenging (and sometimes dangerous) task. We had to depend on each other. Trusting your buddy was essential for success. These experiences drew me closer to other guys than any lecture in graduate school ever did. I see AT as very similar. I (David Scheinfeld) first discovered the therapeutic potential of wilderness adventure as an adolescent canoeing with my father in the Boundary Waters, Minnesota. The tranquility intermixed with physical challenge created a new opportunity for self-reflection and connection that was difficult to obtain in other settings. I returned from those outings with new insights, confidence, and a passion for personal growth. Most importantly, I felt closer to my father and vice versa.

Adventure therapy can be modified to work with almost any kind of client, and it does not require that the participants be in tip-top shape. We have taken men on AT retreats that had diabetes, had heart conditions, were older than 60 years of age, were obese, and had severe mental illness. As necessary, we changed the activities so that the members could still participate. For example, we allowed a man with a heart condition to drive himself to a destination, while the other men completed a solo cross-country hike to that same place. While he missed out on the hike, he participated with the other men in discussing the task each man was to reflect on during the experience, "What does it mean to be truly alone?"

Over time we've come to utilize two general methods for facilitating AT. In the first approach, we let the clients move through the adventure experience (e.g., climbing a peak) with little to no facilitation, letting their group experience naturally provide impetus for therapeutic insight. Often we will facilitate a process session after the experience to help them take further meaning from their experience. In the second approach we implement structured therapy activities that incorporate the adventure activity or the wilderness environment. Gass, Gillis, and Russell (2012) respectively refer to the former as *The Mountains Speak for Themselves* and the latter as *The Therapist Works with the Mountain*. On retreats we often use both approaches. The next two sections will provide you case examples of how these two methods operate with men's groups.

THE MOUNTAINS SPEAK FOR THEMSELVES: JOHN'S STORY

John, a 45-year-old male military veteran with major depression, went to see a therapist twice, but stopped going because he didn't see how only talking about his problems would help. John was often irritable and reported "feeling numb." He struggled to get out of the house. His therapist suggested he try a men's wilderness retreat that I (David Scheinfeld) was conducting. John had vivid memories of enjoying time in the north woods as a young man canoeing, exploring, and hiking. He figured, "Why not give this wilderness retreat a shot?" After two days on the retreat, John began to feel comfortable opening up to the other men. He found it reassuring when he heard several other men talk about their own struggles with depression. In fact, he noted that some of the most helpful realizations occurred when he spontaneously talked with other group members while they were hiking, cooking, and hanging around camp.

While John and the group were ascending a peak, I noticed that he began to feel overwhelmed by emotion. He told me later that the climbing reminded him of when he was an active young man enjoying his life. He hadn't felt enjoyment or a sense of purpose in a long time. He stopped in his footsteps and broke down crying as he realized how depression had gripped his life. All the men came over to console him. We held an informal process group on the side of the mountain. With the group circled ready to listen to John, he began to talk about his frustrations and sadness. Several other group members acknowledged that until then they had found it hard to relate to John, because he seemed withdrawn and angry. The guys expressed their appreciation for John's increased candor and openness. We all immediately felt closer to him. He later told me he felt like a heavy weight had been lifted from inside. John still talks about that moment on the mountain as a turning point for him.

At the summit John felt a rush of rejuvenated energy, a new part of him seemed to come alive as he yelled "ooh-rah!" He proceeded to hug all the other men in the group. He seemed to have a bitter-sweet moment as he began to experience happy and sad emotions. Later, he said, "at least I am feeling again."

In our experience men like John who are more resistant to therapy, often relate better with the *Mountains Speak for Themselves* approach because it is less overt and structured. As we see from John's AT experience, he was therapeutically engaged through a combination of the adventure activities and unstructured group therapy processes. We find this multidimensional approach particularly effective with men, because we are not just talking. We are commensurately engaging them on cognitive, emotional, interpersonal, and behavioral levels. This approach also provides more autonomy for the men to make meaning of their therapeutic experiences, which often better aligns with their preferred learning styles.

THE THERAPIST WORKS WITH THE MOUNTAIN: USING STRUCTURED ACTIVITY

To shed light on the more structured, *The Therapist Works with the Mountain* approach, we will share some examples of our structured activities.

Use of wilderness as metaphor: Talking about feelings or discussing issues can be difficult, foreign, or threatening for men. This is especially true for those men who are unfamiliar or uncomfortable with therapy. Therefore, we utilize wilderness areas and activities that elicit metaphor and encourage self-introspection to get the men in touch with their emotions and inner-selves.

On one AT trip the men were taken to an abandoned ranch house in the middle of a desolate desert valley. Nearby was a broken down fence surrounding a small cemetery, no doubt holding the remains of at least a few of the long-gone and forgotten people who had lived in that place. The participants were asked to write their own obituaries and to gather an item to place on their own graves.

The group then held funeral services for each man. One by one, the men read their eulogies, reviewing what had been most important in their lives and describing the family members who had survived them. Virtually every man cried as he completed his turn. Being next to the graveyard in the vast desert brought a sobering genuineness to the experience; they were alone in the wilderness confronted with death.

One man, Mark, had been notable throughout the weekend for his bravado. He seemed to want to "one up" any man's story with one of his own, with him as the tragic figure at the center of the anecdote. When he read his obituary he revealed a different side. He cried as he described himself as being thought of by his family as a loving and devoted husband and father characterized by his humility. In reality, he had been a domineering and sometimes abusive figure with his wife and children. His obituary, as he later acknowledged to the group, was aspirational, describing how he wanted to be remembered, not how he truly was acting. Afterwards, Mark and the other participants were asked how they might want to live differently since they now had a "second chance."

While this exercise promoted the expression of emotion, it also gave promise of renewal and opportunity. We believe that these men may not have experienced this level of internal intimacy without being separated from home, in the wilderness, next to an old gravesite.

Promoting emotional expression: One of the most common reasons people seek therapy is to help them deal with loss. Sometimes it is not the loss of a person or a material possession, but other factors that are more difficult to identify (e.g., loss of freedom, independence, youth, etc.). Since men often find it difficult to access, label, and express their emotions, they may be more restricted in their abilities to identify and cope with a range of different losses. We frequently see men who have sustained a major loss such as the death of a child or the end of a marriage, yet they seem unable to connect with the emotions that typically accompany such events.

In the AT context men may more readily access and express their emotions. Indeed, in our experience it is common for men to cry during an AT retreat, and exceptional when they do not. These tears are often associated with unfinished grief about loss. Therefore, on retreats we always include at least one activity that helps men examine their losses.

Just before the sun began to set the men were led to an out of the way narrow canyon. The men all scrambled onto an enormous boulder that was lying in the middle of a dry streambed. The boulder was surrounded by a stand of charred, dead trees seemingly standing sentinel over the spot. The facilitator began by noting that all of us tend to live our lives without sufficient awareness of what is most precious to us. The men were asked to make a list of the ten most important things in their lives: people, abilities, relationships, etc.

Afterwards, the facilitator noted that, unfortunately, we do not get to retain all that is important to us. Life inevitably has its losses. Therefore, the participants had to pick three items on their list that they will have to give up and to share that decision with the group. While this discussion evoked a good deal of sadness, some participants anticipated that this might be part of the experience, thus they "hedged their bets" by including some items on their list that were not vitally important to them. The facilitator then added that in life we often don't get to choose what we are willing to give up and what we get to retain. So that in addition to the three things they had chosen to give up, they also had lost items number 2, 3, 5, & 7 on their lists. This evoked great emotion from virtually every member of the group, and tears flowed so freely that tiny rivulets flowed down the pockmarked boulder. As a closing to the exercise the men were reminded that the challenge is not to prevent all loss, but to live life with the awareness that nothing is permanent. Following the exercise, the men returned in silence to the campsite.

Of course, this exercise would probably not be appropriate for persons who suffer from chronic or acute depression, but it could be "softened" in such instances. Dealing with loss remains an important goal for almost any therapeutic endeavor. We have also often employed the use of writing a letter to a loved one as an exercise to deal with loss. These letters have sometimes taken the form of a "Dear John" note to the participant. At other times they have been a goodbye letter from the participant to a third party.

QUALITATIVE RESEARCH FINDINGS

These case examples corroborate findings in our recent qualitative study on AT with men's groups (Scheinfeld, Rochlen, & Buser, 2011). Similar to John's case example, we found that men's interest in participating in a therapy experience immediately peaked when they heard there would also be opportunities for adventure. They reported that the physical separation from home helped them gain clarity and focus more on personal issues. We found that a deep sense of trust rapidly emerged among the group members because of the interdependence, support, and teamwork required to live in the wilderness and communally engage in the adventure activities. One of the more profound realizations we had is that the combination of shared adventure activities complemented by structured group therapy sessions provided more time and alternative outlets for the men to express themselves emotionally and interpersonally. For men, this is especially important, because it is often hard for us to create a space where we feel safe to open up and be vulnerable.

THE AT PROCESS: BRINGING IT ALL TOGETHER

Let's take a closer look at how we create the therapeutic process for the *Mountains Speak for Themselves* and *The Therapist Works with the Mountain* approaches. It is important to remember that you can merge elements from both approaches.

Mountains Speak for Themselves: We choose adventure activities (e.g., team initiative, backpacking, etc.) that engage men with both their environment and one another. During the adventure activities we find moments for unstructured therapeutic process sessions after they undergo a noteworthy experience. We encourage men to initiate these unstructured process groups whenever something significant surfaces. Alternatively, if they find themselves sharing notable reflections as a dyad while hiking or cooking etc., we encourage them to bring those themes up with the group when they deem appropriate. We find that men become vulnerable more readily when we create an environment that encourages them to simply go with the experience. Then in an informal and unstructured manner, share the insight from their experience.

Additionally, the small group setting coupled with interactive adventure activities creates a unique social microcosm; the small group format allows for interpersonal tendencies to surface, while also leaving room for them to practice new ways of relating with themselves and others. As a result, we (therapists and the group members) are afforded unique perspectives that shed light on the men's interpersonal styles and coping strategies. Ultimately, one on one or as a group, we continually help the men make connections between behaviors and emotions exhibited during the AT experience and those they present in their family and community environments. This approach allows experiences to unfold in the AT context, with an unstructured process session initiated by therapist or client post-experience.

Nature provides an important separation from the urban environment that is worth noting. We have found that nature itself is often therapeutic. Time and time again we hear the guys talk about the wilderness as a place that provides aspects of tranquility, contemplation, and greater intra- and interpersonal awareness. We find that the wilderness often provides a restorative function through lowering clients' stress level. To further promote connection with the environment, we ask clients to leave behind any and all technology. This lack of technology in a natural setting decreases distractions that men often use as unhealthy coping strategies (e.g., tuning out to an iPod or video game). In turn, they are given greater opportunity for self-reflection and rest for the mind. We strongly encourage AT retreats be held in remote wilderness areas to reduce distraction and bring greater focus to the intra- and interpersonal therapeutic process.

The Therapist Works with the Mountain: Using this approach, we preplan structured theme-based activities (e.g., anger management exercises) during the AT retreats. We encourage clients to utilize and practice the insights and new skills learned from the themed activities during the AT retreat. For men, this is a unique opportunity to have an extended period where they can safely experiment with new ways of relating. Additionally, as the trip unfolds, we incorporate structured reflective activities (e.g., journaling) to help the men think more deeply about their behavior and emotions during the AT retreat. These are critical because they help the men integrate and remember what they experienced, reflected upon, and learned from the adventure activities and the group setting.

IDEAS FOR INCORPORATING ADVENTURE AND THERAPY

Importantly, if it is not possible to get out into the remote wilderness, you can still provide powerful adventure-based therapeutic initiatives. Every therapist has at least a few favorite activities that might be employed in AT. We ourselves have borrowed ideas from our own experiences in outdoor education, experiential education, scouting, sports, and the military. You should recognize that the same exercise performed outdoors or around a campfire may have a very different impact than it does in your office.

Rather than using a standard set of experiences on each AT retreat, we prefer to design new exercises and activities for each occasion. These experiences are developed based on the particular psychological issues of the participants.

In addition, since we utilize wilderness areas for our AT offerings, we use the actual geography of the area to accentuate or highlight aspects of the activities. Our exercises commonly require the completion of a task, perhaps physical, sometimes mental. They are planned in advance with specific guidance for what the participants are to do. At the same time, though, the activities are ambiguous about how the participants might respond. Think of them like Rorschach cards; the stimuli are planned in advance, but each person has a unique response to them.

Camping and hiking have long been passions of ours, and thus we have sought to combine them with our therapeutic work. But in considering your own approach, be expansive and creative in incorporating recreational interests and hobbies into therapeutic venues. Traditional AT activities include: team building initiatives, ropes courses, rock climbing, mountaineering, backpacking, hiking, canoeing, kayaking, sailing, white water rafting, snowshoeing, skiing, and winter camping. Additional examples of some potential AT activities include: group initiatives in an office or park, walking or sitting with clients in a natural setting, long-distance bike rides, martial arts, horseback riding, weightlifting, and team sports.

The primary components when considering an experiential activity for therapeutic purposes are:

- Is it an activity you enjoy? You want to have a reasonably good comfort level with the activity before trying to get others to do it.
- Can you make it safe for participants? You will need to take precautions to make sure the activity can be done safely...this may rule out hang gliding.
- Can your intended audience participate adequately? For example, if the activity requires physical stamina, are your participants healthy enough to perform the activity?
- Will the activity lend itself to reflection and insight? Almost any activity can be therapeutic if the therapist adequately processes the experience with the clients.
- Does the activity take the client outside of their normal experience and expectations? The best learning occurs when clients are no longer in their comfort zone. They are then less able to respond with their standard defenses and are more open to incorporating new information into their understanding.
- Will the activity or the wilderness setting lend itself to metaphor? The learning by doing/experiencing component of AT provides fertile ground for integration of metaphor to promote insight. Metaphor often allows for a deeper emotional and personal connection to the activity (see http://kinestheticmetaphors.com).

THE NUTS AND BOLTS OF AT

We now want to turn to the nuts and bolts of how to plan and implement AT as part of your practice. We will describe general issues to consider as well as some exemplars of particular things to remember.

Experience of the facilitators: Ideally, the facilitators are reasonably well-skilled at the activities that will be undertaken. You don't have to be a world-class expert, but you have to at least be able to show others how to accomplish the task. If you are only middling in ability at the activity, you might consider collaborating with an expert. For example, you might hire a fishing guide to demonstrate tying fly lures while you as the therapist focus on talking about the prerequisite skills of patience in fly fishing.

Recruitment of participants: When you first offer an AT retreat, you need a large pool of potential participants. Start with activities that will be successful even if you have a small group. Consider the minimal number you need to be successful in the activity and in making the logistics work.

Interactions between leaders and participants: In AT you may spend extended periods of time with your clients. Essentially you are a therapist and a participant that continues to maintain therapeutic boundaries. You may share in physical tasks, prepare meals, or even take turns going to the bathroom. Although this may seem initially awkward, our experience is that the men often develop a greater sense of trust in us as they see us as more real, down-to-earth, and like them. Before the event explain to your clients how your role will be different.

Confidentiality: AT abides by similar confidentiality norms and safeguards as group therapy. We explain limits and guidelines regarding confidentiality to potential attendees as we would with any client, but we stress ways that participation may pose particular challenges. For example, the nature of AT activities often requires extended and more intimate contact with fellow participants.

Equipment needed: Usually to provide AT experiences to your clients you will need some specialized equipment as well as experience in using that equipment. You don't want to try rappelling with your men if you don't know how to tie a knot! Depending on the activity, the participants might be asked to provide equipment themselves. For men who cannot afford or do not want to buy equipment, we provide basic gear (e.g., tents and backpacks). In addition, as facilitators we plan the logistics and bring all equipment needed for the group as a whole such as cooking gear and lighting. You won't have everything figured out the first time you try such an activity. You have to be willing to be flexible, improvise, and learn—wonderful examples for your participants to witness. Also, making mistakes (preferably small ones) can be rich opportunities to model how to handle mistakes and disappointments.

Safety/liability: If you are engaging in activities in which participants might be injured you must consider medical, safety, and liability concerns. As a facilitator, it is imperative to be trained in at least basic first aid and cardiopulmonary resuscitation (CPR). If you are leading trips into the wilderness we strongly recommend that you acquire specialized training in Wilderness First Responder first aid (a basic internet search will highlight a variety of companies that offer this certification).

To reduce your liability we recommend that you consult with an attorney regarding consent waivers and extended liability insurance. Most problems can be prevented with good planning. Make it your business to know about the physical fitness and limitations of potential participants. Have participants complete a form that describes medical issues and diagnoses, medications that they are taking, allergies to consider, physical limitations, and dietary restrictions. If you are unsure that a person can safely participate in the activity, either decline to include them or modify the activity if possible.

Emotional issues: In addition to the physical risks of AT, you should not underestimate the potential emotional effects of these events. Frequently, there is more expression of emotions (sadness, shame, anger, and fear) than will be seen in the therapy office. You must be prepared to guide participants in constructive ways of expressing and experiencing these emotions, particularly if they emerge suddenly or unexpectedly. Emotions stirred up by an AT experience often become the topic of meetings with participants subsequent to the AT event. If you don't have ongoing meetings with the participant members, create some sort of follow-up mechanism (phone calls, emails, etc.) to check on how the participants fared afterwards.

Schedule: AT requires a great deal of work prior to the event. In order to get adequate participation, you must set the date for the event in advance, taking into consideration such factors as weather and holiday schedules. For example, in Texas where we reside, it is simply too hot in the summers to try such activities as desert hiking. As a facilitator you have to create a schedule of activities that is reasonable given the abilities of your participants while at the same time allowing you sufficient programming time to accomplish your therapeutic objectives.

CONCLUSION

AT utilizes familiar elements of group therapy in a novel setting to enhance the impact of psychotherapeutic experiences. It is especially appealing to men because of their socialization to challenge themselves both physically and mentally. This approach feels less like therapy to men while at the same time enhancing their willingness to be self-disclosing and emotional, key features of the therapeutic experience. True enough, this approach is more demanding of the therapist, but it can be incredibly rewarding and powerful for everyone. To be effective, AT must be much more than a series of experiential activities. The most important aspect of AT is the psychological processing of the experiential activities. The facilitators must give adequate time for processing the experience, post-activity.

AT is not a panacea or a replacement for other therapeutic endeavors. Yet we have consistently found that it does accelerate the psychological learning of participants in a way that is both unique and less threatening.

REFERENCES

Brooks, G. R. (2010). *Beyond the crisis of masculinity: A transtheoretical model for male-friendly therapy.* Washington, DC: American Psychological Association.

Gass, M. A., Gillis, H. L., & Russell, K. C. (2012). *Adventure therapy: Theory, research, and practice.* New York, NY: Routledge Publishing.

Scheinfeld, D. E., Rochlen, A. B., & Buser, S. J. (2011). Adventure therapy: A supplementary group therapy approach for men. *Psychology of Men and Masculinity, 12*, 188–194.

CHAPTER 8

Creating Experiential Weekend Retreats for Men

Matt Englar-Carlson and Mark A. Stevens

Whether it is in a bar, at a bowling alley, on a playing field, in front of a TV, at a coffee shop or around a pool table, historically men have found traditional gathering spots to share stories and connect. Often these traditional meeting spots provide an important type of ritual for men where they can unpack some of their stress about work and family, unwind, laugh, and blow off steam. Many traditional gathering spots may also contribute to reinforcing cut stereotypes of men and masculinity and be unfulfilling in terms of deeper personal connections. Sure, it is fun to hang out with other guys drinking beer and watching football, but in other ways traditional male gathering rituals allow a very narrow sort of interaction. In a sense, these gatherings only privilege one way of men connecting, but we believe that many men are fully capable and desire opportunities to deepen their relationships with other men and oneself. There is nowhere in the "Hangout with the Guys" manual that allows times to deeply explore topics like relationship concerns and divorce, depression, loneliness, shame, fears about death and multiple losses, sexual dysfunction, not having friends, and getting old. Also, traditional men's gathering places are pretty hetero-normative, so there is little room for gay and bisexual men to be fully present. We believe that men want to deeply connect with each other and experience the risks, fears, and thrills of living authentically in the moment with other men. This chapter is about creating those types of alternative gathering spaces for men where relationships and experiential learning are valued.

Over the past six years we have been creating and facilitating what could be considered an "outside of the masculinity box" gathering spot. Our gathering spot in Big Sur, California at the Esalen Institute has lots of similar dynamics to being around a TV, watching a sporting event, and feeling the energy of guys being in the room together. There is laughter, teasing, complaining, joking, and eating and, of course, something a bit different than typical male gathering spots. There is a humanistic touch to this gathering spot. There is both strength and vulnerability, and a willingness to engage without the typical armor of homophobia and competition. We attract all types of men, but over the years many participants themselves are in the helping professions (i.e., psychologists, counselors, nurses), so there is an aspect of our group on "helping the men that help others." In this chapter we share the stories, the setting, and the strategies that contribute to making this "same time next year" men's gathering a unique and healing opportunity for those that attend. Further we highlight the transformational snapshots of men coming together in an intimate and powerful weekend retreat. Our goal is to also stretch the reader into considering the wealth of nurturing, caring, and connection a group of men can create when given the invitation to push beyond their own perceived boundaries. While exploring the dynamics of our group, this chapter will offer ideas about ways the reader can create their own experiential weekend retreats for men.

THE IMPORTANCE OF THE SETTING

Weekend retreats need to have an attractive setting where guys want to come. It is hard for many men to get a weekend away from home due to work and family responsibilities and demands. Further, for many men, it is hard to ask for time apart to take time for oneself. It may feel self-indulgent or selfish in light of other strains and pressures from work and family. It helps to have a place that feels special and unique, as it strengthens the rationale for attending and getting out of town.

Creating a destination weekend event for men requires a fair amount of work and planning. There are many locations that can work: campsites, retreat centers, and resorts. We believe a key component is finding a spot that accentuates and reinforces the goals of the weekend. Having a communal space to eat, hang out, and talk without other competing distractions is useful. Ideally, participants should be unplugged from their smart phones and actually spend time with each other.

The location for our men's retreats is pretty special. You cannot be a student of humanistic and transpersonal psychology without having some reference back to Esalen Institute in Big Sur, California. Set along the cliffs above the Pacific Ocean, Esalen conjures up images of wonder, splendor, beauty, freedom, and endless possibility. Matt first came here in 1989 as an undergraduate at the University of California at Santa Cruz on a late night bus excursion offered by the Recreation Department that would drop students off at 2am to soak in the hot baths and return to campus by morning classes. At the time, those trips felt like an outer body experience of wonder that he still has a hard time grasping.

Mark first came to Esalen in 1978, sneaking into the baths overlooking the ocean, never imagining that he would one day become a workshop leader with Matt in this beautiful spot.

ENVISIONING A SPACE FOR MEN TO DEEPLY CONNECT

Matt and Mark have played together, written together, shared meals with extended family, swapped boyhood stories, taken many bike rides, and have developed a deep and caring friendship. On a bike ride, Matt mentioned to Mark of an opportunity and a desire on the part of Esalen Institute to offer some programming aimed at men. We had just finished editing a book on psychotherapy with men, which gave us some "credibility." With a sense of this being a long shot, Mark and Matt talked about a vision for a weekend men's retreat at Esalen. We knew right away we wanted to propose something that would be experiential, creative, engaging, and healing for men.

From the onset, we wanted something on the smaller and more intimate side, and thus limited the workshop to 15 participants. It is important at this point to know a little more about us. We are pretty "touchy, feely" guys and work to create deep, emotionally connected relationships—and we wanted to offer an experience that would allow men to form deep connections albeit in a short period of time.

We landed on the theme of "Men as Nurturers." We knew that men had lots of personal stories that often went unspoken. We wanted to create an experience for men to share these unspoken stories about being a nurturing man, and we wanted them to develop new skills and ideas about how to further their nurturing side. Juxtaposed on this objective was the desire for the men to feel a connection with the other men in the group, thus allowing and giving permission *in vivo* for the participants to give and receive nurturing. We knew from our academic and clinical work that many men feel isolated and deeply desire a safe space to share their inner world lives with other men in a full and free manner. So, sharing untold stories and connecting in "outside the masculinity box" type of ways became our paradigm and desired outcome for our future and yearly workshops.

In planning your own group, ask yourself what types of connections do you want to promote? What themes or goals do you have for the weekend? How do you and your co-leader embody those themes and model them for others?

THE MEN AND HOW THEY GET TO US

Getting men to sign up for a weekend experiential retreat is not easy. You will have your work cut out for you. A men's weekend is not like the *Field of Dreams*—offer it and they will come. In fact, truth be told, we offered our retreat the first year and nobody came. That experience taught us to offer the retreat and then work your butt off to get men to take the risk and make the time to focus on their own needs.

So who would want to come to spend a men's weekend at a place like Esalen? A natural, beautiful, outdoor setting calls for men to slow down, self-nurture, eat healthy, self-reflect, and be vulnerable. While you might envision hippies or counterculture hanger-ons, we have had the full range of men as participants. We initially targeted men in the helping professions as we thought they would find this group and the theme attractive. This turned out to be crucial for our experiential retreat. Understandably, that includes many psychologists, but also nurses, entrepreneurs, accountants, graduate students, dancers, business leaders, bankers, florists, business consultants, and men who are retired. These men have been some of our own friends, and friends of the group members. The men who have returned each year have gotten close to each other and maintain contact throughout the year. All of these factors create a group with many layers of connections and relationships. The take home message here is: be strategic in recruiting people. If you do not get enough participants the group does not happen. Take the time to target participants, make personal invites for people to come, and tell them to bring their friends.

Without a doubt, the men who are interested in a weekend experience represent a certain segment of the population. We are not likely to attract too many culturally conservative *National Rifle Association* (NRA)-loving men. Rather many of our participants are growth-retreat veterans. We think a big draw for many men open to personal growth is the fact that men want to be around other men. A returning member explained this, "In addition to all of the important advantages of being in a group, going through this experience in the company of men is invaluable for me… These are men I admire. Men willing to tread where the real scary stuff lies."

Other men had their wives read about the workshop, and they are the ones that signed them up. A few of the men in our workshops arrived planning to attend a different workshop, but they ended up having dinner with us or some of the returning men at the meal before the opening session. That meal or conversation itself was transformative, and they decided to join our group. Another participant recalled, "I ended up talking to these guys at dinner, and they were so excited to be together. The more I sat there, I realized this was exactly what I needed in my life, so I decided to join them for the weekend."

Many of the participants in our early workshops were men recruited by us or by other returning group members. Most of the group members had such a powerful experience; you could hear it in their voices as they spoke. They returned home and talked about the experience with their male friends. Over time it seems as if the group has sold itself and the percentage of returning group members has continued to be high.

Recruiting participants is a process that takes foresight. Consider trying to offer a men's group in places where other types of workshops/retreats exist, but none have specifically been targeted for men—put your line in the river and see what happens. Don't be afraid to talk up the group with influential people (wives, partners, adult children) who can persuade men to come. Finally, *never* underestimate that men want to come, rather *acknowledge* that what makes it hard is to admit wanting to come and then following through.

WORKSHOP THEMES

We loosely organize each workshop around a theme—the theme becomes the starting point and we develop the theme over the weekend. A theme also provides a portal or lens for men to explore some of the current concerns and struggles in their lives and meaningful relationships. We began with an initial theme of offering a men's group that examined men as helpers. From that workshop other ideas began to flow from us and from workshop participants. As we have become more secure with our participants and know that the group will run each year, we have become bolder in our ideas. The key is to create a theme that will appeal to the population you are planning to attract. Below we briefly review past themes by presenting some of the text from our advertising of each workshop (that is why it is presented in future tense).

Exploring the Journey of Men in the Helping Professions: An Experiential Workshop (2008, 2009). This workshop will explore the personal and professional journey as a man (father, son, mentor, friend) and as a helping professional (therapist, counselor, teacher, bodyworker). How do we support others, and how do we get the support we need? Through storytelling and creative examination of our clinical work, participants will have the opportunity to find connections between their own gender-role socialization journey and their work as a nurturing man. This course will examine experiences of when it is difficult to be a man in a helping professional role.

Re-discovering Boyhood Passion (2010). Many men experience a longing to feel closer to other men in a setting that allows them to share common experiences and stories. This workshop is focused on participants' exploration of how they find meaning in the dreams, desires, and activities in their lives that cultivate and maintain passion. Through storytelling, reflection, and creative examination of our own lives, participants will have the opportunity to remember their passions of boyhood and explore how those passions have been kept alive and/or lost. Participants will have the opportunity to find connections between their own journey from boyhood into manhood and how it has influenced their current lives, hopes, and dreams.

Exploring Male Friendships (2011). The stories of male friendships are quite powerful and profound, yet often not fully examined. This workshop is designed for male participants to bring to life their memories and experiences of their friendships with other men. Stories of friendships of the past and present, friendships lost, and friendships sustained will find their way into the room and be examined for the meaning and ways these friendships have shaped the participants' lives. Participants will have the opportunity through a variety of creative means to share friendship stories filled with feelings and experiences of joy, wonder, competition, homophobia, pain, gratitude, rejection, loss, curiosity, and loyalty.

Men and Creativity (2012). The energy of masculine creativity can be healing and rewarding. We invite you to come to Esalen and join with a group of other men to (re) discover or tap into your life-long desires to express your creative self. Allow your creative energy to emerge. Come listen in a non-judgmental way to your inhibitions that may be holding your creative self from blossoming. Come feel the support of other men as they encourage you to express your creative self. Whether you come by yourself or with a friend, this workshop will balance thoughtful reflection and risk-taking with humor, fun, and an enthusiasm for deepening the relationships of the participants in the group.

Learning to Live with Our Changing Bodies (2013). As we men age, our physical achievements, limitations, and future potential can become core themes of our daily lives and personal narrative. Over time, injury and illness, and fitness and wellness, influence how a man experiences his masculinity and self-worth. Many men report having experienced only internal conversations about their relationship with their bodies. Making those internal conversations more public can be enlightening and enriching. What type of relationship did we have with our bodies as we were growing up? Were we tall enough, athletic enough, muscular enough, and handsome enough? How did we feel about other people's perceptions of our bodies and physical features? How did those self-perceptions and external perceptions impact our ways of being in the world? How have we learned to cope with the physical changes and limitations of our bodies? A rare conversation among men, this workshop focuses on examining men's bodies over time. Feel free to bring any photos or other artifacts that speak to the story of you and your body.

IF YOU WERE A FLY ON THE WALL: PROCESS AND CONTENT OF THE WORKSHOP

We wanted to give a clear idea of how each weekend is structured. You can create your own, but it is often helpful to have a template. Our group's time runs from late afternoon on Friday until after lunch on Sunday. During this time we have 10 hours of time set aside for the group, and the rest of the time is open (though many group members spend time together). We want to walk you through a typical weekend in our group and share some experiences and exercises.

Friday night: you say hello. As previously mentioned, some men in our workshops know each other through long-term friendships and working relationships and others know no one. As facilitators we to try to "even the playing field" by making the relationships existing in the room transparent. Transparency offers a message to the group, "we are here to play fair." This is often not the expectation men have when coming together in a group of other men, whether that is at work, on the court, or in the boardroom. Some of the usual ways in which facilitators start a group would be recognized. We go over ground rules, ask for additional ground rules, and preview the weekend. We all sit in a circle on the floor with pillows and back chairs. The space between participants is usually a little closer than in most settings where men come to gather (except in a crowded bar with parallel drinking going on).

We are creative with our introduction transitions. A mainstay exercise has been a 20–30 minute guided imagery that could be viewed as an induction to the setting, the group itself, and the weekend as a whole. We help the men feel and picture the transition from the place they are leaving (i.e., the world of work, deadlines, cell phones, and endless responsibility, etc.) to the peaceful and reflective space they are entering. The windows are open, and the crashing waves of the Pacific Ocean become the live music in the background. The men are grounded with their attention on their breathing and being in the present moment. Messages of congratulations are offered for the choice, risk, and sacrifice made to come to this workshop. Hopes, dreams, and reservations about the weekend are encouraged to be listened to and felt. Then the men share their experience of the exercise. Permission for self-care and leaving behind a hyper-responsible life are often the themes that emerge and motivation for coming to the workshop. Fears or a feeling of hesitation of being with other men are commonly voiced and shared. Ice has been broken, and something unique is unfolding.

We also developed another getting started ritual. On a very large piece of newsprint, we have the title of the workshop and ask men to associate what that title means to them. It is a creative and free-flowing process, and an easy way for everyone to get involved. This exercise is often filled with smiles, nods, and, sometimes, intense laughter. We keep the newsprint in a very visible place to be seen throughout the weekend. We end the first evening sharing one or two words that describe their mood, feeling, or state of mind. Words such as: anticipation, energized, connected, hesitant, optimistic, glad, surprised, inspired, and hopeful are examples of what the men say after the first evening together.

Saturday: the full monty. We have two big blocks of time to work with the group on Saturday. By now, many of the men have been to the hot springs baths together during the previous evening, shared a meal or two and bonded outside of the "official" workshop time. Saturday is what we call the working day. As we open the morning as a group, we have found a nice ritual to say hello and reconnect in our official space. We check in with one another over 1–2 minutes by saying hello only with our eyes. No words, but usually there are inviting smiles and grins. Men talk about this experience as being difficult, yet feeling very intimate and maybe a little embarrassing (perhaps just suppressed joy).

Before meeting, we, the leaders, have created and planned a variety of experiential exercises. We offer the participants the opportunity to explore their own lived experiences of the theme of the workshop within the growing relationships in the group. That being said, we are also flexible and allow the energy of the group to guide us. For these exercises we often try to use the beauty of the outdoor setting to break out in dyads or small groups to complete some task. Participants can sit in the garden, go to the beach, sit in the trees, and engage in small group exercises. Words, bodies, music, nature, writing, drawing, and games are utilized to help enhance the opportunities for connections and insight. After a set period of time we all come back as a large group to process the activity.

At the workshop on Men Re-discovering Boyhood Passions, you could hear from a distance "Olly, Olly Oxen Free" as a group of the men decided to play hide and seek. At the Men and Creativity workshop, the group, one by one, made a noise and soon the whole group became a symphony of sound. At the Men and Male Friendship workshop, the participants wrote letters to male friends and read them out loud. At the Men in the Helping Professions workshop, one participant related how he was such a caregiver all his life that he did not care enough for himself. This became a more emotional and intense experience for him, and then group encouraged him to make a public declaration. Before we knew it, he was hanging off the balcony screaming down to the Pacific, "Hey Hot Tubs, I have been a fucking nurturer all my life and I am taking care of me now!" At the last workshop on Men and Creativity, the group was directed to notice where they were feeling blocked in their bodies. We translated these blockages into parallels with personal problem solving. Using a group psychodrama / gestalt approach, the members helped each person unlock their creative problem solving potential. We challenged participants to use their words, tears, noises, and bodies to express the blocks. They were held, swayed, and encouraged by other group members. As facilitators we suggested and helped guide the energy and intervention, and invited men into the space. It was one of the most powerful, creative, and therapeutic group encounters we have witnessed.

We encourage the participants to lean into any discomforts, push through any resistance, and then experience their feelings and reactions in the supportive space of being with other men. Our day ends with the ritual of checking out with a word or two describing what the men are experiencing and feeling. We often hear words such as: connected, safe, nurtured, welcomed, energized, wow, peaceful, joyful, and alive.

Sunday morning: and we say goodbye. By now Matt and Mark have spent time in the baths checking in with one another and ideas for Sunday, and our ideas at this point are usually different from what we originally had planned on paper before the group began. We start with the ritual of saying hello with our eyes. This time the connections are much easier, softer, and longer. The tension associated with this type of intimate contact has noticeably evaporated for most of the men. Eyes are smiling with connection, interest, and "glad to see you." Typically, we offer and solicit ideas from the group on how they want to spend their last few hours together. There are often some left over issues that the men want to talk about or often an invitation to a guy in the group they might be concerned about or want to hear more from. There is a ritual of taking a group photo. Time is dearly protected to say goodbye and share the meaning of the workshop with one another. Observations and interpersonal feedback are often shared between the men in the group. Hopes and dreams for one another are shared with non-greeting card sincerity. There are lots of laughter, tears, and hugs. The male energy can be felt in the room.

We have ritualized an ending to the official workshop. With arms around each other we sing a song called "Listen, listen, listen to my heart song. I will never forget you and never forsake you." Looking into each other's eyes, swaying gently, we sing this song in unison. We end by humming just the melody.

OUR PARTICIPATION AS FACILITATORS

The participants know we are the facilitators and often appreciate that we are the leaders. Many participants whose professional lives involve mental health work thank us for carrying the "weight" of being facilitators and note how much they enjoy being in the passenger's seat. A returning psychologist remarked, "For me, as one who usually leads men's groups, it's an opportunity to take care of myself instead of just helping others." Yet as facilitators, we cannot avoid (nor should we) being a quasi-participant of the group. We share similar experiences; we are friends and colleagues with some of the participants, and we are also men desiring what the participants want from the workshop. At times we participate in the exercises, primarily the ones involving saying hello and goodbye. We appropriately self-disclose without putting us into the "center" of the discussion—but we use our experiences and examples as a model for engaging or deepening the process in the room. While the workshop is incredibly healing and therapeutic for us as well, we are not the primary participants. We may share personal stories during those times, but we feel we have found a comfortable boundary of engagement and context driven professionalism. Each leader has to find their own way with their level of comfort with disclosure and engagement. Give time to consider the extent of your boundary before you lead your group. Also, since our workshop is a seven hour drive, we (Mark and Matt) have plenty of time before each weekend and after to plan, debrief, and give feedback to each other about how the weekend went. The debriefing period is particularly useful as a place for us to systematically process the weekend and prepare for next year.

WHAT THE MEN SAY ABOUT THEIR EXPERIENCES

Overwhelmingly, our participants indicate having a positive reaction to the retreats. One member commented on why he comes back each year, "The facilitators, group members, the format of the retreat, the location, the relationships built with others, a weekend with men where everyone is real and connects in a real meaningful way, my own self growth, let go of stress, the ability to explore my life with other men and help others...I can't think of not attending a retreat."

Many men noted being surprised that a weekend workshop could be so meaningful and that issues can be explored in such depth. One participant noted, "I go to be with good men as often as I can, to remember what I want to be about and to reinforce the masculine part of me that nurtures others and myself. I am reminded that men caring for each other are far more powerful than men waging war, or trying to 'get ahead.' Oh, and raw curiosity. One can never tell what will happen!"

For many of the returning members this weekend has become a yearly ritual to anticipate and build into their lives. One member commented, "I personally gain a weekend to regroup, connect with others, explore my own issues, and I come back refreshed to better work with my own clients, make friendships and connections." Another added, "I need this each year. The men's weekend is now part of my life." Others come with their friends and colleagues, and the weekend has become a standing "date" that they use to maintain and deepen the relationship.

A common comment from some members is surprise that a group of men can connect in such intimate and caring ways, as it has not been their experience to find a group of men like that. A new member said he was genuinely skeptical that he would fit in at first, since the men in the group seemed so connected, but then he "took a risk to share something that I was not planning on sharing, and the group picked me up, supported me, and was dumbfounded with how powerful it was for me."

OUR ENDING AND YOUR BEGINNING

Our experience leading retreats has revealed to us that men simply want to be with each other in a safe and supportive setting. While endless variations of exercises and interventions exist to facilitate the experience, our recommendation is to:

1. Encourage men to share stories in order to develop connections with each other.
2. Emphasize a holistic approach of moving men from the brain to the body, emphasizing self-awareness, and fostering a passionate approach to life.
3. Allow for extended time so men can interact in various ways over the weekend.
4. Utilize outdoor space so that participants can use their encounters with the environment as metaphors and images for how they can better frame their lives.
5. Reinforce the importance of men shedding their tendencies toward over-responsibility so they can reengage with the playful and compassionate aspects of themselves.

CHAPTER 9

Getting Wired

Connecting With Men through Technology

Ryon C. McDermott, Christopher R. Smith, and Jack Y. Tsan

I (Ryon) was recently attending a staff meeting when the *liquid-crystal display* (LCD) projector stopped working. A few of us (the only men) frantically stepped up to fix the machine without much of an idea of what we were doing. When we couldn't figure out the problem, we felt strangely ashamed. This feeling was further heightened when a female colleague pointed out that the device had simply become unplugged!

This anecdote, while comical, reflects an interesting angle of male gender role socialization and points to a larger societal trend. Men are taught that they should be the masters of all things electronic. Indeed, numerous popular-press and scholarly articles have illustrated that men, on average, tend to use and enjoy technology more than women (e.g., Bialik, 2011; Fallows, 2005; Su, Rounds, & Armstrong, 2009).

Clearly, some men appear to have internalized the belief that they should appreciate and understand technology. Men who hold this belief may also adhere more rigidly to traditional male values and norms. Feminist scholars have argued that traditional masculinity is intertwined with a technological worldview and has been since the industrial revolution (Benston, 1988).

While there may be negative consequences to these beliefs (e.g., making a fool of oneself at a staff meeting), we believe that this technological worldview holds tremendous promise as an "inroad" to providing therapy with men. In the present chapter, we will share our experiences using specific technology to work with men, especially those resistant to traditional counseling approaches. In particular, we will focus on two important applications: (1) using technology as the treatment and (2) using technology as a bridge to treatment.

TECHNOLOGY AS A TREATMENT: MEN AND BIOFEEDBACK

Just as men are socialized to appreciate technology, they are also taught to restrict and control vulnerable emotions. This point has been emphasized in research, theory, and in several chapters of this book. Chris and I (Ryon) have noticed that some guys even begin to lose touch with the physical experience of emotion. Men who are extremely disassociated from these experiences tend to become overwhelmed with emotions. This often happens because these men don't notice the affect until it reaches a critical level or breaking point.

To address this particular issue, we have found that the technology of biofeedback is an excellent way of helping them reconnect their minds to their bodies. This technique often accomplishes this goal in a way that men appear to appreciate. In the sections to follow, we share examples of how we use biofeedback with men. We will also suggest ways to use this technology in your own work.

Biofeedback Defined

According to the Association of Applied Physiology and Biofeedback (AAPB, 2011), biofeedback involves using precise equipment to measure brain waves, heart rate variability, breathing, muscle activity, and/or skin temperature to provide individuals with concrete ways of viewing and changing their physiological reactions.

Although the AAPB definition sounds complicated, the principle is relatively simple. Through biofeedback equipment, clients learn how to manage their stress, anxiety, or emotional experiences by receiving feedback from their physiological reactions.

Biofeedback is used by a variety of health related specialties. In mental health, it is most often used to manage anxiety or stress by helping anxious clients learn how to relax. Clients continue to practice until they no longer need the feedback to change their physiological reactions. In this way, biofeedback can lead to a profound sense of agency over one's experiences of anxiety and stress.

A wide variety of programs and devices can be used. The three most common systems are first-person videogame formats, real-time graphical output systems, and portable devices that emit sounds indicating how well someone is changing his or her physiological reactions. While it can be tempting to purchase an elaborate and expensive biofeedback system, we have seen excellent benefits from the most basic, inexpensive systems.

Personally, we prefer the graphical output devices. The real-time graph is useful for demonstrating changes in a client's reactions. In contrast, the videogame-style systems provide feedback through an animated object (e.g., a pool of water that recedes as you become more relaxed). Furthermore, you may find that the videogames do not appeal to some traditional men, because they are often steeped in feminine imagery (e.g., displays outlined in flowers).

Biofeedback With Men

We have noticed that two types of men seem to be especially amenable to the use of biofeedback: guys who might be less inclined to see the benefits of emotion-focused work in therapy and guys who tend to be more intellectualizing in their presentation. In your own work, you may have encountered these men, many of whom are far from sold on the benefits of therapy or the problems with emotional restriction. For these men, the combination of immediate feedback, being slightly removed from negative emotions, and the simplicity of focusing on physiological indicators all make biofeedback appealing and effective.

Biofeedback With Anxious Men

Most of our biofeedback work with men has focused on anxiety using technology displaying heart rate variability. I (Chris) recall one instance with Stephen, a young man who presented as extremely anxious. Stephen lacked awareness of his anxiety until it became so intense that it could not be ignored. Unfortunately, this also meant that anxiety impacted his performance, especially in testing situations.

After some discussions with Stephen about his goals for therapy, I presented the option of biofeedback as a way to increase his feelings of mastery over his anxiety. We agreed we would begin with practicing deep breathing and calming thoughts while monitoring his progress through biofeedback. We typically spent 20 to 30 minutes together. My role was essentially "coaching" him on how to relax while he was hooked up to the machine. Then, I would leave the room for the remaining time. This approach helped him achieve a sense of mastery over these techniques.

With individuals like Stephen, we are able to provide opportunities to use the technology and then check in on their progress through therapy. After only a few biofeedback sessions, it was clear that Stephen had learned how to decrease and increase his anxiety at will. Stephen also appeared to be more connected with his body and the physical sensations of fear associated with anxiety.

Biofeedback and Men's Emotions

By increasing men's awareness of how emotions are connected to physical sensations in the body, they may begin to reconnect with their experience of emotions. You might find that the mindfulness skills inherent in biofeedback make it a natural gateway to having deeper conversations about emotions. In particular, we often use biofeedback as a way to help men learn about their connections between thoughts and feelings.

One aspect of biofeedback we truly appreciate is that both therapist and client can easily see a record of the emotional reactions over time. From a *cognitive behavioral therapy* (CBT) perspective, this can be an important tool to emphasize the links between thoughts and physical experiences in real time. For example, you can notice a change in heart rate and then ask, "What was going on for you here [pointing to the change]? What were you thinking or feeling?" You might also try asking the client to think about negative versus positive thoughts and instruct him to notice the changes in his physiological indicators.

Biofeedback and the Therapeutic Alliance

In addition to helping men reconnect with their emotions, we have found that biofeedback helps strengthen the therapeutic alliance, especially for treatment-resistant men. Often the procedure provides quick results, which the men we work with seem to appreciate, and fits nicely with how men are taught to problem solve. Moreover, we feel extremely satisfied when our clients feel like therapy is working, and biofeedback has been identified as a highly effective treatment for anxiety and stress (Lehrer, 2007).

We believe that biofeedback also strengthens the alliance in other, less apparent ways. Specifically, it takes abstract concepts like "feelings" and makes them more concrete. In our experience, many guys appreciate being able to work with emotions in a tangible way. We see this as a way of meeting clients' needs in a manner that respects their culture of masculinity and their readiness for further work.

For instance, I (Ryon) recall working with Juan, a young Latino who came to counseling feeling stressed and overwhelmed by school. Juan became visibly nervous and resistant when I tried to help him identify how his thinking was related to his emotions. When we explored this further, I was struck by how he could not describe his feelings. Juan, like so many other men, appeared to be struggling with normative male alexithymia (Levant, 2001). In other words, he had never developed the vocabulary (English or Spanish) to describe his emotions.

After our first few sessions, I found myself feeling somewhat frustrated with Juan and myself, in part because of the lack of discussion around emotions. I noticed that I was working harder than Juan, and I knew that I had to adjust my approach. I suggested biofeedback as an alternative, and he agreed to participate.

During our first biofeedback session, I was amazed at how different our dynamic had become. Compared to previous sessions, Juan appeared to be engaged in therapy and actively working toward his goals. We connected over the process of biofeedback, and he identified that he was often tense without realizing why. He learned to relax by using deep breathing and mindfulness approaches with the help of the biofeedback system. In turn, he noticed an important decrease in feelings of stress and being overwhelmed by school over time.

Although Juan never learned exactly how to speak about his emotions, he did learn how to modify his feelings by taking control over his experience of stress and anxiety. Thus, rather than forcing Juan to speak the language of emotions, I was able to work with him using a language he already understood and appreciated. This opened the door for a deeper connection between us.

Ethical and Practical Considerations

While we believe that biofeedback offers promise for working with men, it is also important to note relevant challenges. Mainly, effective use of biofeedback requires extra training. There are currently no state laws requiring biofeedback training, but ethical practitioners will adhere to the standards for training to assure that they are conducting themselves appropriately. Various certifications are available for individuals who wish to be trained. The Biofeedback Certification Institute of America (BCIA) is an excellent resource (http://www.bcia.org) for further information.

TECHNOLOGY AS A BRIDGE TO THERAPY

My colleagues have just described a promising approach for using technology as an intervention. What I (Jack) describe here is different in that I will focus on using technology as a "bridge" to treatment in its more traditional (and varied) formats. This use of technology is central to addressing the logistical demands that might otherwise prevent men from seeking therapy.

Currently, I use technology to help veterans. For many civilians, like me, veterans symbolize honor, bravery, and courage. I have heard the stories of their sacrifices, and I have seen them struggle when mental health issues impact their performance at work, school, or family relationships.

At the same time, I have seen the successes of therapy and the positive impact it can make on their lives. Yet, so many veterans, especially men, do not seek the help they often desperately need. In the sections below, I will share how technology can be a powerful ally in that battle.

Using the Internet as a Resource

Internet websites, such as Web MD or Men's Health, may be some of the first places that men search for information about their behavioral or mental health concerns. Having reviewed the contents of these websites specific to common behavioral and mental health conditions, I have found them to be good resources for potential clients.

For example, when I met David, a married veteran in his mid-20s, I was struck by his ambivalence about being in counseling. I recommended that he look into the empirically-validated benefits of counseling via various websites that summarize this work.

While a simple scenario, David's situation represents how external information from reputable sources online can push men to overcome barriers, including stigma, that get in the way of seeking help. By providing directions for helpful information, men may feel empowered to research their issues, thus making them more invested in treatment.

Other times, I can tell that men have done their own research about mental health issues before they even come to see me. I particularly remember Jim, a veteran in his early 20s who had been deployed in Iraq. He told me he sensed the stigma of seeking mental health services as a military man, but the information gleaned on the Internet helped him recognize that getting help was more important. I've found that many men are seeking information on the Internet before they check out a psychologist's office.

In addition to developing a sense of investment in one's treatment, using the Internet to research one's mental health concerns and treatment options may help reduce some of the mystery/fear surrounding therapy. You can do some Google, Bing, and Yahoo searches for common mental health issues (e.g., anxiety, depression, bipolar, etc.) in order to see what guys in your area find when they search for their own concerns.

I also recommend searching the Internet for guy-friendly resources that can help men make decisions about whether therapy is appropriate. Searching for things like "therapy benefits for depression," or "does therapy work?" can lead to some very good sites.

Bridging the Distance: Telemental Health

Technology can also be used to reach men who might not ordinarily be comfortable or able to meet in person. Specifically, I deliver some of my services to clients without ever seeing them in person, a process commonly referenced as Telemental Health (Mallen, Vogel, & Rochlen, 2005).

There are essentially four types of Telemental Health currently available: (1) text-only, (2) voice-only, (3) text and video, and (4) voice and video. I've used all of these communication approaches and seen many benefits. Voice-only is the easiest to use, because you only need a phone. Below, I'll share with you some tips, recommendations, and personal experiences to consider if you want to explore any of these approaches.

The Therapeutic Alliance

The number one myth I hear about voice-only Telemental Health is that it can impact the therapeutic alliance. Despite the physical distance in Telemental Health, I have found that I'm able to develop strong therapeutic alliances with my clients over the phone. My experiences are consistent with research demonstrating that Telemental Health has little to no negative impact on the therapeutic alliance (Day & Schneider, 2002).

I have even noticed qualitative differences between face-to-face and telephone interactions for my male clients in terms of their ease of sharing sensitive and vulnerable disclosures. In a typical face-to-face session, it may take up to four visits before a male client shares something vulnerable and potentially "unmanly." Over the telephone, this type of disclosure has occured as early as the second or third session.

A recent example further illustrates this point. Robert, a veteran in his mid-30s, reported to me that he was having sexual performance problems. Although men have disclosed vulnerable information to me in face-to-face sessions, the surprising thing was that Robert was very open and answered all my questions without hesitation in the first few sessions on the phone.

Cases like Robert are fairly typical of my work with men through Telemental Health. The ease with which he and many others appear to be able to self-disclose suggests that there may be aspects of Telemental Health that are especially suited for working with men. Specifically, I believe that the physical distance inherent in this format can help some men feel safe enough to break through traditional male roles that may otherwise impede face-to-face therapy.

For instance, Robert grew up in an environment immersed in a military culture where weakness was seen as a liability. The physical distance of Telemental Health services may have allowed him to discuss vulnerable parts of his masculinity without having to display any signs of "weakness" in person. I found that when Robert felt comfortable opening up to me, our therapeutic alliance strengthened considerably.

In your own Telemental Health work with men, you might try embracing the physical distance between you and the client. As a therapist, it can be relieving to not have to worry about making eye contact while taking notes, sitting a particular way, or being judged by your appearance in some fashion. I sometimes feel myself being more relaxed using such approaches. You might find Telemental Health to be somewhat liberating, and chances are this mirrors the way your client feels on the other end of the phone.

Video Teleconferencing and Secure Messaging

Compared to the voice-only systems, video teleconferencing (i.e., voice and video) is more advanced. This technology requires fast, secure Internet connections, web cameras or video broadcasting devices, and the necessary software (e.g., Skype, Yahoo video chat, Google Chat with video capabilities, or V-Tel systems). These systems may not be as accessible to you and your clients as telephones. I have also had my share of problematic sessions due to poor signal strengths or other technical difficulties. Still, this kind of virtual distance therapy is clearly the wave of the future and is becoming more prevalent.

I have had the unique opportunity to run mental health behavior groups using V-Tel systems in which multiple outpatient facilities connect to each other. Despite the novelty of the approach, I have not observed any major differences in group cohesion between V-Tel groups and live groups. The men eagerly observe each other on the video cameras, and they often comment on how interesting it is to be using such innovative technology. It has been touching to watch these men support each other through this unique format. For those who are thinking about running group treatment for men using video-conferencing technology, developing strong group cohesion is absolutely possible.

In addition to the V-Tel systems, many facilities also have secure messaging. Veterans are able to access a secure website and type a message to a therapist as a way of seeking help in times of crisis. While I have not conducted therapy solely using this modality (i.e., text-only Telemental Health), I have noticed that many of my male clients use this service. I believe it allows them to ask for help in a way that avoids feelings of shame or vulnerability, which may otherwise get in the way of seeking services directly.

A recent case illustrates this point. Jonathan, a 20-year-old platoon sergeant who served in Afghanistan, reached out for help by contacting us through our secure messaging system at a time when the office was closed. Jonathan typed out his struggles (e.g., feeling on the edge, going from 0 to 60 in a split second over the small stuff, and feeling extremely down). The next morning, Jonathan's primary care team and his doctor immediately relayed the message to me. I contacted him, and we talked over the phone.

In speaking with him, I recognized that he served an important leadership role as a platoon sergeant and felt responsible for the lives of the soldiers he commanded. Coming back to civilian life had been extremely challenging, as he had been dealing with the loss of his friends in combat and was questioning whether he belonged in this civilian world. I also felt his ambivalence about therapy, and he described how difficult it was for him to reach out for help.

Personally, I believe that men like Jonathan, who have sacrificed so much, deserve to be given the highest honor and respect. I am saddened at times, because I know that many people are not aware of the sacrifices that these men make. I am also aware that asking for help can be very difficult, even for men who are courageous in every sense of the word. I appreciate the efforts the Veterans Association (VA) system has made to make it easier for men to seek help, and I wonder whether Jonathan would have reached out had he not been able to confidentially type out his concerns using a modality that, in many ways, circumvents the vulnerability that may be present when asking for help face to face.

Balancing Work and Therapy

Regardless of the type of system used, Telemental Health meets the unique demands of men with difficult jobs and busy schedules. I recall working with William, a married trucker in his 40s. He told me that he was often on the road and had difficulty getting weekly time off from his employer to seek mental health treatment for his depression. He was also concerned that his employer might fire him for taking too many days off for doctor visits.

Clearly, getting access to traditional face-to-face psychotherapy, which often requires weekly visits, can be extremely difficult for men like William. One solution that worked was to use his lunch break for voice-only Telemental Health psychotherapy. William appeared to greatly appreciate the convenience of therapy over the phone, and this helped set the stage for a strong working relationship.

I feel empowered when I can help men like William, because they are able to focus on their treatment rather than the logistics of how to access services. Sometimes the logistical demands of getting to therapy (e.g., time missed at work or transportation) are enough to deter potential patients from even trying. The VA has recognized the tremendous benefits of technology for increasing access to mental health services. They maintain a presence on Facebook and offer a veterans crisis line via telephone or Internet chat (http://veteranscrisisline.net/). There is even an iPhone application for posttraumatic stress disorder (PTSD) issues that clients with smart phones may be able to use (http://itunes.apple.com/us/app/ptsd-coach/id430646302?mt=8). If you are working with veterans, do consider these resources.

Ethical Considerations and Therapeutic Concerns

Provision of Telemental Health services can be challenging, and there are ethical considerations to recognize. Below are a few that I consider to be most salient. One of the first is client safety. For example, when working with clients at a distance, it is important to establish a system in which you can connect with other mental health providers or with a client's local emergency health care system when needed. This is particularly important in the rare event that your client is at imminent risk for harming himself or others. This is also something you will need to talk about with your client. In most cases, you always have 911 as an option, but you may, with the client's permission, enlist another provider, friend, or family member.

A second challenge is to address privacy and security issues. When Telemental Health is offered over the Internet, there are currently no 100% absolute secure lines, although developers are working on this problem. Hence, whatever our clients share with us during sessions is always at the risk of being discovered. To the best of your ability, ensure that electronic data is encrypted. If you don't know how to do this, ask, get help, or figure out the process that best ensures the confidentiality of your client. Likewise, make sure your clients are aware of the limitations in using these technologies as part of the informed consent process.

A third challenge is the ability to practice across state lines. I am fortunate to work in the federal system, and it has helped my clients in the transitioning process during the transfer to another federal facility in a different state. Some states offer reciprocity for licensees, but ultimately it is the responsibility of the provider to examine how best to coordinate care and if the provision of services across state lines is within the scope of one's practice. It's helpful to contact your state's licensing board to see how they handle issues of distance therapy in another state.

Finally, should you consider the practice of Telemental Health, ongoing training will be important in order to stay on top of the latest developments in the field, especially regarding some of these ethical issues. For more information about training and resources you can refer to telehealth.org, www.americantelemed.org, and it might be helpful to check out an article published by APA on Telemental Health (www.apa.org/monitor/2011/06/telehealth.aspx).

SUMMARY

As the preceding sections illustrated, integrating technology into our therapy with men has been tremendously valuable. You can use technology as a form of therapy with men to help repair the consequences of emotional restriction and losing touch with one's body. You can also use it as a way of meeting the unique logistical demands of male clients.

Personally, we appreciate the ways in which integrating technology into therapy fits with men's gender role socialization. Technology, such as biofeedback and Telemental Health, allows us to work with men who might not be able or willing to seek counseling. For these reasons, we hope that you will consider exploring the potential uses of these technologies in your own work.

The views expressed are those of the authors and do not necessarily reflect the position or policy of the Department of Veterans Affairs or the United States government. All client names have been changed to protect their identity.

REFERENCES

Association of Applied Physiology and Biofeedback (2011). About biofeedback. Retrieved from http://www.aapb.org/i4a/pages/index.cfm?pageid=3463

Benston, M. L. (1988). Women's voices/men's voices: Technology as language. In C. Kramarae (Ed.), *Technology and women's voices* (Vol. 3, pp. 12–23). New York, NY: Routledge.

Bialik, C. (2011). Who makes the call at the mall, men or women? *The Wall Street Journal*. Retrieved from http://online.wsj.com/article/SB10001424052748703521304576278964279316994.html#project%3DNUMBERS_GUY_1104%26articleTabs%3Darticle

Day, S. X., & Schneider, P. L. (2002). Psychotherapy using distance technology: A comparison of face-to-face, video, and audio treatment. *Journal of Counseling Psychology, 49*, 499–503. doi:10.1037/0022-0167.49.4.499

Fallows, D. (2005). *How women and men use the internet*. Washington, DC: Pew Internet and American Life Project.

Lehrer, P. M. (2007). Biofeedback training to increase heart rate variability. In P. M. Lehrer, R. L. Woolfolk, & W. E. Sime (Eds.), *Principles and practices of stress management* (pp. 227–249). New York, NY: Guilford Press.

Levant, R. F. (2001). Desperately seeking language: Understanding, assessing and treating normative male alexithymia. In G. R. Brooks and G. Good (Eds.), *The new handbook of counseling and psychotherapy for men* (Vol. 1, pp. 424–443). San Francisco, CA: Jossey-Bass.

Mallen, M. J., Vogel, D. L., & Rochlen, A. B. (2005). The practical aspects of online counseling: Ethics, training, technology, and competency. *The Counseling Psychologist, 33*, 776–818. doi:10.1177/0011000005278625

Su, R., Rounds, J., & Armstrong, P. (2009). Men and things, women and people: A meta-analysis of sex differences in interests. *Psychological Bulletin, 135*, 859–884. doi:10.1037/a0017364

CHAPTER 10

Coaching Men

A Direct Approach to Intimacy and Sexuality

Jim Benson

I'm dining at a Manhattan restaurant the evening after I've led a two-day workshop on relationships, intimacy and sexuality for men. I'm telling my companions about the techniques I used in my one-on-one sessions with three different workshop participants. One of them says, "That sounds like coaching to me." She mentions that she and two of her friends at the table participated in a coaching program in the San Francisco Bay Area. "You should check it out," she adds. When I got back to California, I did.

And that's how I started on my path to becoming a coach.

What exactly is coaching? Here's a short definition that I like from "the coach's coach," Myles Downey: *Coaching is the art of facilitating the performance, learning and development of another* (Downey, 2003).

However you define it, it seems that coaching attracts a greater percentage of men than does therapy—more than twice as many. Recent data from the International Coaching Federation (ICF, 2008) states that the male/female ratio of coaching clients is 45/55, while the male/female ratio for those who voluntarily enter psychotherapy is much more skewed toward women (Addis & Mahalik, 2003).

Later in this chapter I'll offer my theories about why a greater percentage of men are drawn to coaching. I also have a number of suggestions for introducing coaching techniques into an existing therapeutic practice. But right now I want to talk about sex.

SEX AND RELATIONSHIP COACHING

My particular arena of coaching—sex and relationships—turns out to be an ideal focus for this book. First of all, for nearly all men, having good sex is *very* important. When they run into difficulties, they are highly motivated to make changes. Also, many guys facing sexual challenges might shy away from therapy, but those same men seem to be more comfortable talking with a sex and relationship coach like me, who they perceive as less psychologically judgmental.

Men confide in me about issues like their lack of confidence in bed, premature ejaculation, and expectations from partners that aren't being met. Difficult conversations? Absolutely. But just *having* the conversation begins the healing process for many men, simply because they've never talked about these issues with anyone.

Because I am known as a sex coach and promote myself as such, men often seek me out to specifically address their sexuality concerns. With these guys, talking about sex is relatively easy. Even with general coaching clients, though, I usually take the first step and ask about their sex life. Is it satisfying? Do they want more from their sexual encounters? Any hang-ups or problems? My own comfort and sincere curiosity, combined with my belief (often made explicit) that sexuality is reflective of an individual's overall health and integration, orients my client to a non-shaming atmosphere regarding sex. Together we look at their sex life simply as one part of their life situation.

Providing a safe, comfortable context in which men can honestly explore their sexuality is key, whether or not they have come to me specifically for sex coaching. I've found there to be a few fundamental elements to providing this context:

1. *My own self-management.* If I'm met with an aspect of a client's sexuality I find jarring or hard to understand—a particular fetish or fantasy, or protracted infidelity, for example—I need to be fastidious in addressing and digesting my own response. My capacity to remain welcoming and non-shaming is essential for a successful outcome. If I find that I cannot hold this kind of equanimity (my client harming others for sexual gratification, for example), I will share this with them and discuss referral.
2. *Initiating sexual vocabulary.* Clients are often initially reluctant to speak openly about specific sexual issues. So if they start off with, "Sex is over pretty quickly," I ask, "Oh, so are you ejaculating earlier than you'd like?" There's often an audible sigh of relief on the other end of the line, now that I've spoken so directly to what was formerly unspeakable. I'll continue to lead the way: "Is it mostly when you're fucking, or also when she's going down on you?" I establish a vocabulary that is casual and very man-friendly as soon as possible in our session. For instance, I use words like *cock*, *pussy*, and other "dirty" words in lieu of more clinical terms. I also listen closely

to each client for their own sexual words and phrases, which I add to our growing shared vocabulary.

3 *Normalizing pleasure, emphasizing success.* Tito, a 29-year-old Latino with a foot fetish, carried a heavy burden of shame when he initially broached the subject with me. Here's how I proceeded in our session.
   a I asked genuinely curious, judgment-free questions to get more detail (frequently using affirmations like "Cool!" or "Great!" with each new disclosure).
   b I acknowledged him for his bravery and vulnerability in sharing his sexual history.
   c I affirmed his fetish by letting him know that there is no "normal," and that, rather than encouraging him to overcome or bypass his kink, my goal was to help him accept, celebrate, and fully "own" his kink.
   d I asked if he'd ever had a successful "foot" encounter with a partner from which to build upon. He could indeed recall a very enjoyable night during which his fetish was in full expression, and we expanded his potential for greater fulfillment with that experience as a foundation. (If he hadn't, we would have explored ways for him to find an appropriate partner with whom he could share his desires.)

4 *Appropriate self-disclosure and humor.* To help move clients toward greater self-acceptance, I regularly use humor, as well as disclose some of my own sexual trauma and "kinks." Obviously, you'll not want to make inappropriate jokes, nor will you want to disclose parts of your sexual history that you haven't fully come to terms with yet. But I find that showing my humanity to clients can teach them important lessons, and can also help them become more vulnerable in our sessions. And my playful attitude toward sex encourages them to hold their issue more lightly than they have been doing so far.

As I help men begin to understand and heal their sexual and relationship issues, "side benefits" typically appear. Some clients make changes to their diet, return to their meditation practice, or become more assertive in addressing problems at home and work. Sometimes it's because I've directly encouraged them to do so (since I'm also trained in life coaching), but just as often it's because they're beginning to respect themselves in a new way. I'm giving them the information and guidance they're seeking about sex and intimacy, but at a deeper level, I'm walking with them on the path to greater self-acceptance and self-love—which, of course, affects *every* area of their lives.

A CASE STUDY

In order to better understand my approach to coaching and its effectiveness in working with male clients in particular, I offer a recent case example.

Jamie, 27, lives in a rural town in the Pacific Northwest. In our initial interview I ask if he's ever been in therapy. He says he's not sure that there are any therapists in his area, and if there were, he wouldn't want to run into someone around town with whom he had a therapeutic relationship. Jamie works for a small non-profit organization. He's introverted and conflict-avoidant, which has been impacting his relationships with family and friends, and has kept him from meeting the kind of women he's interested in.

Over the course of our six-month coaching term, I helped Jamie in a number of areas. In nearly every session we discussed topics he had never spoken about with anyone.

First, I assessed how satisfied Jamie was in a number of different areas in his life. It turned out that he was struggling with some personal relationships. I helped him understand how to have an authentic, direct conversation with his parents and co-worker by describing how he might do it, and then I asked him to role-play it with me. I also found out what physical health practices he was currently doing, and what he might want to do in the future. As a result, he started going to the gym three times a week and enrolled in a yoga class in a nearby city.

To work on his intimacy issues, I encouraged him to start conversations with women after the yoga classes. We discussed how he might meet women in ways that were aligned with his introversion and values. After about two months of working together, he shared his experience of the somatic symptoms of being rejected by women. I encouraged him to allow and then magnify the sensations. He emerged from this "process coaching" feeling more stable and secure in himself. A month after this he was dating three different women, and soon after, he chose one of them with whom he wanted to "go steady." Jamie then shyly asked me for a plan to help him become a better lover, which I designed with him.

Around this time I heard a dramatic change in the quality of his speech. He hesitated less and spoke with more authority and conviction. I pointed this out, and encouraged him to use this new strength to explore what changes he'd like to make in his work life. He decided to ask his supervisor for more responsibility and more money, and we co-created a way for him to present his case. It turned out that his boss couldn't give him what he wanted, but the process helped him commit to explore new employment possibilities.

Not all of my coaching relationships unfold as steadily and smoothly as my work with Jamie, but most successful ones do follow a particular progression. Over the course of four to six months, guys who were struggling with a presenting sex or relationship issue see a clear improvement or progress toward their goal as well as other positive changes in their lives.

COACHING ≠ THERAPY ≠ CONSULTING ≠ MENTORING?

"Therapy," says psychologist Michael Cavanagh, "seeks to comfort the afflicted. But in coaching, however, the coach is often called upon to afflict the comfortable!" (Cavanagh, 2009).

In contrast to therapy's medical-model roots, coaching traces its origins to mentoring traditions around the world; to sports coaching (Tim Gallwey's *The Inner Game of Tennis* is the seminal tome here); to contemporary business management theory and executive training programs; and to personal growth workshops that emerged in the 60s and 70s from (surprise!) California.

"Pure" coaching—what I learned in my life coaching training—is not the same as consulting or mentoring. In pure coaching, the coach asks questions designed to draw out the client's own wisdom. Pure coaches can coach a client on any subject without knowing much about the subject matter itself. But people seek out consultants and mentors because they have expertise in particular areas.

These days, even "pure" coaches have areas that they specialize in, and more and more coaches are doing the job that consultants and mentors do—they just call themselves "coaches." One of my colleagues was a chief executive officer before he became a business coach. Another coach I collaborate with studied nutrition and led women's groups for a decade before becoming a women's health coach.

The distinctions between therapy, coaching, consulting and mentoring may become less significant as time rolls on. Programs like San Francisco's Interchange Counseling, for instance, are on a mission to bridge the counseling–coaching gap. Founder Steve Bearman's one-year training is designed to give tools to coaches to make them more aware and skillful in working with clients on psychological, emotional and interpersonal levels. The program also helps mental health professionals be more coach-like, directive and results-oriented in their work (S. Bearman, personal communication, April 18, 2012).

The bottom line is that, whatever it's called—coaching, mentoring, witchcraft, mumblety-peg—if it helps guys create positive change for themselves, use it!

HOOK 'EM WITH COACHING

I believe there are many men who have the sense they might be able to change their lives in a positive way, but wouldn't consider going to therapy. Coaching can be an effective hook to enroll guys who are new to the idea of personal growth.

Ron, 36, is a middle manager of an alternative energy company in Colorado. He has been sexual with a total of three women: a drunken one-night stand in his early 20s; a five-year relationship; and his current wife of six years. He called me three months after learning his wife had an affair with her co-worker. Her complaint—as he tells it—is that he isn't emotionally available, and the sex is lousy. Not surprisingly, Ron is having a lot of confidence issues.

"I'm glad that we're talking on the phone instead of meeting in person," says Ron, in our first session. "Talking about all this sex stuff would be too much for me to do in person." I ask him if he's currently, or ever has been, in therapy. "Eight years ago I was in couples therapy to try and rescue my first relationship. The therapist was a woman

and she always seemed to side with my partner. I never trusted her and refused to go back after a few sessions." When I ask Ron why he's coming to me instead of a therapist, Ron laughs, "Because I don't think I'm screwed up enough to need a therapist! Seriously, I'm not big on self-reflection. I am big on getting results, and that's why I thought coaching with you might be a better approach for me."

In his own way, Ron points out a number of reasons why some men prefer coaching to therapy. Here's how I would distinguish them:

Coaching doesn't challenge most men's sense of self. At certain points in their development, some men are simply not comfortable with (or able to do) deep, exposing, emotional work: it's too confronting to their concept of themselves. There's a social component as well: guys will more readily tell a friend that they're getting coaching instead of counseling because they're afraid their mental health will be questioned. These men will choose a coaching relationship because they don't want to be burdened with the (sadly outdated) stigma that "because I'm in therapy, something is wrong with me."

Coaching aligns with the traditional masculine value of achievement. Many men who might have difficulty contacting and expressing feelings (traditionally, the realm of therapy) might be eager to be invited to the party through the side door by working with a coach. Coaches frequently help their clients design measurable goals and track their progress—including "homework" that has been co-designed with the client. It's the kind of challenge that can motivate many results-oriented guys (like Ron) to begin the process of change.

Coaching on the phone—at least in the "sex and intimacy" arena—helps men feel "safer." Every man I've worked with has had some amount of shame and performance anxiety regarding his sex life, and phone sessions seem to offer the hesitant man an ideal blend of "lack of threat of embarrassment" and "freedom to speak."

In addition to the reasons from Ron's example, here are four more theories about why guys who want to make changes in their lives are more likely to call a coach than a therapist.

Coaching has the potential of positive associations with sports coaching. Guys who had a favorite coach when they were younger might easily accept the idea of a personal coach just for them. Guys who didn't have positive associations might want to correct their trauma by hiring a "good coach." Either way, there's the archetype of a strong, fiercely loving figure that offers the "fathering" that many men—especially younger guys—are craving in our increasingly fragmented Western culture.

Coaching is hot right now. Rising stars in corporations are often assigned a coach to help prepare them for advancement within the organization. It's an indication that they're worth an investment, and that the company believes in their potential. Who wouldn't like that—inside or outside the corporate environment?

Coaching offers short-term solutions. Cognitive-behavioral and solution-focused therapy aside, most therapeutic clients benefit from years of weekly meetings with their therapists, building the secure attachment and the deep holding environment necessary for change. Most coaching engagements, in contrast, last from four to six months—very appealing to men who like the idea of achieving results within a specified amount of time.

Coaching doesn't require face-to-face meetings. Although most psychotherapists offer supplemental phone contact and occasionally make use of Skype or other video technology for out-of-town clients with whom they have established relationships, many coaches work entirely on the phone. This kind of flexibility eliminates travel time and lets clients enjoy a session from any location. I've had dozens of coaching clients I've never met in person. (Although, truthfully, I've met a lot of men who prefer face-to-face meetings to phone sessions.)

COACHING FOR ADDICTS AND THE MENTALLY ILL

Is coaching for everyone? Definitely not. Anyone diagnosed with a mental illness will be better served with other forms of support (such as psychotherapy or psychiatry), but I've teamed up with a therapist to work successfully with a high-functioning bipolar client. Coaches, please note: it is unethical to pursue psychological work with clients when you have not been trained to do so. And you *must* refer mentally ill clients to a qualified mental health practitioner.

Also: when I first started coaching, I noticed that a couple of my clients were getting very limited results. They would initiate change but lack the staying power to concretize those changes over time. Further investigation revealed that they had active addictions (alcohol and drugs). In both cases, I stopped our work together and recommended that they enter a recovery program before proceeding with coaching. I now ask questions regarding addiction as part of my initial intake with clients.

The bottom line is that clients must be not just willing but *able* to make the changes they want in their lives.

INTRODUCING COACHING TO YOUR EXISTING MALE CLIENTS

We all want to feel effective in our work with men. It doesn't take much to shift your practice to include more aspects that might appeal to men, as well as encourage them to stay. Here are some steps for you to consider if you're interested in becoming more "coach-like" in your therapy practice.

Begin by discerning your best candidates. Some men may simply be better served through therapeutic modes—like encouragement to feel feelings, trauma recovery, an unconditional loving presence—rather than being supported toward particular goals. But if you sense a man wants more than that, and think that the coaching angle could work for both of you, then introduce a few coaching principles over time. Keep the process explicit and gradual, so as not to negatively impact the therapeutic bond.

In a session, start by tracking your own impulses. Notice when you are drawn to guide a client toward a specific action. Then check it out with yourself. Can you tell if it is truly an intuitive insight? Or is your own projection or counter-transference muddying the waters? Sometimes I'm completely transparent with a client and say something like: "I notice that I have a strong impulse right now to offer you an action you could take. I could be totally projecting my desires onto you, and you also may not be interested in hearing anything that sounds like advice. What say you?"

Here's another direct approach you might try: "I'm feeling inspired to work with you more as a coach than your therapist right now. Is it OK with you if we try that? It means that I might be more directive with you, or that I might ask more challenging questions, or I may encourage you to take steps towards your goal. What do you think?"

If the client is game, consider asking mildly confronting, open-ended questions like, "What's the next step you could take right away?" or "Who, besides me, could support you in this?" "So, what *is* the vision for your life?" Sometimes when a client says to me, "I don't know," I reply (as a kind of mental aikido), "What if you *did* know?"

If your client is locked into a particular way of thinking, you might suggest "Blue Sky Brainstorming." Tell them that you'd like to see if there are some other ways they might look at this issue, or alternative directions for them to consider. Make it collaborative and inviting: "Let's brainstorm some ideas here. If you could make it any way you wanted, what would this situation look like?" Then throw some of your ideas into the ring with theirs. Male clients seem to especially like brainstorming.

Let's say that your client has agreed to take a specific action over the next week. It's nearing the end of the session. Consider getting him to commit to that action. There are a number of ways to do this, but the simplest is for him to write it down—two copies, one for you and one for him—and have him sign and date both copies. Some clients might experience this as too threatening, but consider using it if a verbal commitment didn't work from the week before. Other clients will take such commitments very seriously and rise to the challenge.

When you review the client's actions or commitment in your next session with him, make sure to acknowledge him if he was successful in accomplishing his action: "Robert, I want to acknowledge all that it took for you to move past your inner resistances and outer obstacles to reach your goal. From my perspective, you've done a great job here."

In the next session, help the client deepen his learning. You can do this whether or not they accomplished their goal. Ask him, "What are you taking away from this?" "How were you 'well-used' in this process?" "What new qualities have emerged in you?" Then add what you noticed to his list.

As you begin to expand your coaching repertoire, you'll get to experience navigating between the roles of task-master, cheerleader, and loving parent. You might find it helpful to buy a couple of books or a home study program about coaching to help you get a feel for the territory. Good ones are *Co-Active Coaching* (Whitworth, Kimsey-House, & Sandahl, 1998), *Coaching for Performance* (Whitmore, 2002), and *Life Coach in a Box* (Stanton, 2006).

THE NEXT STEP

Some therapists and counselors get very enthusiastic about adding coaching tools to their sessions, and some want to have a coaching practice that stands side by side with their therapeutic practice. If this is you, here are my suggestions on how to proceed.

First of all, *get coached yourself*. Hire an experienced, qualified coach and work with them for six months. Then, to experience a different working model, let that coach go and hire a new coach—one who was trained in a different coaching program than the first one—for another six months. Repeat as often as you like. I found this method extremely helpful for me on both the personal and professional levels. One way of insuring that you'll be getting high-quality coaching is to work with a coach who holds a PCC (Professional Certified Coach) or MCC (Master Certified Coach) credential with the International Coach Federation (ICF).

In your first session with your coach, tell them that in addition to working with you as a coach, you'd like them to mentor you in your new coaching practice as well. Ask them to explain what they're doing with you while they're doing it. Consider hiring a therapist–coach as one of your mentors—someone who has already made the transition you want to make.

Next, enroll in a reputable coaching training so you can experientially learn the craft of coaching. Most basic coaching programs offer 100–125 hours of training, and are offered either in-person or on the phone. Again, look for ICF-accredited coaching programs to give yourself the best chance of a quality education.

Consider putting out your shingle as a coach. That might mean changing your work description to something like "Therapist and Men's Coach." When new clients call, you can ask if they're interested in coaching or therapy—or ask if it even matters to them. You might experiment with working with some of your new coaching clients strictly on the phone and see how you enjoy that.

Be clear in your initial meeting with a client if you're going to be doing coaching or therapy with them. If either you or the client is unsure, use that initial meeting to find out.

GOING ALL THE WAY

Some therapists engaged in this process end up preferring their coaching work to their therapeutic work, and stop accepting new clients who are mentally ill. They increase their hourly rate (sometimes as much as double or triple their therapist's rate), stop filing insurance paperwork, and focus solely on high-functioning clients.

There are entire books and programs dedicated to helping you build your coaching practice. Your mentor coaches will have lots of ideas for you as well. In the meantime, here are some ideas for you to chew on.

I suggest that you define a niche for yourself. Is there a particular male demographic that interests you, or one in which you have specific expertise? Guys in their 20s? Men transitioning out of the corporate world? Recovering addicts? Gay men? Limiting your audience will make you more attractive to that same audience.

As you begin to put yourself out there, go with your strengths. If you're a good speaker, make recordings and podcasts, get interviewed on radio shows, and book speaking gigs. If you like to write, start a blog and publish consumer (non-academic) articles. If you're a people-person, join networking groups. If you're a closet techie, do the best practices to get your site ranked high by search engines.

Consider coaching groups of men—in your chosen niche—via teleconference. I took a training in how to lead group coaching programs and found it very helpful. Remember to think big: you can attract men from all over the world to join a group you're leading.

Another step many coaches take is to create products and sell them: e-books; CDs or MP3s; DVDs or downloadable videos. Products mean passive income that can build over time. I can also recommend that you establish partnerships and affiliate relationships with people you trust. I formed an alliance with a company who marketed personal-growth programs and products to men. They helped me convert an in-person sexuality seminar that typically attracted 20 participants into a teleseminar that registered nearly 10 times that number of men. I gained valuable reach into a new market as a men's sex and relationship expert.

WRAPPING IT UP

When you add coaching skills to your psychotherapeutic toolkit, you're creating a win–win for you and your potential male clients. The men win—those guys who might avoid a strictly therapeutic relationship with you—because they're invited into an out-of-the-box environment that holds more potential for their self-actualization. You win because you can serve more men—perhaps *a lot* more—by doing more of what you love to do.

REFERENCES

Addis, M. E., & Mahalik, J. R. (2003). Men, masculinity, and the contexts of help seeking. *American Psychologist, 58*(1), 5–14.

Cavanagh, M. (2009). Coaching from a systemic perspective: A complex adaptive conversation. In D. Stober, & A. M. Grant (Eds.), *Evidence based coaching handbook* (pp. 313–354). New York, NY: Wiley.

Downey, M. (2003). *Effective coaching: Lessons from the coach's coach*. Independence, KY: Cengage.

International Coaching Federation (2008). Global Coaching Study, Executive Summary. Lexington, KY.

Stanton, C. (2006). *Life coach in a box: A motivational kit for making the most out of life.* San Francisco, CA: Chronicle.

Whitmore, J. (2002). *Coaching for performance: Growing people, performance and purpose.* London: Nicholas Brealey.

Whitworth, L., Kimsey-House, H., & Sandahl, P. (1998). *Co-active coaching: New skills for coaching people toward success in work and life*. Palo Alto, CA: Davies-Black.

PART III

Populations

Intervening With Male Sub-Groups Who Share Identities, Perspectives, and Experiences

CHAPTER 11

A Holistic Approach to Counseling Military Men

Jerry Novack and Scott A. Edwards

> We sleep soundly in our beds because rough men stand ready in the night to visit violence on those who would do us harm.
>
> Winston Churchill

As we write this chapter, America has been at war for more than 10 years. Millions of military men (and women) have deployed to Iraq, Afghanistan, and all areas of the world. Some have been sent multiple times. This intense and prolonged military activity has resulted in military and civilian therapists seeing more men with connections to the military than they once may have.

Military service men can sometimes be challenging clients. We know from experience. Having worked with these men for years, we have learned that trust and alliance with them is not easily earned. We have both had our moments of struggling with how to best help these men who are sometimes mandated to treatment, frequently resistant, and often disinterested. Frequently, these men avoid discussing their military experiences with anyone, let alone a therapist who might not really understand them. Many have even been instructed to deny the presence of mental health symptoms by senior leaders.

Still, despite these difficulties and challenges, we have been fortunate to enjoy a fair margin of success working with these heroes in various settings. We have consulted with each other and other colleagues regularly in order to determine exactly what does and does not work with military clients. In these talks we have uncovered a core commonality in how we effectively reach service men in our work.

Though it might seem simple or obvious, we work from this basic assumption:

We are all changed by our experiences, and military service—especially deployments and active combat—are profound experiences. As a result, military men are impacted in some way—good, bad, or otherwise. In fact, there would be cause for concern if they were completely unchanged by their military experiences.

Some people (us included) would consider this the very definition of learning; change as a result of experience. As simple and obvious as this supposition might seem, it affords us several advantages in our work with military men. We do not find these same advantages in a purely symptom/pathology focused approach.

This approach ensures that our diagnoses are based on assessment of the client's symptoms, not his military experiences. It offers us a real appreciation for the ambivalence that military men might experience entering treatment. This approach helps us quickly build strong alliances with our military clients. This therapist lens requires us to consider context and holism in our work with them. It also allows us to focus on meaningful growth instead of just symptom reduction. This concept is genuinely outside the box, but we hope that it will become more common. Finally, this approach lends itself nicely to working with the service men's significant others and families. It is this approach and the related suggestions and interventions that form the basis for this chapter.

THE PTSD PITFALL

Many soldiers, marines, airmen, and sailors suffer no injuries as a result of their service, but some suffer from severe physical and mental health injuries. We are filled with a combination of gratitude and sadness when we meet these brave warriors. In our conversations with these men, they tell us they would much rather contend with physical injury than to face what are commonly referred to as the "invisible" wounds of war. This might help explain the strikingly high suicide rates among men who have returned from Iraq and Afghanistan.

The paradox is that while almost 80% of West Point Seniors expect to develop PTSD as a result of deployment (Matthews, 2009 as cited in Cornum, Matthews, & Seligman, 2011), research suggests that fewer than half of men returning from deployment meet criteria for any diagnosable disorder (Tanielian, Jacox, Adamson, & Metscher, 2008). It can be very tempting to diagnose a military service man with PTSD based on solely his exposure to traumatic experiences, but doing so has serious ethical implications and can threaten the effectiveness of the therapy. This happened to Gary.

Gary came to see me (Jerry) at his university's counseling center for help with his marriage. He served in Iraq, and was in several firefights there. He had been injured by an improvised explosive device (IED) made from an aerosol can. Skeptical about counseling, like many vets, he had tried therapy before and was told that he had PTSD, and he had to be treated using a specific protocol

(Cognitive Processing Therapy). Although Gary was mildly uncomfortable around aerosol cans, he demonstrated no other symptoms of PTSD (or any other diagnosable disorder).

My work was centered on his marriage. Ultimately, Gary saw that experiences from his family of origin had contributed to the way others reacted to him. I helped Gary realize that he was the *scapegoat* in his family. He got in trouble in an effort to draw attention away from other family problems. This role became habit for him and he continued it in his military unit and his marriage. He recognized that his enlistment was partially motivated by a desire for more structure than he had at home. He also recognized that his marriage was emotionally abusive. He eventually divorced his wife and reported great improvements in his wellness.

PTSD and mild traumatic brain injury (mTBI) can be tricky to accurately diagnose. Often, the symptoms that point clinicians to PTSD or mTBI are irritability, poor sleep, difficulty concentrating, and the like. While these are, in fact, symptoms of PTSD, they are also common reactions to life stressors. We have noted that, as military men ourselves, we could be diagnosed mistakenly with PTSD based on our own reactions to stress. Importantly, just because a military man has had some exposure to trauma and demonstrates these symptoms, does not mean that he meets criteria for a disorder. In situations like this, assess your military clients diligently, as most will not meet the specific criteria for PTSD, TBI, or any other clinical disorder.

AMBIVALENCE AND SKEPTICISM

Research shows that men are unlikely to pursue mental health services whether they are in the military or not. Yet, in addition to the expected masculine concerns about being "crazy" or "weak," military men often face real consequences for admitting to mental health symptoms. Weapons handling, security clearances, entrance into many schools (e.g., sniper, special operations), and eligibility for some occupations (e.g., aviation) can be threatened by the presence of mental health concerns.

While conducting assessments for the Army National Guard, I (Jerry) began each session by asking the soldier what brought him in to my office. Frequently, he had no idea. He only knew that his commander or supervisor told him to attend the appointment. In one instance, following a 10-month paper trail, it was revealed that the soldier had endorsed "trouble sleeping" (one of the "SIGECAPS" symptoms of depression popular in military assessments) during a mass assessment event. It turned out that the service member had just moved into a new apartment and did not have air conditioning. He had trouble sleeping because he was uncomfortable—not because his deployment had "damaged" him.

Sometimes male service members who present for therapy have been faced with an ultimatum. In some ways this parallels how men must often make decisions about attending couples counseling or face losing their partners. He might be "command directed" to treatment. Sometimes, loved ones have told the service member that he risks losing relationships with them unless he gets help. In the absence of an ultimatum, a male soldier who self-refers for treatment is likely in such intense distress that he is unable to function well in everyday life. Whatever scenario brings a male soldier to therapy, expect him to be skeptical and hesitant about engaging in counseling at first.

Steve was a tough, battle hardened, "iron major." Injured in battle by a fragment in his neck, millimeters from his spinal cord, Steve applied pressure to his own wound while caring for other wounded men. He worried that his military career was over when he came to counseling at his wife's behest. He said, "I don't know what the hell I'm doing here—it's probably a death notice on my career, but I love my wife and kids and they say I'm not the same, so here I am. Fix me, Doc. Apparently I'm broken." I (Scott) assured Steve that he did not seem "broken," but in fact may have changed—in some ways for the better. I also suggested that his family might have changed while he was away, too. It seemed clear that Steve did not meet criteria for any disorder. He was instead contending with grief over friends lost in battle, challenges reintegrating with his family after deployment, and fear for his career because of these troubles—difficult challenges for anyone. I validated Steve's concerns and shared my interest in preserving his career if I could. We discussed his sense of self as a man, a father, a husband, and a soldier. Steve had changed as a result of his experiences, but his core values and beliefs remained intact. I helped him share these changes with his family while building on existing strengths. Understanding Army culture and being aware of common stressors in deployment and in civilian life, all in the context of Steve's beliefs and values, were keys to success with him.

Importantly, it takes time to fully understand a warrior's motivation for coming to therapy. In working with these men, have patience and empathize with their ambivalence about being there. We have both experienced angst and uncertainty when we sought personal and marital counseling. We relate—and we think that helps. When we can appreciate their concerns about seeking help and demonstrate our genuine desire to be of service to them, we find that these are goal-oriented men who work diligently with us to overcome their obstacles. Draw on your own experiences to connect with military men. Also, take time to discover what criteria, timelines, and consequences are involved with the warrior's treatment. It is unlikely that the service member will know these details, and getting this information can be complicated.

More suggestions: be explicit about the fact that you are in no hurry to diagnose or otherwise label the service man. Let him know that you prefer to really understand how his life experiences, military and civilian, have contributed to him being the man he is today. Assure him that all people, military and civilian, even the therapist (you), excel in certain areas and struggle in others. Share that you intend to help him capitalize on his existing strengths while examining his struggles and helping him work towards his goals for his life and relationships. We have found that very overt statements like these (as long as they are honest and heartfelt) help navigate ambivalence and facilitate treatment.

INTERACTING IDENTITIES

By avoiding unwarranted fixations on PTSD based solely on a man's military experiences, we are freed clinically (and cognitively) to consider the importance of context in each warrior's life. The fact is that every soldier, marine, airman or sailor plays many roles in various environments. In addition to their identities as warriors, these clients are also sons, fathers, brothers, marital or romantic partners, friends, employees, bosses, and community members. Understanding that various roles can mean different things is critical. Keep in mind that, whatever their meaning to the client, these roles likely interact with one another in complex ways. This attention to interwoven identities helps us develop a rich, multifaceted connection with that client. In doing so, we get to appreciate potentially important factors that might have been missed if we focused exclusively on a man's military experiences and erroneously relate all his difficulties to the potentially traumatic ones.

True enough, examining every potential role and identity might be impossible and is certainly beyond the scope of this chapter. However, we will discuss three identity pieces—masculine identity, a warrior ethos, and family system involvement—that military men tend to have in common.

MILITARY AS A CULTURE OF MASCULINITY

There is no question, the military culture is a decidedly masculine one (Godfrey, 2009; Godfrey, Lilley, & Brewis, 2012). Masculine qualities such as emotional stoicism, toughness, and aggression are prevalent and commonly rewarded. In an environment concerned with war, these qualities can be important, adaptive survival skills. Military clients likely value traditionally masculine qualities in themselves and others.

We love this kind of work. Although men sometimes struggle with issues of emotion and intimacy, they are often great friends, loyal family members, hard working employees, protectors, and providers. It has been said by many, and we agree, that the cornerstone to helping men in therapy is not to change the men into "better clients," but to change the therapy to conform to masculine clients' needs. Most notably, Kiselica and Englar-Carlson (2010) have identified 10 male strengths that they consider positive aspects of traditional masculinity and often refer to in their clinical work. They are:

1. Male relational styles
2. Male ways of caring
3. Generative fathering
4. Male self-reliance
5. The worker/provider tradition of men
6. Male courage, daring, and risk taking
7. The group orientation of men and boys
8. The humanitarian service of fraternal organizations
9. Men's use of humor
10. Male heroism

While every man is different, several of the strengths above have paid particular dividends in our work with men. We use *male relational styles* and *humor* to facilitate closeness in our relationships and build rapport with our clients. We have both conducted sessions with men while shooting "hoops" using a basket suctioned to an office door, listening to music, or playing checkers. Humor has proven an equally effective grounding technique after particularly intense sessions.

Further, *male self-reliance*; *male courage, daring, and risk taking*; *the group orientation of men and boys*; and *male heroism* frequently emerge as important themes in our work with warriors. At a bare minimum, these strengths help create a more balanced and honest understanding of the client than a pathology-focused approach might. We have yet to meet the man that is "all bad" or "all good." All people have strengths and struggles. When many service men present for treatment, they are so focused on their difficulties that they overlook their strengths. Highlighting these strengths has proven an important step in building rapport and achieving the clients' therapeutic goals. Sometimes, when men recognize these strengths as part of their military service, they can use the same strengths and abilities to improve their relationships and their lives.

HARNESSING THE POWER OF THE WARRIOR ETHOS

> Honestly, I have wanted to do this since I was about eight years old. I love it. It is all I have ever wanted to do. It is who I am.
>
> SSG Ray Lowry as quoted in Winslow (2012)

In his book, *The Heart and the Fist,* Eric Greitens (2011) detailed his experiences serving as a social justice advocate and a Navy SEAL. He explained that while visiting wounded warriors in the hospital, he would often ask them what they wanted to do after leaving the hospital. He found that wounded veterans wanted to return to their units, ships, and duty stations. Needless to say, many of these men had been injured in ways that would prevent them from returning to active duty. Greitens recognized that, despite their injuries, "warrior" remained central to their identities.

Of course, not all military men will feel strongly about their identity as a warrior. It is important to not assume that this identity will mean the same thing to all military men. In fact, some might view this part of their identity negatively. As the next three vignettes illustrate, regardless of the service man's opinion about his service, we recommend that therapists recognize the potential impact of this identity piece and attend to it in the therapy.

James came for help with severe depression, anxiety, and conflict with his partner. In sessions, I (Jerry) found myself mired in James' hopelessness and negativity. Needing something with more traction, I noted that James seemed happiest when he spoke about his life as a soldier. While deployed, he felt better than he could remember feeling before or since that time. James took great pride in his identity as a warrior. He felt strong, loyal, capable, focused, and altruistic. Service men are all individuals who bring their own set of abilities and values to the job. By approaching his schoolwork, physical and mental health, and relationships as missions, James found that he could apply the qualities that he valued in his military experience and achieve success as a civilian. James was able to reconnect with the sense of meaning, purpose, and satisfaction that he experienced while deployed.

Similarly, after returning from deployment, Adam had difficulty transitioning back to family life. In asking about his experiences, I (Jerry) learned that Adam took great pride in his role as unit leader. He valued his ability to look after his men and his accountability to them and their families. Through continued exploration, Adam saw that the qualities and values that he brought to being a unit leader were his. He did not have those qualities by virtue of his job. He had his job because he possessed these qualities. By taking ownership of this truth, he was able to apply those values and qualities to his family life and gain a sense of fulfillment by caring for and being accountable to his wife and children.

Joe, on the other hand, regretted his service. He enlisted after 9/11 hoping to participate in the "Global War on Terror." In his experience, though, the government used him in an operation that had little to do with combating terrorism. What's worse, Joe felt tossed aside after being injured in combat. As he saw it, his brothers-in-arms had forgotten about him the instant he was no longer useful to them. By examining Joe's willingness to face danger and fight for what he believes while still validating and appreciating his disappointment in his lived experience, Joe was able to make meaning of his service. Ultimately, he summoned his courage and values in addressing family issues, repairing relationships with his parents, and leaving a failing relationship.

A man's soldier or warrior identity can easily become intertwined with his identity as a man in a masculine environment like the military. While there is nothing inherently wrong with interacting identities, in the case of wounded or retired service men, such interactions can contribute to emotional distress and identity confusion. We help these warriors identify which qualities they want to integrate into their enduring sense of identity and explore options for applying those qualities in their new roles. Also, retired and/or injured service men can consider which qualities no longer serve them well and work to grieve those parts of themselves, transcend old definitions of self, and create a new reality.

Clients with negative perceptions of their military service can be particularly challenging, especially when the service member has a duty commitment left to fulfill. In our work, we have found that an existential shift is often required for warriors such as these. Therapists can help the client differentiate what he does not like about his military experience from the values and character strengths that inspired him to serve. The key for clinicians in these situations is to help a man discover the elements of his military identity that do fulfill him and give him meaning, then help him apply them to his work and to other areas of his life.

UNIT INTEGRITY: THE MILITARY FAMILY

Family dynamics often play a vital role in whether a military man thrives or struggles. We are sometimes struck by how the same man will have outstanding relationships with his unit, attending to their needs and holding himself accountable for them, while struggling to connect with his own partner and children. We do not try to explain this phenomenon. Yet, we have had some success working with it.

We take our time and explore the client's relationships in his unit. We learn about his role in the unit, and his approach to fulfilling that role. Sometimes we spend several sessions learning about the service man's rewarding experiences there. Once we have thoroughly "field stripped" these positive relationships, we will share our curiosity about what is different in his home life. If he can have strong relationships in his unit, then he is capable of engaging in meaningful ways. As is often the case, the "problem" is seldom with him specifically, but with the system. On the other hand, when a service man has not had a great experience in his unit, we detail what he would want those relationships to look like and explore possibilities for creating those dynamics in his family. Whenever possible, we make it a priority to include a service man's family in his therapy. Consistent with research on military families, we have found that the families' opinions about the service man's work, father–child relationships, and the families' openness to new experiences can be important themes in the work. We attend to these factors, as well as individual family situations and characteristics in our work.

Deployments are tough on families. Partners, children, siblings, and parents can sometimes go long time periods without knowing if the service man has been hurt or killed. If there are children in the family then the service members' partners become single parents while the service men are away. Still, families that take pride in military service tend to function best. When the service man, his partner, children, parents, etc. believe that his work requires meaningful sacrifices for noble reasons, they seem to manage deployment-related transitions better than families that do not.

Researchers have shown father–child relationships prior to deployment seem to predict family adjustment to deployment and post-deployment reintegration (Shaw, 1987). Though not directly related to deployment, military families that value cultural diversity and enjoy cross-national and international networks of friends and loved ones also tend to thrive. People who enjoy new experiences, foods, and customs tend to tolerate military life better than those who prefer the familiar. They thrive in life satisfaction, relationship satisfaction, and other important domains.

We suspect that men in same sex relationships might experience challenges different from those mentioned, but there is still little known about these relationships in a military context. More research is needed to understand the way military experiences impact gay men and their families.

We have noted that military men will often discuss the importance of their units, not assuming much, if any, credit for their accomplishments and successes. We make a point of helping them recognize the importance of their family units as well. By helping family members find meaning in the man's service, while validating their fears and political perspectives; facilitating father–child relationships; and helping families find joy and adventure in new experiences, we work to promote healthy adjustment for the entire "unit."

Scott's work with Charlie provides a rich example of some of these themes. I (Scott) met with Charlie and his family after he had been back from war for about 12 months. He was experiencing anger and frustration at home. Though he had always enjoyed a close relationship with his children, he found that he could no longer get along with his oldest son. His son said that Charlie was always telling him what to do and didn't trust him to make decisions, and that he hated the military because it "messed our family up." Charlie felt his son had become belligerent and disrespectful. He had been proud of how well his son had been helping around the house and caring for the younger kids while he was away. I challenged Charlie to look at his son as an aspiring young leader. When Charlie viewed his son as he might a junior enlisted airman, he was able to embrace his son's growth and look for ways to foster increased responsibility. All Charlie needed to do was apply his unwavering commitment to his men and unit to his own family's cohesion.

POSTTRAUMATIC GROWTH

> Out of difficulties grow miracles.
>
> Jean de La Bruyère

Men who experience very difficult military events often recover from the trauma and do well in life. We have found that many grow emotionally and interpersonally from the experience. However, therapists fixated solely on trauma and symptom reduction might miss valuable opportunities to help facilitate this growth. For us, it is nice when we can help a marine, soldier, airman, or sailor achieve a baseline absence of symptoms. Still, it's so much more rewarding when they tell us that they are actually thankful for their trauma, because their lives are now richer for it. We believe that posttraumatic growth (PTG), not just the absence of symptoms, should be the therapeutic goal when working with military men. It saddens us to consider this approach "outside the box." Yet, we find PTG a rare consideration in both research and clinical arenas.

PTG is "positive personal changes that result from [trauma survivors'] struggle to deal with trauma and its psychological consequences" (Tedeschi & McNally, 2011, p. 19). It is distinct from resilience. Resilience suggests that an individual who experiences trauma possesses coping abilities that minimize the trauma's psychological consequences. Paradoxically, more resilient people experience less PTG than less resilient people do. Those with more severe PTSD symptoms generally experience greater PTG. The key to growth after a trauma seems to be in the struggle to process and make meaning of the event. To that end, we embrace this struggle openly, excited to help warriors use their male strengths to frame their experiences in the context of heroism, humanitarian service, and courage. Be warned, though: patience is key. We have found this process takes time. Still, as research suggests, the "working through" process seems necessary for achieving growth.

Matt had deployed to Iraq for nearly 18 months as part of a special Combat Search and Rescue (CSAR) team. He conducted more than 100 difficult missions while overseas. Many of the missions involved receiving rocket and small arms fire while flying overhead in his team's MH-60 Blackhawk. He saw the death of "many enemies and more than a few friends." When he returned, he was reintegrated into his unit where his commander "urged" him to seek mental health treatment. Matt explained, "I guess he figured anyone who got into that kind of trouble had to be broken."

I (Scott) interviewed Matt and his wife. He admitted that he had been struggling with intrusive thoughts and disrupted sleep and other symptoms when he returned from war 15 months earlier. He went to the Veterans Affairs Medical Center (VAMC) for six months where he was diagnosed with PTSD and treated with medication and a paltry schedule of prolonged exposure therapy.

Matt admitted that the treatment had helped him, and his wife agreed he had made substantial gains through "a lot of really hard work and many sleepless nights." By the time he got to me, most of the hard work had been accomplished. He had regained "85% control" of his thoughts and behaviors, and his emotions were not as unpredictable as they had been.

Our work together focused on existential issues, incorporating his experiences into his sense of self, and helping him and his wife revitalize their sex life. Matt's wife attended every session. Matt worked hard with me for six months. He no longer shut down when he talked about witnessing the death of his platoon sergeant. Yet, he still struggled with the thought of it. I knew our work was ending when Matt said that he would never want to re-experience what he had been through, but he was a stronger and better man because of it. His wife said that Matt enjoyed life more, was more attentive to her needs, more involved with their children, and more patient and compassionate. She noted that his faith in God seemed stronger, too. Matt demonstrated that people could suffer and struggle through difficult experiences but often come out better for it. In fact, with the right guide, PTG should be considered the norm. By the way, their sex life improved too!

CONCLUSION

In this chapter, we have shared our experiences using a strength-based approach that assumes military experiences always impact men, but it does not assume they necessarily impact men negatively. It is an approach that discards the notions that difficult experiences are equivalent to a PTSD diagnosis; that all symptoms overlapping with PTSD must be treated with a trauma-focused approach, and that PTG is an exception. We have examined how issues of masculinity might influence counseling with military men and offered suggestions for treatment. The importance of individual identity factors, family, and social supports and possibilities for strengthening those supports were stressed. Finally, we have explored the value of both resilience and PTG in pre- and post-deployment therapy. It has been our experience that creative, strength-based approaches to individual and family therapy will help military service men feel welcomed and comfortable in treatment and achieve wellness beyond what they might have imagined possible.

REFERENCES

Cornum, R., Matthews, M. D., & Seligman, M. E. P. (2011). Comprehensive soldier fitness: Building resilience in a challenging institutional context. *American Psychologist, 66*(1), 4–9.

de La Bruyère, J. (1885). *The "Characters" of Jean de La Bruyère.* London: John C. Nimmo.

Godfrey, R. (2009). Military, masculinity and mediated representations: (Con)fusing the real and the reel. *Culture and Organization, 15*(2), 203–220.

Godfrey, R., Lilley, S., & Brewis, J. (2012). Biceps, bitches and borgs: Reading *Jarhead's* representation of the construction of the (masculine) military body. *Organization Studies, 33*(4), 541–562.

Greitens, E. (2011). *The heart and the fist: The education of a humanitarian, the making of a Navy SEAL*. New York, NY: Houghton, Mifflin, Harcourt.

Kiselica, M. S., & Englar-Carlson, M. (2010). Identifying, affirming, and building upon male strengths: The positive psychology / positive masculinity model of psychotherapy with boys and men. *Psychotherapy Theory, Research, Practice, Training, 47*(3), 276–287. doi: 10.1037/a0021159

Shaw, J. A. (1987). Children in the military. *Psychiatric Annals, 17*(8), 539–544.

Tanielian, T., Jacox, L. H., Adamson, D. M., & Metscher, K. N. (2008). Introduction. In T. Tanielian & L. H. Jacox (Eds.), *Invisible wounds of war: Psychological and cognitive injuries, their consequences, and services to assist recovery* (pp. 3–16). Santa Monica, CA: RAND Corporation.

Tedeschi, R. G., & McNally, R. J. (2011). Can we facilitate posttraumatic growth in combat veterans? *American Psychologist, 66*(1), 19–24.

Winslow, T. (2012). Indiana aviation: Consistent support through persistent conflict. *Indiana Guardsman, Spring, 8*, 11–17.

CHAPTER 12

Working Outside the Box With Incarcerated Men

Mark E. Olver and Therese Daniels

We make a living by what we get, but we make a life by what we give.
Winston Churchill

As an undergraduate, I (TD) took a class on psychopathology where I learned the basics about mental illness. Thinking I might eventually be a therapist, the class scared the hell out of me. I thought, "Just let me work with some 'normal' people with 'regular' kinds of problems." It didn't quite unfold that way.

As a graduate student, my first practicum was a summer placement at a treatment center for federally incarcerated individuals. As I had enough experience working in "secure settings" having spent almost 16 years in the Canadian Armed Forces, it was not my first choice. Honestly, I was afraid of working in a prison with "evil men who had committed horrendous crimes." And I thought, "What do I know about prisons, or working with men?" I did a lot of self-talk to convince myself that I could handle working with criminals. I asked myself, "How bad could it be?" I told myself, "I can do anything for a few months." I drew strength from having worked with men in the military.

Adding to the complexity of the situation was the gender factor. In the early 80s, allowing women to work on aircraft was a new concept. And the men didn't like women in "their space." They assumed we wouldn't be able to do the job and it seemed like they were waiting and watching, hoping that we would fail. The off-color humor took some getting used to—and then I found my own voice and started to match their jokes with my own comebacks. Having three older brothers and training with male athletes during my years of competing came in handy. So I figured that working with men who were incarcerated wouldn't be all that different. That was my thinking before I found out that I was to work on the sex offender unit! "Please not the sex offender unit." But 12 years later, I'm still working with sex offenders on the same unit and look forward to coming to work *almost* every day.

As the years passed, I came to realize that the men on the unit were like a lot of other men I knew. They weren't slimy and sleazy as I thought sex offenders would be; rather, they were men who had made some bad decisions and whose freedom had now been taken away from them. As I listened to their histories, I was struck by the extensive abuse in their childhoods. It was not unusual to hear that they had been sexually abused within the family unit or in foster homes and had then been sent to a boys' school or reformatory only to have been sexually abused by older boys or by staff (oftentimes priests and/or guards). It was the norm rather than the exception. While I didn't condone what they had done, I could understand how they got to this juncture in their lives. That central insight helped me become more comfortable and I'm sure made my interventions more effective.

I (MO) completed my first practicum on the same unit and treatment facility as Therese. It was the only forensic placement being offered, so, by default, it became my first choice. I too was initially intimidated by the thought of working clinically in a maximum-security psychiatric facility. And I was definitely unsure as to what to expect when working with sex offenders. My doctoral research supervisor, who worked at the facility, wanted to adapt a risk instrument he developed so that it could be used with sex offenders. The placement and the research topic, both on sex offenders, just seemed to coincide, and in some respects you could say I just sort of fell into this field.

I also learned to see these men, in many respects, as quite ordinary—not the monsters depicted by the media. All had made some terrible decisions in their lives. Some had committed worse crimes than others, and some had more serious personal problems. But ultimately, they were people, first and foremost, with rights, feelings, and interests, loved ones and, usually, hopes for a better future. I immediately saw the value in holding respect and humility for each man I worked with, with the recognition that they were more than simply the worst personal mistake they had made in their lives. Over the years I would work with offenders in various settings, youth and adult, and have continued to do so even after settling into my current academic position.

The program we have worked in is a 48-bed inpatient sex offender treatment program for offenders assessed as at least moderate to high risk for sexual violence. The program treats individuals with special needs, including those who are learning disabled, brain injured, or seriously mentally ill. In this chapter we share some of the stories and lessons learned from working with this population and with incarcerated men in general.

ISSUES OF TRANSFERENCE AND COUNTERTRANSFERENCE

The truth is, men who are incarcerated are often very challenging clients. Many are highly resistant and distrustful of the treatment process. These men, especially sex offenders, have often done horrible acts that have brought them to prison. Their reasons for entering treatment are frequently not based on their own motivation to understand why they committed crimes or their interest in changing their behavior. More often, their treatment interest and involvement is based on their hopes in attaining an early release.

A detailed discussion of transference and countertransference issues in working with offenders is well beyond the scope of this chapter. However, we do want to highlight some common key issues. One is the high number of female therapists, nurses, and other service providers working with adult male offenders. This seems to exacerbate the men's issues of power, dominance, sexualization, and intimidation towards females, primarily therapists and facilitators.

We often have to have open discussions with the patients about a number of topics that are not easy. These include sexual fantasies, inappropriate jokes or remarks, personal questions, making threats, violating one's personal space, or even rearranging or scratching their genitals while having a discussion with a staff member. These uncomfortable conversations can stir up any clinician's issues around sex and aggression. In addition, graphic abuse or brutal crime descriptions can easily trigger countertransferential reactions. This is even more common if the patient demonstrates antagonistic or disruptive behaviors, or when there is a denial of personal responsibility.

For me (TD), some cases are harder than others. The graphic details of the patients' sexual offending history impact me more than the particulars of their own experiences of being abused. When I started working in this facility after my initial practicum, I had a recurring nightmare related to feeling unsafe. New staff are surprised when I mention the nightmares; but knowing the effects of working in this environment, and knowing you are not alone is a documented antidote to burnout (Nathan et al., 2007).

One of my solutions was to take Tai Kwan Do, which boosted my confidence that I would be able to protect myself if necessary. I do not discourage the rumor that I have a brown belt, since I have enough training to protect myself. Thankfully, there are also no more recurring nightmares. I have found that ultimately having open and meaningful conversations that are "real" with each of the patients will go much further to protect you than any form of martial arts. Frank, open, and respectful communication (which also serves as good role modeling), empathy, and validation can go a long way.

Disappointing Fred

I (MO) am reminded of an angry and volatile young man in segregation at a different institution, named Fred. He had appealed a psychological assessment that denied him parole. I had the task of completing the new assessment. In the end, Fred was quite clearly not suitable for early release, but I felt the need to inform him in person and also to warn the correctional staff that I would be giving him bad news. One correctional officer smiled to another and mightily shook a can of pepper spray. I hoped this wouldn't be necessary. I handed Fred the copy. He inhaled sharply, stared down at the table, and voiced some incoherent utterances of disbelief, anger, and disappointment. Finally he read the report. I sat there and watched as his demeanor changed. Fred let me know that he found the report to be more balanced, accurate, detailed, and fair than the previous assessment. Although he did not like my conclusions, he understood how I arrived at the conclusions and eventually accepted them. I could have assumed an unhelpful combative stance or argued back and forth which may have culminated in intervention by security. Instead, Fred was able to use the skills we have worked on in treatment to manage his disappointment.

USING HUMOR AND BEING HUMAN

When I (TD) reframe a patient's "bad behavior" into "What is he trying to tell me or why is he doing this behavior at this time?" I can usually find a crack in the exterior that opens up a promising conversation. It may be that what the patient wants is unrealistic in this moment, but maybe we can make a plan for how to get there from where we are. I have found that Miller and Rollnick's (2002) motivational interviewing has been very helpful as a way to get both of us on the same side of the problem. One of the motivational techniques that always stayed with me was asking the client what kind of a report he would like to read at the end of the program. When he describes this "glowing report," I can honestly say, "I would love to write that report. What needs to happen so that I can write that for you?" and now the ball is back in his court. We are on the same side, but the outcome is his responsibility.

Using humor, as pointed out by Chris Kilmartin (2013) in this book, is another way to align with incarcerated male clients. We have found that humor helps to break the ice, and can be used to challenge a patient and get the process moving forward when he becomes "stuck." Particularly when I am struggling with some kind of resistance or we are not on the same page, and it seems like the river is widening between us, I may use the line from the movie *Jerry Maguire*, when Tom Cruise screams, "Show me the money... Help me to help you!" and the patient almost always breaks a smile.

I (TD) use music and song in much the same way, when appropriate. For example, when the guys are learning to identify feelings, I may have that infamous chart with the picture of the faces with emotions in front of them. As I'm waiting, I may start singing, "Feelings, nothing more than feelings" and I usually comment, "I better not quit my day job." This breaks the stress. They laugh, and they seem to know they are not being judged because they are struggling with identifying what they are (or were) feeling in a given situation. With the mood lighter, we get back to the task.

I (MO) recall a young man who was engaging in some horseplay in group and dumped a cup of hot coffee down the shirt of another, more passive, group mate while the other facilitator's back was turned. I pointed this out and we discussed his behavior. The young man seemed to avoid me afterward and to take the matter personally. I saw him playing guitar one day thereafter and asked if I could join him. He seemed surprised, but nodded, and so I grabbed another guitar and played along with him. We knew some of the same melodies and I asked him to teach me some bars of one of his favorite songs. He seemed to appreciate the implicit message that my handling of the incident was one of holding him accountable and practicing new skills; it was not personal. We developed an amicable working relationship, sharing this common interest.

PICKING THE RIGHT METAPHOR OR ANALOGY

As authors, we were quite pleased to see the topic of working with metaphors and analogies being covered in this book (McKelley, 2013). Below are a few of our experiences with this helpful approach.

Chainsaws and Assertiveness

Abstract concepts don't seem to work well for many offenders. Many men describe themselves as "meat and potato kind of guys." We find that using analogies that the men can understand, and attaching the more obscure point to the analogy, helps in teaching a concept or getting a point across. For example, I (TD) use my chainsaw experience when teaching assertiveness. Most of the guys have used a chainsaw and they know when I talk about the orange case, I am referring to a Husqvarna model—so now we have some connection and they are interested in hearing more about my chainsaw. We recall learning how to cut down a really small tree (almost shrubs) before cutting down a "real" tree. This usually leads into stories about the difficulty in cutting down a larger tree—not making a big enough notch in the big tree only to have it collapse onto the blade. Now we can talk about the fear and the adrenaline and how they solved this problem. This is a perfect segue into learning about assertiveness. It takes a lot of practice. It usually doesn't come easily. We discuss how being "tongue-tied" or feeling inadequate in communicating appropriately (rather than aggressively) is similar to feeling nervous or cautious (or downright scared) using a chainsaw for the first time.

Pumpkin Pie and Why?

Analogies are also used to simplify important concepts and make them more understandable to the men we work with. I (TD) was in charge of preparing Josh, a 22-year-old developmentally delayed man, for his meeting with the Parole Board. The stakes were considerable. During this meeting they would ask him questions and then decide if he could be managed in the community. We had to ensure that Josh knew his "rules": no parks, no playgrounds, no babysitting, no touching, and no exposure. The first three he always remembered, the last two were far more difficult.

Further, the bigger challenge was helping Josh to understand the concepts of his statutory release date (SRD; which occurs when two thirds of the sentence is complete) and his warrant expiry date (WED; when the full sentence has been served). To help him grasp this timeline I used the concept of thirds by picturing a sliced pumpkin pie. This seemed to make complete sense. When I checked back a couple of weeks later, all Josh remembered was the pumpkin pie (and the vanilla ice cream he likes to have with his pie). All the attached meaning was gone.

Renovating the House

We also encourage patients to create their own analogies to help them better understand treatment concepts. Paul created one such analogy involving a dilapidated old house to describe his process of personal improvement while undergoing intensive treatment. Paul was raised on the East Coast of Canada and other men relate to Paul's analogy either because they know the East Coast weather or because they are familiar with run-down houses in need of extensive repair. Paul said, "We're all a work in progress. We can't expect miracles to happen overnight ... unless it's on a home renovation reality TV show!" He went on, saying, "We have to work at it a little at a time. First scrape off the old layers, then prime it on a nice day, then add coat upon coat of paint until it is just like new again. You can move to the inside when the weather outside gets bad, room by room until everything is sparkling." In reference to a long-term patient who had been making considerable strides in treatment, Paul commented, "He's been renovating his 'home' for over a decade now." When our patients can create their own analogies, this makes treatment concepts more meaningful and useable for them.

Volleyball Bumper

We find that analogies can also be used to convey a message with greater therapeutic impact. Chris was a sex offender who struggled with applying treatment concepts. He was still relying on his old coping strategies to deal with stressors and was soon to be released to the community. I (TD) was doing some individual work with Chris to help him broaden out his plans for release or "Safety Plan." I knew that he was a strong athlete and really liked playing volleyball. He was always animated when sharing the latest story about what happened in the most recent game. Having played volleyball myself in high school, I knew the lingo of the game. One day I said, "I hear you're a good volleyball player." His chest puffed out with pride and he joked that he was better than good. I said, "So you serve overhand" and he replied, "Of course." "And you know how to set and how to spike" and he retorted, "I'm the best on the team." So I asked him, "What if you were the team captain and there was a guy wanting to play but you knew that he couldn't serve overhand, he couldn't spike, he couldn't set, and he couldn't even bump the ball very well?" Chris sneered and said, "No way man! He ain't coming on my team." So I said to Chris, "You know what? When it comes to your 'Safety Plan', you're a bumper!" Well, this immediately got his attention. "Who me—I'm a bumper? No way, I'm not a bumper!" This conversation, while partly in jest, opened up the doorway for me to speak Chris' language and motivate him to put more effort into his release plan.

REDUCING RELIANCE ON SPOKEN AND WRITTEN LANGUAGE

One of the most pressing obstacles we have found working with this population is the spoken and written word. Frequently these men lack the language skills to verbally express their inner experience or to describe "what's going on" in the moment. Using interventions and strategies that are mainly verbal is strongly discouraged, particularly when working with intellectually delayed offenders. In our experience, this method shuts down therapy before it even begins. It was a big challenge for us to muster up creative resources to find alternative ways of helping these men develop useful tools that draw on their strengths and compensate for their verbal limitations. Below are some cases that illustrate these challenges and our solutions.

Head to the Hills

Harold is 62 years old, 250 pounds, and diagnosed as mildly mentally retarded. He is designated a "dangerous offender." Harold has big issues with authority figures and has received over 300 institutional charges. He has a long history of being abused sexually since childhood. Harold is also hard-of-hearing and has numerous reasons why he is not wearing his hearing aids (we are still not winning this battle!). When he first arrived, I could hear him yelling and threatening someone as I entered the main unit door. His behavior was unmanageable and he was at risk of being sent back to his institution. Such a move would likely result in Harold spending many months in segregation if we couldn't get his behavior somewhat under control. Despite his claim that "I don't trust nobody," he was willing to give me (TD) a chance because his best friend, who had previously spent about three years here, said to him, "It's okay, you can trust Dr. D. She's good people." And because Harold was motivated by the impressive changes he had seen in his friend, he let me into his life.

As much as Harold tried to tell himself to "shut his mouth" and "walk away," he would jump to conclusions, overreact, and start swearing and threatening to harm someone. After one outburst, he was almost on the bus back to his parent institution when he begged me to do something to keep him here. We started doing "therapy" together. Yet we didn't talk about what brought him to prison or what kinds of trouble he found himself in; rather we talked about his childhood years. Given the extensive abuse he reported, I asked him about the good times he remembered. He started talking about old TV shows like *Green Acres* and *The Beverly Hillbillies*. I remembered these shows too, but he actually had the tunes and the words like "Green Acres is the place to be..." We were able to come up with two slogans ("Zip it!" and "Head to the hills"), with accompanying hand movements (zip across the mouth and then quickly slide the right hand over the left to indicate getting outta here) that really fit his experience. He mastered these two rules and started reporting back to me all the times he wanted to hurt somebody but that he "zipped it and headed to the hills." Since we started 17 months ago, Harold has used these interventions successfully to remain in treatment and feel proud of his self-control.

PROVIDING "FACE-SAVING" OPPORTUNITIES AND THE POWER OF REFRAMING

Sometimes situations arise where patients are at risk for being embarrassed or even shamed. In such cases, we try to provide an "out" that allows him to preserve his dignity and self-esteem. That is, we try to create face-saving opportunities, which we find also helps to promote trust and therapeutic engagement.

The Smoke Break

George had great problems with self-control and was referred to our center because he was difficult to manage in the regular institutions. We saw similar challenges in our work. He parroted whatever was said in group, but never followed through. One day in session, I (TD) challenged him on his most recent outburst. George pushed back his chair and stood up, ready to storm out. Before he left, he yelled that he hated being treated like a child and being "sent to his room every time he was bad." Okay, so now we finally had something. When asked what would work better for him he said, "I know I get on people's nerves.

Why don't you just tell me I need a smoke break? Then taking a time-out won't seem like such a punishment." With further discussion, he shared that he wanted to start each day with a clean slate. He agreed that if he was told to take a smoke break, and he went to his house (i.e., "cell") for 30 minutes, then he could freely return to the unit until the next time he "needed" a smoke break. And so on. This strategy was miraculous. George accepted being told to "take a smoke break" and reengaged appropriately after the 30 minutes was over. George learned to manage his behavior by having his smoke breaks. Within 10 months, he was released to the community and has maintained his freedom for over seven years now.

ISSUES OF TRAUMA AND VULNERABILITY

An immediate priority for these men is to complete sex offender treatment as this is designed to address their risk factors. However, I (TD) also receive referrals for additional treatment to help men address abuse issues that could be interfering with their treatment progress. As such, I have adapted the Cognitive Processing Therapy (CPT; veteran/military version) that has been found effective for posttraumatic stress disorder (PTSD) and other corollary symptoms following traumatic events (Chard et al., 2009; Resick et al., 2010). Although CPT is typically conducted over 12 sessions, we usually need several more sessions (group or individual) to complete the work. Patients with multiple traumas and/or very limited cognitive functioning usually receive CPT on an individual basis. Harold, from an earlier example, required 39 individual sessions to successfully complete CPT; all of his practice assignments were done in session.

Stuck Points

The common thread among the men is that each has experienced or witnessed severe violent and/or sexual abuse from various sources (e.g., parents or others in caregiving roles, foster homes, residential schools). The men complete the Post Traumatic Checklist (specific; PCL-S) before each session to allow us to evaluate the number and severity of symptoms experienced between sessions. They also write an Impact Statement explaining why they think this traumatic event happened, and describe its effects on their life in the areas of safety, trust, power/control, esteem, and intimacy. We look for "stuck points" associated with the trauma (often based in shame and blame) that, up to this point, interfered with healing from the abuse (e.g., "It was my fault the abuse kept happening because I didn't tell anybody.").

Once the Impact Statement is completed and we are talking openly about what deeply matters and affects these men, the number and the intensity of symptoms decreases significantly. There seems to be a different quality or level of self-blame, however, when the men have been abused by other men. They often question their sexual orientation. The message seems to be, "If I experienced physical pleasure, that means I am responsible for it, or enjoyed it." As one patient related, "I kept going back to my abuser even though he was doing these things to me, but I was disgusted." We found that when the men could talk about their "stuck points," they could change the messages they were telling themselves. Those men in our group sessions were comforted and relieved by knowing they weren't the only ones who had been abused.

CONCLUSIONS

In writing this chapter, I (TD) asked the men I've worked with what they considered to be the most helpful aspects of our work. A key item seemed to be working with respectful, trustworthy, and down-to-earth staff. Staff members who didn't "use big words," and could use creative devices to illustrate treatment concepts without heavy reliance on language. The men also appreciated the use of humor to diffuse stress and found witnessing the success of other patients helped give them a glimmer of hope. Finally, the men identified the clear structure and expectations of the program to be helpful, and they appreciated receiving a certificate in the end to validate their achievement.

What these men outlined was very much consistent with some of our own beliefs about what might be effective in connecting with them in a therapeutically meaningful way. In this chapter we have illustrated a number of these strategies, particularly for incarcerated men with intellectual delays. Creative, often more concrete or nonverbal strategies that are both sensitive to their cognitive limitations and build on their individual strengths seemed to be most effective. We have found that being sensitive to how these men perceive their progress is significant since it allowed them to build on what they do well and assisted them to change what wasn't working. Many times we have been stumped about how to connect with a patient or how to help him understand the material. "Thinking outside the box" is critical and a necessity with the men we work with in this environment. Schafer and Peternelj-Taylor (2003) state that, "the ability to establish therapeutic relationships and maintain boundaries is among the most important competencies required by forensic mental health nurses" (p. 606). We would go further and suggest that the ability to establish therapeutic relationships and maintain boundaries is among the most important competencies required by *all* staff members working in the health services field and, particularly, within the forensic treatment setting.

The opinions and conclusions presented here are those of the authors and do not necessarily reflect those of the Correctional Service of Canada.

REFERENCES

Chard, K. M., Reisck, P. A., Monson, C. M., & Kattar, K. A. (2009). *Cognitive processing therapy – therapist group manual: Veteran/military version*. Washington, DC: Department of Veterans' Affairs.

Kilmartin, C. (2013). Using humor and storytelling in men's work. In A. B. Rochlen and F. E. Rabinowitz (Eds.), *Breaking barriers in counseling men: Insights and innovations*. New York: Routledge.

McKelley, R. A. (2013). Pushing haystacks and cracking steel balls: Using metaphors with men. In A. B. Rochlen and F. E. Rabinowitz (Eds.), *Breaking barriers in counseling men: Insights and innovations*. New York: Routledge.

Miller, W. R., & Rollnick, S. (2002). *Motivational interviewing: Preparing people for change, second edition*. New York: Guilford Press.

Nathan, R., Brown, A., Redhead, K., Holt, G., & Hill, J. (2007). Staff responses to the therapeutic environment: A prospective study comparing burnout among nurses working on male and female wards in a medium secure unit. *Journal of Forensic Psychiatry & Psychology, 18*, 342–352.

Resick, P. A., Monson, C. M., & Chard, K. M. (2010). *Cognitive processing therapy: Veteran/military version*. Washington, DC: Department of Veterans' Affairs.

Schafer, P. E., & Peternelj-Taylor, C. (2003). Therapeutic relationships and boundary maintenance: The perspectives of forensic patients enrolled in a treatment program for violent offenders. *Issues in Mental Health Nursing, 24*, 605–625.

CHAPTER 13

Making the Connection With Male Teenagers

Dave Verhaagen

Robert Fulghum's book claimed, *All I Really Need to Know, I Learned in Kindergarten* (1988). Maybe I'm a late bloomer, because I feel like everything I really needed to know about therapy with teenagers, I learned in my first year out of graduate school. That year was so intense, so rock and roll, that I crammed a near lifetime of learning into those 12 months. One guy in particular challenged me so strongly that his lessons have stuck with me more than two decades later. I want to share his story with you, and then give you four big takeaways that have helped me connect with teenage boys in therapy over the years.

Fresh out of internship, I took a job as a psychologist with the Willie M. program, the product of a class action suit mandating treatment for teenagers who were not only mentally ill, but also violent. This included guys who had committed carjackings, rape, and multiple assaults, even murder. For a guy like me, whose career of violence consisted of a single 30-second fight with Gary Rudiger in the sixth grade, this was uncharted territory, to say the least.

Within the first few weeks of starting my job, a delusional, mostly unhinged 16-year-old named Jarrod, who had violently attacked multiple people, was assigned to me upon his release from a psychiatric hospital. He had lived on the ward for over a year, an eternity in inpatient terms, which only served to underscore how ridiculously dangerous he had become. His case manager, Ron, picked him up that morning and drove him straightaway to the mental health center for our first session.

From the first second I looked at him, I could tell that we would not be having a sit down conversation. My first clue was the fact he was skateboarding down the hall. *Do they let you have a skateboard in the psych hospital?* I remember thinking.

After I caught up with Jarrod, he agreed to take a walk with me.

"Jarrod, my name is Dave Verhaagen. I'd like to be your therapist," I said as we walked down the sidewalk around the back of the building.

"Mmmmm," said Jarrod, not looking at me. I wasn't sure what that sound meant.

"Sometimes when I'm trying to get to know someone, I ask them to describe themselves in a few words. What words would you use to describe yourself?"

"Cool," said Jarrod without hesitation.

"You're a pretty cool person?"

"Mmm-hmm," he said, meaning "yes."

"What other words would you use to describe yourself?"

"Can we go back inside now?"

We had reached Jarrod's load limit. He was done.

"Sure, but first can you think of any other words you would use to describe yourself?" I asked trying to eke another minute out of our time together.

"Cool," he said again without hesitation.

"Okay, let's go back inside." I thought he might be able to hang in there a little longer if we could just sit down.

At the time, my office didn't have a door on it (why was never really clear to me), so I couldn't meet anyone there for therapy. I asked Jarrod to follow me down the hall to a small TV lounge. Once we were in the room with the door closed, Jarrod became quickly agitated, his eyes darting wildly. He ran around the room like some kind of crazed lizard in a jar.

"Jarrod, please come sit down so we can talk," I said calmly.

"You shut up! I ain't listening to you!" came his not-so-calm reply; he looked entirely deranged.

Jarrod rummaged through the TV cart, then he dug underneath it. All of this was like watching a video in fast forward.

"Jarrod, come sit down..."

He wheeled around holding two big metal bars, both about a foot long. They were components from the TV cart that were never assembled, just laying there to be used against me as weapons in the hands of a flipped-out teenager. He stared at me and then started swinging the bars around martial arts style. He began to walk toward me in a clear attempt to intimidate me. I didn't change the expression on my face, but inside I was imagining what it would feel like to be beaten bloody by metal bars.

"Jarrod, you need to give me those bars," I said calmly, staring at him.

He kept walking toward me, swinging the bars faster.

"I'm going to count to three. If you haven't given me the bars by the time I say 'three,' I will take them from you any way I can." I was improvising. I had already violated the cardinal rule of working with aggressive teens: don't let a big violent kid swinging metal bars get between you and the door.

He kept approaching me, swinging the bars wildly.

"One..."

He stared at me, still swinging them so fast they looked like silver blurs.

"Two..."

He was still moving toward me, now making slashing movements with the bars. *This is going to be really ugly*, I thought to myself.

Let me pause to tell you I am a pretty skinny guy. I am not known for my imposing physical presence. (I once broke a finger making the bed.) By contrast, Jarrod outweighed me by 30 pounds, if not more. Plus he's psychotic. So this was not a happy moment for me by any means.

"Three!"

He immediately stopped swinging the bars and quickly handed them to me like a button had just been pushed in his brain.

"Here!" he said, looking terrified as he released the metal head-caving bars into my hands. Then he jumped into a chair, as if ready for the session to begin.

From this moment, I recognized the real deal with Jarrod: if he felt threatened, even by the smallest thing—a new person, a new environment, anything—he lashed out. But when you set the limit on him, he would invariably comply.

Our first order of business was to get his therapeutic foster home equipped to handle him. This was no easy task. Allan and Mary Walsh were turkey farmers in rural North Carolina who had agreed to be trained as therapeutic foster parents. They were good, old-fashioned salt-of-the-earth types who had raised good kids themselves, but none of their life experiences had prepared them for Jarrod. Within the first week of arriving in their home, Mary called me, frustrated almost beyond words.

"He won't give me a moment's rest!" said an exasperated Mary.

"What do you mean?"

"He can't leave me alone for two seconds. He's like a little puppy dog."

"That's got to be tough, I'm sure," I said.

"You don't understand. He won't even let me go to the bathroom. He's knocking on the door every five seconds, asking, 'Mary, are you in there?' Well, where else am I gonna be?"

However, this annoyance was nothing compared to the shock of finding Jarrod sitting in the kitchen one evening slowly and methodically stabbing the table with a knife, looking like a deranged Jack Nicholson in *The Shining*.

"Quit that!" Mary told him.

And he did.

Mary found him to be crazy but loveable. Allan thought Jarrod just had a behavior problem. Allan's solution was that hard work would cure all of the boy's ills, so every day when Jarrod came home from school, he had to help shovel turkey poop out of the turkey houses. Allan maintained a firm hand with Jarrod and was dismayed at the "no corporal punishment" rule of our agency.

"They say I can't beat him," said Allan, "but I *can* beat him....one time!"

One day Ron brought Jarrod to my office for his appointment. By unfortunate coincidence, there was a police car in the parking lot at the same time they drove up. Jarrod stared at the police car, then ran full speed into the building. He ran down the hall to me.

"David! David!" he screamed.

"Jarrod, be quiet!"

"Why did you call the cops on me?"

"What?"

"You called the cops on me! I'm going to make a run for it!"

"Tell me what you are talking about," I said, completely confused.

"The cops. Out front. You called them on me, didn't you?"

"No," I said plainly.

"Oh," he said, his volume dropping almost to conversation level.

"Jarrod, why would I call the police on you?"

"Because I had a bad day at school and I thought you must've found out and called the cops on me. Are you sure you didn't do it?"

"No, Jarrod, I wouldn't call the cops on you."

"Cool," said Jarrod, composing himself.

Jarrod was terrified of the police. Sometime later, he and Ron were driving back to the Walsh's house. When they stopped at a red light, Jarrod noticed a police car directly behind them in the passenger's side rearview mirror. Immediately, he jumped out of the car and began running at breakneck speed across a parking lot. Ron had to park the car and chase after him on foot as the cops watched this little scene unfold.

Jarrod was a bundle of anxiety, always looking like he was about to jump out of his skin. I realized later that the reason he had gone after me that first time was because he was terrified of being alone with a man. He was constantly on his guard against people hurting him. No one really knew why.

Therapy was slow-going for him. We had to spend the first few sessions talking outside behind our building, later he would come into my office and talk with my (newly installed) door open. Finally, he got comfortable enough to come in with the door closed. Even with this, he was always on the verge of exploding with anxiety. If I had a transcript of those first behind-closed-doors sessions, they would read *in their entirety* like this:

"Good to see you, Jarrod."

"Good to see you, David."

"What do we need to talk about?"

"I've been feeling a little worried."

"About what kinds of things?"

"Everything."

"Well it's good to talk about your worries."

"You're right. Thanks, David. Thanks for the help. Good talking to you."

Then he would jump to his feet and run out of the room. If we went for five minutes without him bolting, it was a marathon session. Despite this, we were at least making some forward motion. Jarrod was coming in the room and we were able to talk for a few minutes. We were doing fine until our big setback.

It came at the end of one five-minute session. As we stood up to leave, I reached out to shake his hand. When our hands met…*bzzzt*!…a little static electricity. Jarrod jerked his hand back and looked at me terrified as if I were a witch doctor who had summoned fire from the heavens. From that time on, he refused to shake hands with me. In fact, every session he would bring up this traumatic event.

"Don't shock me, David!" he would say each time we met.

"Are you going to electrocute me today?" he asked me once.

This obsession with me shocking him dominated the next couple of meetings, even when I tried to redirect him. After a few times of this, it occurred to me that this whole weird fixation *meant something* to him. I decided to put it out there to him.

"Jarrod, what's the deal with this shocking thing?"

"Nothing. I just don't want you to electrocute me."

"Electrocute?"

"Yeah. Don't electrocute me."

"Have you ever been electrocuted?"

"Yeah…by you."

"I mean besides that. Really electrocuted."

Jarrod shifted in his chair.

"I don't know."

He said it in a way that I immediately knew I had just hit pay dirt.

"Tell me what happened."

"My daddy…" he began, his eyes widening a little as the scene played out in his head. "My daddy used to hit my fingers with a hammer when I was bad."

"What else?"

"One day when I was really bad—I don't know what I was doing, but it was bad, I think—he threw me onto the electric fence. And I got caught in it. I couldn't get out."

Jarrod looked up at me and I could tell that he had just revealed the important thing in his life. He'd been telling it to me for weeks but I didn't hear it.

I came to find out that his father was so violent that when social services came to take Jarrod away from him, they brought the police with them for protection. *When the police come, they take you away.* Later on in his life, when the police came for Jarrod himself, they had taken him away for over a year. *When the police come, they take you away*. For months, we'd been thinking of Jarrod as paranoid and crazy when he was really just scared.

"What do you want most out of life?" I asked him once.

"I don't want anybody to hurt me," he said.

Luckily, Allan never gave him that beating. In fact, Jarrod came to trust and respect him. He clearly trusted Ron, letting him drive him around the county for appointments and interviews and activities. He came to trust me. Not all at once, but gradually it clicked for him that these people were not like his dad. They wouldn't hurt him.

The more he trusted, the more he talked; the more he talked, the less scared he became. He did well in school and he let Mary have her peace in the bathroom. He became, in essence, your average turkey poop-shoveling teenager.

Jarrod and I developed a great relationship, something I could not have imagined possible when he was contemplating smashing me to a bloody pulp with those metal bars. We sat and talked, though never longer than about a half hour or so. He even let me joke around with him. Once after a session, when I could tell he was doing well and in a playful mood, I came toward him in the waiting room with my index finger pointing at him, scuffing my shoes as if to generate the largest static shock ever documented, sure to create a blast that would rip a hole in the side of the building. He jumped from his seat and sprinted out of the front door.

"You better not shock me!" he yelled over his shoulder.

Only this time he was laughing.

WHAT I LEARNED FROM JARROD

Most of my clients now just smoke pot, punch holes in the wall, steal their parents' car in the middle of the night, and that sort of thing. The majority of them aren't nearly as emotionally-disturbed as Jarrod. But what I learned from him about working with teen boys has shaped my practice to this day. Let me give you my four takeaways from my year with Jarrod.

It's the Relationship, Stupid

For most of us, our therapy training was nearly all about theory and technique. We got the theoretical underpinnings, followed by the therapeutic action steps so we could put it all into practice. What we didn't get was an acknowledgment of how central—how vital—the *relationship* was. Yes, the therapeutic relationship was important, we were told, but what we weren't told was that it was *the thing*.

I'm not bad-mouthing technique; I use a ton of it. But no amount of good technique would have helped Jarrod without a trusting, genuine, and respectful relationship. The therapeutic relationship is the house; the techniques are the furnishings. The therapists I know who are most skilled at working with adolescent males are, without exception, exceptionally skilled in the relationship aspects of their work. They come from various theoretical backgrounds, but they all connect in authentic, empathic ways.

In Skovholt and Jennings' (2004) review of the qualities of peer-nominated master therapists, they found interpersonal and intrapersonal qualities, more so than technical mastery, separated the goods from the greats. That's been my experience in clinical practice, as well. One of my colleagues who works with younger teens jokes that he knows only one therapeutic technique (perhaps a mild exaggeration), yet there is a waiting list to see him for individual therapy and huge demand to get into one of his groups. Why? Because he connects with honesty, humor, and authenticity.

I started as a cognitive-behavioral guy (and still claim that tradition), then evolved into more of a motivational interviewing guy when I realized I needed a better approach with resistant clients, especially substance abusers. What I like so much about motivational interviewing is its emphasis on genuine empathy, equality in the relationship, and respect (Miller & Rollnick, 2002; Naar-King & Suarez, 2011).

Recently a school administrator asked me what made me successful in my work with teenage boys, a population that leaves many scratching their heads. I told him I just tried my best to be genuine, honest, and respectful. In other words, the relationship is king. The journal *Psychotherapy: Theory, Research, Practice, and Training* devoted an entire special issue to an exploration of the relationship factors in therapeutic outcome. In their final conclusions, they stated, "The therapy relationship makes substantial and consistent contributions to psychotherapy outcome *independent of the specific type of treatment*," (Norcross & Wampold, 2011, p. 98, italics added). To break it down specifically, their stringent evaluation of the research found empathy, alliance, cohesiveness (in groups), and soliciting feedback from the client was "demonstrably effective," and positive regard, goal consensus, and collaboration were "probably effective." Going a step further, they found that adapting the relationship to specific client characteristics only serves to enhance the effectiveness of therapy. They conclude by saying, "The therapy relationship accounts for why clients improve (or fail to improve) at least as much as the particular treatment method" (Norcross & Wampold, 2011, p. 98).

Janet Edgette writes in *Candor, Connection, and Enterprise in Adolescent Therapy* (2002), "The assumption (or hope) that a therapist can influence genuine change within a reluctant teenaged client in the absence of a meaningful relationship is a problem that rests behind many disappointing interactions between therapist and client" (p. 8). My own experience lines up with this. The therapeutic relationship is ultimately more important than therapeutic technique. Technique is not unimportant; it just isn't as important.

It's Good to Lighten Up

One of my clients, an 18-year-old college student, told me how depressed he had been during the past week because he felt tricked by an ex-girlfriend. "She called me over to her apartment late Tuesday night," he explained, "and *finagled my wiener into her.*" I exploded in laughter. Even though he was serious about feeling awful about it, his phrasing was so crudely funny, so crass, and so fantastically descriptive that I couldn't help but react. He smiled because I had appreciated his intentionally funny phrasing.

Since Jarrod, I have seen the benefits of humor in therapy, whether it's appreciating the humor of my clients or joking with them myself. When done well, humor can be a way to connect with clients and even help move them forward toward therapeutic goals (Salameh & Fry, 2001; Selekman, 2005; Verhaagen, 2010).

In my own experiences in using humor with teens, a few keys stand out. The first is that the style of humor is important in making this approach work in therapy. Rod Martin has uncovered four humor styles: affiliative, self-enhancing, aggressive, and self-defeating (Martin, 2006; Martin et al., 2003). *Affiliative humor* is positive, self-accepting, and used to enhance relationships. This style of humor is associated with all kinds of good outcomes, including greater emotional stability and higher self-esteem. *Self-enhancing* humor involves the good-natured ability to laugh at oneself. People often use this to cope constructively with stress and other difficulties. It lends itself to a more optimistic outlook on life and less depression. *Aggressive humor* involves sarcasm, put-downs, and other humor at the expense of others. People who use this style of humor a lot, predictably, tend to be more hostile and interpersonally aggressive. Finally, *self-defeating humor* involves self-disparagement and generating humor at one's own expense. People who do this are often more depressed, more neurotic, and have lower self-esteem.

The therapeutic application here is obvious: affiliative and self-enhancing humor can be helpful and therapeutic, while aggressive and self-defeating humor styles are not. I used humor often with Jarrod, as I do with most of my clients. I chose the example of me scuffing my feet to "electrocute" him as an example because it's slightly complex. On the surface, it seems fairly aggressive and done at his expense. Am I making fun of his trauma? Am I being a little mean? Here's where the relationship comes into play. Absent a solid relationship, doing that would have been wrong, perhaps even cruel. In the context of the relationship, it is a different message: *We have a shared experience. We both know this is funny because of what we have talked through, what we have been through together. This relationship is safe. I'm not really going to hurt you.*

He got it and, more importantly, he appreciated it. Joking with him was one of the keys to making a connection with Jarrod. It built trust, it signaled authenticity, and it connected us to each other.

You Don't Have a Magical Office

Years ago, I had a client who would scarcely talk to me in my office, but would chatter on non-stop if we were anywhere near his car. Many sessions, we would just go and lean up against his car for the better part of an hour. I have gotten comfortable with meeting kids where they can do their best work and make their most progress.

The same was true with Jarrod. I had little choice but to start my therapeutic relationship with Jarrod outside of my office. For starters, he was in constant motion. I also didn't have an office door for about a month. Our relationship started outside of the office out of necessity, and while we eventually got comfortable enough to meet in a traditional therapy setting (i.e., an inside office), many of our sessions—all or in part—involved walks, sitting outside, watching him skateboard for a while, or any number of other out-of-the-office activities.

In the research, there has been an increasing awareness of the benefits of out-of-office therapeutic experiences (Brooks, 2010; Hill, 2007; Scheinfeld, Rochlen, & Buser, 2011). Traditionally, we have been taught that therapeutic relationships have good boundaries (which they do) and those boundaries include the *place* where therapy occurs. The message is that therapeutic work occurs here, in this space, within these walls. I see the wisdom in that to an extent, but I have come to see greater benefit of being flexible with the geography of therapy. This is because I have increasingly realized that it's not really the place; it's the relationship with the therapist that is truly therapeutic. And that relationship can occur outside of the four walls of your well-appointed office. Yes, keep good boundaries, but feel the flexibility to move out of office as needed, especially with those restless teenage boys.

Being Uncomfortable Sucks, But it Can Make for Great Therapy

I would be lying if I didn't tell you those first weeks with Jarrod were as nerve-racking as hell. Would he attack me the way he had attacked those other folks before he went into the psych hospital? Would he do something dangerous in the community while he was on my watch? There were more than a few times when I felt my stomach tighten up as his session approached.

The truth, though, as I have reflected on it, is that the whole experience made me a better therapist. It forced me to reflect on myself, to be as genuine as I could be, and to be more thoughtful about what I was doing. There is a great danger in trying too hard with teenage clients—trying too hard to be liked or to be cool or to be engaging—but there is little danger in being more authentic and self-aware. A little discomfort can go a long way.

This lesson that started in my therapy experiences with Jarrod has carried over into other aspects of my life, as well. At times, I've found myself uncomfortable as a parent, a husband, a boss, and a friend. These relationships, while all immensely rewarding and important, are also, from time to time, sources of great discomfort and frustration. And while I've never been threatened with swinging steel bars in any of these relationships, there is often a sense that even more has been at stake. Being willing to tolerate tension and discomfort has made me, I hope, a better dad, a better spouse, a better employer, a better friend, and even a better member of my community.

Yes, being uncomfortable sucks, but it can make for great relationships and it can make you a better therapist. Don't seek it, but embrace it when it comes. Working with teenage boys can be tough and often highly uncomfortable, but you can be all the better for it.

REFERENCES

Brooks, G. R. (2010). *Beyond the crisis of masculinity: A transtheoretical model for male-friendly therapy.* Washington, DC: American Psychological Association.

Edgette, J. S. (2002). *Candor, connection, and enterprise in adolescent therapy.* New York: W.W. Norton & Company.

Fulghum, R. (1988). *All I really need to know I learned in kindergarten: Uncommon thoughts on common things.* New York: Villard Books.

Hill, N. R. (2007). Wilderness therapy as a treatment modality for at-risk youth: A primer for mental health counselors. *Journal of Mental Health Counseling, 29*, 338–349.

Martin, R. (2006). *The psychology of humor: An integrative approach.* Waltham, MA: Academic Press.

Martin, R., Puhlik-Doris, P., Larsen, G., Gray, J., & Weir, K. (2003). Individual difference in uses of humor and their relation to psychological well-being: Development of the humor styles questionnaire. *Journal of Research in Personality, 37*(1), 48–75.

Miller, W. R., & Rollnick, S. (2002). *Motivational interviewing: Preparing people for change, second edition.* New York: Guilford Press.

Naar-King, S., & Suarez, M. (2011). *Motivational interviewing with adolescents and young adults.* New York: Guilford Press.

Norcross, J. C., & Wampold, B. E. (2011). Evidence-based therapy relationships: Research conclusions and clinical practices. *Psychotherapy: Theory, Research, Practice, and Training, 48*(1), 98–102.

Salameh, W. A., & Fry, W. F. (2001). *Humor and wellness in clinical intervention.* Santa Barbara, CA: Praeger.

Scheinfeld, D. E., Rochlen, A. B., & Buser, S. J. (2011). Adventure therapy: A supplementary group therapy approach for men. *Psychology of Men and Masculinity, 12*, 188–194.

Selekman, M. D. (2005). *Pathways to change: Brief therapy with difficult adolescents, second edition.* New York: Guilford Press.

Skovholt, T. M., & Jennings, L. (2004). *Master therapists: Exploring expertise in therapy and counseling.* Boston, MA: Allyn & Bacon.

Verhaagen, D. (2010). *Therapy with young men: 16 to 24 year olds in treatment.* New York: Routledge.

CHAPTER 14

Navigating Multiple Identities With Gay and Bisexual Men of Color

Kevin L. Nadal and David P. Rivera

Being gay men of color, we are very aware of the many rewards and challenges this identity affords us. We have experienced the joy of acceptance of our identities, but also the pain of rejection associated with our sexual orientation, gender, race, and ethnicity.

Fortunately, we have grown to celebrate our multiple identities and have flourished in our personal and professional lives. And, we have developed the resiliency to persevere through the many microaggressions and other indignities we endure on a daily basis from our colleagues, friends, family, healthcare providers, students, clients, and strangers alike. (For example, a common experience is hearing the term "that's so gay" used as a put down or in a derogatory way.) Through it all, we have grown to accept our unique identities and how they interact with the sociocultural context of the environments that we navigate.

Importantly, our experiences are not unique. Every gay and bisexual man of color has to deal with the complex process of navigating various environments, while simultaneously managing his multiple identities. This process is wrought with obstacles that can interfere with optimizing his full potential to succeed in life, and can create or exacerbate psychological dysfunction. In many situations, the services of a psychotherapist are needed. However, many gay and bisexual men of color might be reluctant to seek help for their issues. And, even when a gay or bisexual man of color does seek out a psychotherapist, a cultural impasse might reduce or eliminate the benefits of psychotherapy. Given this, we believe it is essential that psychotherapists attend to various issues that can create and maintain cultural impasses, so as to minimize their harm on the psychotherapeutic relationship.

Drawing from our personal experiences and our therapeutic work, this chapter will identify several key obstacles that can disrupt the positive development of a healthy therapeutic relationship with gay and bisexual men of color. We will start with gender roles and related conflict areas that are particularly salient for this group of men, since issues of gender are intertwined with their sexual orientation, racial, and ethnic identities. Next, cultural stigma is inevitably experienced by gay and bisexual men of color and can inform everything from their help seeking behaviors to ruptures in the therapeutic process. Similarly, we have experienced multiple occasions in which clinicians ignored or minimized the significant roles that race, gender, and sexuality have in shaping the lived experiences of their clients. Finally, there are a few dynamic processes that can create obstacles and may require a unique approach when working with gay and bisexual men of color. These processes include client defensiveness, transference, and countertransference. For each obstacle identified, we include relevant examples and offer solutions that psychotherapists can utilize to effectively make meaningful connections with these men.

Before we discuss these obstacles and solutions, it is necessary for us to recognize several points. First, we assert that when addressing needs of gay and bisexual men of color, we are discussing a wide spectrum of individuals of different races, ethnicities, sexual identities, social classes, religions, nativities, abilities, and so forth. Therefore, while we may make some generalizations about this subgroup, there are a number of factors and intersecting identities that may influence the ways that these obstacles may manifest in psychotherapy, as well as in clients' personal lives. Because of this, we will give specific examples of how each obstacle may look differently based on these diverse identities and experiences whenever possible. Second, we recognize that the identities, worldviews, and experiences of clinicians have an influence on the ways that these obstacles emerge in therapy, how they are dealt with, and how clients react to them. Third, we acknowledge that the perspectives we share are a reflection of our own personal experiences and identities, particularly as early career professionals, men of color, and self-identified gay men, and admit that our recommendations may or may not be applicable or effective for all clinicians who work with men of color. Our main aim is to encourage reflection on these obstacles as a way to foster greater awareness for the unique experiences of gay and bisexual men of color.

OBSTACLE 1: ADDRESSING GENDER ROLE EXPECTATIONS IN PSYCHOTHERAPY

When working with gay and bisexual men of color, it is crucial to recognize that gender roles and gender role conflict may lead to many obstacles in psychotherapy. While gender roles refer to the behaviors, expectations, and values defined by society as masculine and feminine, gender role conflict refers to the experience of psychological distress for men that is often caused by (a) success, power, and competition, (b) restrictive emotionality, (c) restrictive affectionate behavior between men, and (d) conflict between work and family (O'Neil, 2008). Success, power, and competition involve a man's focus on wealth and accomplishments as a means of self-worth; the need to have authority over another person; and the need to triumph or "win" over another person. Restrictive emotionality is defined as a man's inability to express emotions, while also hindering others from expressing their emotions. Restrictive affectionate behavior between men entails a man's inability or difficulty in expressing intimacy and affection towards men. Conflict between work and family includes a man's difficulty in balancing problems at home and at work (Iwamoto & Liu, 2008; O'Neil 2008).

While men of all racial backgrounds and sexual orientations may experience gender role conflict, cultural values and expectations may influence gender role conflict particularly for gay and bisexual men of color in numerous ways. For example, because of the strong emphasis on *machismo* (male dominance) in Latino cultures, Latino men may experience great pressures to be masculine at all costs, to be physically and emotionally strong, and to be providers for their families. As a result, when they may start to question their sexual identities, they may view themselves as deficient or as failures, they may internalize their emotions, and they may view seeking help as a sign of weakness. Similarly, gender role conflict often prohibits men of color from coming out of the closet and developing a healthy sense of identity, often resulting in many men living secret, closeted, or "downlow" lives (Nadal, 2010).

Gender role conflict may have a huge influence on gay or bisexual men of color's experiences in psychotherapy in a number of ways. First, because these men are generally taught to be emotionally restrictive, therapy itself may seem to be counterintuitive to how they have dealt with their emotions throughout their entire lives. For example, in psychotherapy, one of the main goals may be to encourage clients to identify and discuss repressed emotions in order to alleviate any psychological distress. However, if these men have been repressing emotions all of their lives, it may be difficult for them to even identify negative emotions, let alone express or explore them. For example, many of our own gay and bisexual male clients of color have shared with us that emotions were never discussed in the family and that it was encouraged for family members, particularly men, to repress everything. As a result, they grew up in family environments that viewed emotionality as deficient and even forbidden.

Perhaps one recommendation to address gender role conflict with gay and bisexual men of color is to have open discussions about the gender role norms that each client learned in his family and how it may influence his current ability to share or process emotions in therapy, as well as how it may have an influence on the presenting problems in his life. It is also important to meet clients where they are in terms of their emotional capacity. For some clients, it may be necessary to learn to identify emotions first, before expecting them to explore emotions on deeper levels. My (David) work with a gay Asian man nicely illustrates this issue. Although not his initial presenting issue, it quickly became clear that he had difficulty identifying and expressing his emotions. In order to foster our rapport and trust, I found it helpful to be transparent about this issue and my motivation for encouraging exploration of his emotions. From our experiences working with gay and bisexual men of color, we have discovered that taking a "transparent" approach helps to demystify the therapeutic process, fosters trust, and strengthens the connections that we are able to make with our clients.

Another technique that we have found to be helpful is to ask male clients to describe the physiological response that they are having while in counseling (e.g., "Do you feel anything in your stomach or chest?" or "Do you notice any changes in your heart rate or breathing?"). From there, perhaps one can ask clients to articulate what the physical reaction feels like, which eventually may allow the client to label the feeling and explore his hypotheses as to why he is feeling that way. When gay and bisexual male clients of color have difficulty expressing emotions, it would be best to recognize the external factors that may have influenced this behavior (or lack of behavior), instead of pathologizing the client for his supposed emotional shortcomings. Furthermore, in utilizing the Wellness Model, it may be effective to focus on a client's strengths, instead of his deficiencies, in order to build rapport and engage the client in something that may be foreign to him.

OBSTACLE 2: ADDRESSING CULTURAL STIGMA AND CULTURAL MISTRUST

There has been a significant amount of research that has identified the many factors that prohibit communities of color from seeking psychotherapy (see Sue & Sue, 2008 for a review). First, cultural stigma has been cited as a main reason why there is an underutilization of mental health services for many people of color, particularly for men of color (Sanchez & Gaw, 2007). In many communities of color, psychotherapy has been traditionally viewed as an American practice, in that discussing one's problems is often viewed as superfluous, admitting to needing help is a sign of weakness, and turning to religion, spirituality, or alternative forms of healing would be a more culturally appropriate way of coping with one's problems (Sue & Sue, 2008). Furthermore, there has been an emergence of research that has found how cultural mistrust or patient suspiciousness affects people of color's perceptions of therapy. Cultural mistrust refers to the inclination for people of color, particularly African Americans, to mistrust Whites, in many sectors including education and training, business and work, interpersonal and social relations, and politics and law (Bell & Tracey, 2006; Terrell & Terrell, 1981). When unaddressed, cultural mistrust often leads to premature termination in psychotherapy (Sue & Sue, 2008). Furthermore, lesbian, gay, bisexual, and transgender (LGBT) people of color have been found to have especially high dropout rates in counseling and psychotherapy, due to the negative stigmas that they may perceive from their counselors and psychotherapists (Greene, 1997). Perhaps LGBT people of color are unable to trust clinicians, due to the historical treatment of both people of color and LGBT people in the mental health field. Hence it is necessary for clinicians to address stigma and cultural mistrust directly.

We offer a few recommendations for overcoming this obstacle. First, a direct approach could include overtly discussing the client's perceptions of psychotherapy, as well as the ways that one's family and community view mental health treatment. Some psychoeducational techniques may be employed, including teaching the client about what is to be expected, as well as openly discussing some of the cultural barriers that may impede the therapeutic relationship. Furthermore, utilizing strength-based counseling and encouraging the client's strengths and progress can build a stronger therapeutic alliance and keep him actively engaged.

There are many indirect ways that counselors can address cultural stigma and mistrust as well. Openly discussing issues of race, gender, or sexuality with clients allows them to recognize that a clinician is culturally competent and is comfortable with these topics. In doing so, the client may be more trusting of the therapist and may be less likely to drop out of therapy. In our work, we have noticed how our gay and bisexual clients of color "light up" when they recognize that we as clinicians have a comprehension of something that they thought they would have to explain in depth. For example, I (Kevin) remember a time when a young gay Latino client was discussing concepts regarding gender roles in his family, and when I used the terms *machismo* and *marianismo* in response, he appeared surprised that I was familiar with the terms. When I later asked him about how he felt, he said he felt relieved that I understood him and that he didn't have to spend considerable amounts of time educating me about his culture.

OBSTACLE 3: ADDRESSING ISSUES OF RACE, GENDER, AND SEXUALITY IN PSYCHOTHERAPY

As previously mentioned, there are an array of identities that gay and bisexual men of color may hold that can influence their worldviews, personal experiences, and perceptions of psychotherapy. Some clients of color may have highly developed racial identities in that they are very comfortable discussing race, understand the influence of race in their lives, and seek support from others with similar worldviews. On the other hand, some clients may have less developed racial identities and may not be aware of the ways that race influences their lives. At the same time, many LGBT clients may have strong sexual identities, in which they are accepting and celebratory of their sexual orientations or gender identities. Meanwhile, many LGBT clients may have internalized homophobia, which leads them to being uncomfortable with their sexual identities and repress self-hatred as a result. For gay and bisexual men of color, they can hold any combination of their intersecting identities, sometimes being comfortable with one identity, both identities, or none at all.

Perhaps one way to assess a client's racial and sexual identities is to have an open discussion with them about race, gender, sexuality, or other social justice issues and see how they react. If a client were very comfortable with the topic, perhaps he would need a style of psychotherapy which allows him the safe space to process his emotions regarding any of these issues. However, for clients who may not have had opportunities to discuss such topics, it may be a goal for the clinician to initiate such conversations in order for the client to explore their true reactions and feelings. For example, we have noticed that some clients are able to openly discuss their reactions to microaggressions, or subtle forms of discrimination that they experience in their lives (see Sue, 2010 for a review). These clients are able to identify microaggressions as such initially and may spend time in counseling discussing how they felt in the moment of the discriminatory behavior or if they were satisfied with how they reacted. On the other hand, we have also had experiences in which clients described what we deemed as clear microaggressions, but that they were unable to label as such. In these instances, we provided psychoeducation about microaggressions to help minimize internalization of any negative emotions about the incident or further self blame. This is especially important, because many of these men have internalized negative messages about their marginalized identities and it can be useful for the therapist to help identify these messages and help the client internalize more positive messages about their various identities. As aforementioned, having open dialogues about issues related to culture can be helpful in developing rapport with one's clients and in retaining them in therapy. However, having such conversations can be vital in assisting clients, particularly gay and bisexual men of color, in developing healthier identities and psychological wellbeing.

OBSTACLE 4: DEALING WITH DEFENSIVENESS

It has been our observation that many gay and bisexual men of color can be defensive in psychotherapy, for some of the reasons that were mentioned earlier. Perhaps gender role conflict may prohibit them from sharing their emotions, while cultural stigma and mistrust may disallow them from being vulnerable or engaging in the process. For gay and bisexual men of color, we hypothesize that the defensiveness may be due to the pressure they have experienced to maintain a certain image. As a result, when challenging your clients, there may be a number of defense mechanisms that these men may use to protect themselves or alleviate their anxieties. Some of these include: (a) using humor to deflect any negative emotion, (b) being unresponsive or argumentative to feedback or confrontations, or (c) disengaging in the process altogether.

We recommend a few ways to deal with these defensive reactions when they occur. First, as with some of our other recommendations, it may be helpful to approach them directly and have open and honest discussions about your perceptions of them. For example, I (Kevin) remember a gay male African American client who I found to be endearing and insightful, but who often made jokes anytime I tried to use here-and-now processing with him. The first few times, I may have laughed along with him or avoided pointing out this behavior, but, after a while, it became inevitable that I say something. When I called attention to this tendency of his, he admitted that he often used humor when he felt uncomfortable and that others often laughed along with him. From that point on, every time he made a joke, I acknowledged the behavior and we laughed together before he knew it would be time for him to explore the negative feeling his humor was masking. Eventually, addressing humor became a humorous part of our relationship, and the inappropriate or defensive humor ceased.

Another way to deal with defensiveness is to self-disclose. While some psychologists may have difficulty self-disclosing, it may be very beneficial to self-disclose with gay and bisexual men of color because we are asking them to do something they have not previously experienced. So while appropriately self-disclosing, we serve as models that show that we ourselves have done our work to become emotionally expressive and insight-oriented. Furthermore, because of the cultural stigma and mistrust these clients may hold, our self-disclosures help our clients to view us more as humans, which can eventually lead to a stronger rapport and an increase in their trust in us.

Validating a client, particularly when they feel isolated, can be helpful in showing them they are not alone. For example, when working with a gay Chinese American client who was struggling with his sexual identity because of his strict and conservative family, I (Kevin) was able to self-disclose about the difficulties of being gay and from an immigrant family. I was careful not to go into too much detail (so it wouldn't become my own therapy), but rather I focused on my understanding of his experience, as well as pointing out the fact that so many gay and bisexual men of color have similar struggles. Even for therapists who are not gay or bisexual men of color, self-disclosure can be a useful and effective tool to help foster connection. For example, from an interpersonal-relational perspective, a therapist can appropriately disclose about feelings that the client is evoking from them as a way to increase rapport. Again, this helps to equalize the relationship and can make the therapist appear more human to the client, which can shorten the distance between the client and the therapist.

OBSTACLE 5: MANAGING OF TRANSFERENCE AND COUNTERTRANSFERENCE

With any therapeutic relationship, there are so many dynamics that can be formed that can influence the relationship itself and the effectiveness of therapy. First, in maintaining the ethical standards of multicultural competence, it is essential for clinicians to be cognizant of their own attitudes, beliefs, biases, and assumptions, particularly about gay and bisexual men of color. Psychotherapists must recognize value conflicts that they may have with their clients, due to differences in race, ethnicity, or sexual orientation. For instance, some authors have cited how many clinicians may often maintain unconscious biases against LGBT persons and may desire for LGBT persons to be more similar to heterosexual people (Nadal, Rivera, & Corpus, 2010). Managing this countertransference is necessary because it helps clinicians to acknowledge how their own biases may affect their work with their clients in positive and negative ways. At the same time, clients may also hold transference toward their clinicians, in that they may experience repressed feelings about other people in their lives.

It is common for clients to displace feelings about their parents or family members onto their clinician, particularly those of the same gender (e.g., older male counselor/clinician reminds a client of his father, while a female counselor/clinician reminds a client of his sister). Perhaps open discussions about this transference may allow the client to uncover repressed feelings that he may not feel comfortable in discussing with his actual family members. Openly discussing transference may even encourage clients to have actual conversations about these unresolved feelings with other people in their lives, or at least improve their insights about their relationships.

More specific to gay and bisexual men of color are cultural transferential issues that represent stigmatizing and oppressive experiences (Gelso & Mohr, 2001). When there are differences in race, ethnicity, gender, or sexual orientation in the therapeutic dyad, as there most likely will be, the client might consciously and subconsciously transfer unresolved feelings about their oppressors onto a clinician who holds a privileged social identity. For example, a Black bisexual man who is working with a White heterosexual clinician might unknowingly transfer his feelings of anger or inadequacy associated with his experiences with racial discrimination and sexual stigma onto the clinician. It is important for clinicians to be aware of their privileged positions, not only professionally, but also culturally, so that they minimize the potential for recapitulating experiences of oppression for the client. In this example, a clinician who responds in a defensive way to the client's anger might be repeating an oppressive dynamic that the client has come to expect from their interactions with White heterosexuals. Cultural transferential issues can be some of the most difficult therapeutic situations to address, even more so than those involving family of origin issues, so it is especially important for clinicians to consider these issues in their work with gay and bisexual men of color.

CONCLUDING REMARKS

Making meaningful therapeutic connections with any client can be a challenge; however, making these connections with gay and bisexual men of color can bring a unique set of challenges and obstacles. These challenges, when not addressed, can create cultural impasses that disrupt the therapeutic process. But, when anticipated and addressed can demonstrate understanding and empathy that helps to maximize the clinician's ability to develop an effective and meaningful therapeutic connection with their clients. Part of our call to duty as clinicians is to make ourselves aware and knowledgeable about the various challenges experienced by our clients, which in turn should motivate us to develop skills to address these challenges.

Although it was impossible for us to include all the unique obstacles experienced by gay and bisexual men of color, it is our hope that the issues we did touch on piqued your curiosity about concerns that are likely to come up when working with these men. The process of becoming a culturally competent clinician is a lifelong one. Even the most seasoned clinician can benefit from deepening their self-awareness about their biases and assumptions concerning people who are culturally different. Given that relatively little is known about working with gay and bisexual men of color, it is especially imperative that clinicians take initiative in strengthening their knowledge about the challenges experienced by these men and also the strengths that they possess. Our experience has proven that it is possible to make meaningful connections with gay and bisexual men of color, and we attribute part of our success to being prepared to address the unique obstacles that enter the therapeutic space when working with these men.

REFERENCES

Bell, T. J., & Tracey, T. J. G. (2006). The relation of cultural mistrust and psychological health. *Journal of Multicultural Counseling and Development, 34*(1), 2–14.

Gelso, C. J., & Mohr, J. J. (2001). The working alliance and the transference/countertransference relationship: Their manifestations with racial/ethnic and sexual orientation minority clients and therapists. *Applied & Preventive Psychology, 10*, 51–68.

Greene, B. (1997). Ethnic minority lesbians and gay men: Mental health and treatment issues. In B. Greene (Ed.), *Ethnic and cultural diversity among lesbians and gay men* (pp. 216–239). Thousand Oaks, CA: Sage.

Iwamoto, D. K., & Liu, W. M. (2008). Asian American men and Asianized attribution: Intersections of masculinity, race, and sexuality. In N. Tewari & A. N. Alvarez (Eds.), *Asian American psychology: Current perspectives* (pp. 211–232). New York: Psychology Press.

Nadal, K. L. (2010). Sexual orientation and identity development for gay and bisexual Asian American men: Implications for culturally competent counseling. In W. Liu, D. Iwamoto, & M. Chae (Eds.), *Culturally responsive counseling with Asian American men* (pp. 113–134). New York: Routledge Press.

Nadal, K. L., Rivera, D. P., & Corpus, M. J. H. (2010). Sexual orientation and transgender microaggressions in everyday life: Experiences of lesbians, gays, bisexuals, and transgender individuals. In D. W. Sue (Ed.), *Microaggressions and marginality: Manifestation, dynamics, and impact* (pp. 217–240). New York: John Wiley & Sons.

O'Neil, J. M. (2008). Summarizing 25 years of research on men's gender role conflict using the Gender Role Conflict scale: New research paradigms and clinical implications. *The Counseling Psychologist, 36*(3), 358–445.

Sanchez, F., & Gaw, A. (2007). Mental health care of Filipino Americans. *Psychiatric Services, 58*(6), 810–815.

Sue, D. W. (2010). *Microaggressions in everyday life: Race, gender, and sexual orientation*. New York: Wiley & Sons.

Sue, D. W., & Sue, D. (2008). *Counseling the culturally diverse*. New York: John Wiley & Sons, Inc.

Terrell, F., & Terrell, S. (1981). An inventory to measure cultural mistrust among Blacks. *The Western Journal of Black Studies, 5*, 180–185.

CHAPTER 15

Counseling Fathers

Opening the Door for Reflection and Growth

Chen Z. Oren and Dora Chase Oren

Like many dads, I learned most of what it meant to be a father when I became one. I had little "on the job" training and few role models. What I did have was support and motivation to figure it out. Of course, I wasn't sure exactly what it meant to be a good dad, but I had a vague idea of what it could look like. And I knew what I did *not* want it to be.

My own father definitely fit the mold of the "traditional man." He went to the army to fight for his country. He had his own principles and morals. Some made sense; others, not as much. I am not sure he was concerned about passing his values along to us, but he did anyway. I learned the importance of hard work, family, and doing the right thing. Education was stressed. He wanted me to be a professional. He rarely expressed his feelings.

As I write this, I find my sentences about him short and to the point, just like he was. Although he did not really say it, I knew he loved me. He used actions and money to show his love. He worked many hours in his iron-manufacturing factory. Every day, he left in the early morning and came back late afternoon with hands blackened from the day's work. He took a shower and ate the dinner that was waiting for him. Then he fell asleep, typically snoring in front of the TV.

I heard that life changed for him when my mom passed away. He loved her just like he loved his kids. I was young when my mom died and he worried about me being okay. He gave me a book and said it was from mom, who wanted me to be a good student. And I was. He asked me if it was okay if he got remarried, that he wanted me to have a mom. I was six years old and did not understand. I said yes, it was fine. I think he had talked to our small family to get approval about remarrying. His remarriage turned out to be a disaster for both of us. He had many reasons and opportunities to seek professional help, but he never did.

Even when he was sick he did not get help. He died from melanoma. He was not diagnosed until it was stage four and terminal. Why? I have asked myself that many times. All I know is what he said, "I thought it was nothing, just spots on my skin so I did not go to the doctor." My father died six months after being diagnosed. I was in graduate school writing my dissertation.

His death left me with many unanswered questions. Why didn't he take care of himself? He was going to miss everything—my successes, my failures, my kids, my life. He would miss out on being a grandfather. Why did we not talk about the things that were important to him? I knew there was more to my father, parts that were hidden from me. Sometimes I think about how my life would have been different if we had been closer.

Initially, I was not sure where the answers would come from. I was too busy with life to give it much thought. I completed my dissertation, got my doctoral degree, and got ready for internship. When my mentor introduced me to men's issues I realized why I had entered the field of psychology: it was to work with and help men and to specialize with fathers. While there is a growing body of literature on counseling men, I have found little on working with fathers.

Men have experienced a significant shift in the expectations and roles of fathers. Most of this is in the right direction, positive changes. Yet there are significant challenges remaining, namely deepening men's discussions about fathering, both in and out of therapy. I co-edited the book *Counseling Fathers* (Oren & Oren, 2010) designed to bridge the gap between fathers and therapists. This chapter details the strength-based approach that I use in my private practice to deepen therapy with fathers.

Before getting into my suggestions, I'll ask you, the reader, to pause for a moment and reflect on your own father. First, was he there at all? Sadly, many are not. Second, if he was there, think about your relationship with him. How would you describe your father? How does your relationship with him impact you on a personal level? How might it impact your work? I ask myself similar questions and more. How do we better understand fathers? What do fathers need and how can we help them?

I have worked with many fathers who tell me, "I have been trying to be close to my kids but I don't know how." Gary, a 36-year-old father of three, came to me after separating from his wife. His affair with another woman had been discovered and he started therapy after his home was sold. "The house was empty. I did not even help my wife, who was my high school sweetheart, and my kids pack. I felt nothing. That was the moment I realized I needed help. I know I love my kids and wife but I don't know how to show them. To be honest, sometimes I don't know what it means. I bring money, but I always feel like an outsider."

I base my work with fathers on a number of facts and assumptions. In your work, I'd recommend keeping these facts in mind.

- All fathers are men. When a father comes to therapy he carries with him lifelong experiences related to the socialization process of becoming and being a man in the society and culture he was raised. It is important to learn, explore, understand, and work within this socialization process.
- Most men are fathers. There are roughly 70 million fathers in the U.S. (United States Census Bureau, 2012) making over half of adult men fathers.
- Build it and they will come. Fathers do attend therapy and look for help. In my private practice, almost 70% of my clients are men and most are fathers.
- Being a father is important. The roles and expectations of fathers have been dynamic throughout history and dependent on contextual factors (e.g., ethnicities, culture, religion, age). The most current definition of a good father highlights the importance of providing emotional nurturing, physical and financial support to the children and partners, and being involved, engaged, and responsible (see, Oren & Oren, 2010; Pleck, 1997, 2010; Vann, 2007).
- Fathers can be nurturing and expressive. It is a misconception and stereotype often reinforced by gender socialization that men cannot nurture others or express feelings. Many men in their role of fathers contribute to their children's cognitive and emotional development (e.g., Hawkins & Dollahite, 1996; Lamb, 2010).
- Many fathers do not have training or role models and can feel confused or unsure of how to balance their different, sometimes conflicting, roles and responsibilities.
- Mental health providers' own fathers, their perception of fathers, and their definition of a "good father" shape their work. Recognize how your relationship with your father impacts your worldview, including biases, of fathers. It is a process I try to be aware of with every father I work with.
- Finally, I believe a strength-based approach along with traditional psychotherapy works well when treating fathers. My work is based on the growing movement in the field which suggests that men, and this includes fathers, can benefit from strength-based and male sensitive counseling approaches and interventions.

I know traditional psychotherapy did not work for my father and many other fathers of his generation. I heard that when it was suggested to my father that he go to counseling he had many responses. Some included, "No one can tell me what to do with my own family, I can figure things out by myself, I'm not crazy. They wouldn't understand anyway."

Honestly, I think my father was scared of therapy or that he would have been perceived as weak or incompetent. I wish that wasn't the case. Therapy might have prevented many unpleasant experiences; it may have helped him learn how to talk to me. It might even have saved him from dying when he did. I have worked on dealing with conflicting feelings of anger, love, sadness, betrayal, and mostly longing for him. I take comfort in knowing that he was a good man who loved me deeply, but getting help was not on his radar.

My journey with my father, having my own children, and working with fathers has changed my ideas of who fathers are and their potential.

When I give presentations about counseling fathers I start by asking the audience two questions:

1 What is the first thing that comes to mind when you hear the word father?
2 What does it mean to be a father?

The answers to these questions are often interesting and telling: strong, provider, absent, alone, disciplinarian, etc. are common. In the last few years I started to hear different answers: hero, caring, smart, loving, friend. I am happy to see a shift in my generation of fathers. These are the fathers who are seeking help and coming to counseling.

A while back, a well-established maternity shop called me and wanted to explore starting a fathers' group. Groups and classes are a great way to address the interests and needs of fathers. In the men's group I co-facilitate, issues related to being a father often take center stage. The group format allows fathers to get important and varied feedback and to not feel alone.

I found it difficult to form a fathers' group. I was excited about getting the word out through the maternity shop's pretty extensive marketing, but after a few months the shop could not recruit enough fathers to start a group. I was disappointed by the limited response. Fathers can use the support and often feel left out, beginning in pregnancy, a feeling that can stay with them throughout parenthood.

Fathers are often seen as the secondary parent. Further, many men internalize the experience of being isolated in their role as father. We as mental health providers can reinforce the message. Duhig, Phares, and Birkeland (2002) found that fathers tend to be less involved in therapy and attend fewer sessions than mothers and suggested that it is the responsibility of the clinician to engage fathers in the therapy process. How do we bring fathers to therapy?

I learned that attracting fathers to my practice took creativity. As I improved in expressing my interest in fathers and marketing my practice toward this subgroup, my practice expanded. I encourage you to find creative ways to attract fathers. I gear my methods towards educating and advocating for fathers. I also try to demonstrate my passion for working with them. I give presentations, write articles, and contribute to fathering websites. With these efforts, I use male- and father-friendly images and wording. Key point: be deliberate and purposeful in how you market your practice if trying to reach fathers and your specialization.

Kiselica (2003) looked at ways to establish rapport with boys and men when they come to therapy. He recommended being mindful of the setting. This may include having magazines appealing to men, being flexible with scheduling, using humor and appropriate self-disclosure. Many of these topics are discussed in greater detail in this book. Shappiro (2001) said that successful relationships and interventions with fathers were built on male-friendly counseling. In my work with fathers, I am mindful of these principles.

IN THE ROOM WITH FATHERS

Assessment Questions

Once I sit in the room with a father I am aware of the importance of opening the dialogue about the importance of being a father. A number of my father clients who had been in therapy before say they never felt understood by other therapists. Dustin, 32, told me that his last therapist never asked him about being a father or talked about fathering at all.

To be fair, most fathers I work with have presenting problems that seem unrelated to being a father. I ask anyway, questions that focus on the experience of being a father. How would you describe yourself as a father? How would you like to be able to describe yourself in this area? Asking direct questions and starting the therapeutic process in a more structured way can ease fathers' nervousness. Most appreciate my directness and are comfortable going further.

Notably, I ask questions that elicit a discussion about their struggles, needs, and strengths. These often give men permission to talk about what it means for them to be a father and to learn from their experiences. Many father clients tell me that no one has asked these questions nor had they thought about the answers and their impact. Typically, fathers are explored only in the context of their relationship with their children rather than their own experience.

When working with fathers, you need to be patient. Allow your father clients to learn to trust you and the therapeutic process—at their own pace. Unfortunately, I know about the importance of patience and pacing from my own therapeutic failures. When I feel compelled to act, educate, and give advice prematurely, my father clients take notice. At least one of them never came back when I made this mistake. Regretfully, I did not have a chance to process and repair my immature eagerness to help. I learned the importance of taking the time to reach out to fathers. After trust has been established, I use it to explore how fathers can gain confidence in themselves and others and be nurturing in their own relationships.

An important theme in the questions I ask is related to clients' experience with their own fathers. With men's responses, I pay attention not only to the content of the stories but how they narrate the story. Some fathers narrate with anger, some with sadness, some with respect. Still others get defensive and protective.

Look for the internalized messages, behaviors, and attitudes clients learned from their own fathers that often shape their current parenting. I ask clients: Where and how did you learn to be a father? What was your relationship like with your father? Who were your role models? How does the relationship with your father impact your current parenting?

Danny, 35, came to therapy to work on anxiety. He attributed his anxiety to traveling as a national sales manager. Danny had quickly climbed the corporate ladder, but still worried about his job. He saw everything he did as not good enough. He did not say much about his four-year-old and recently born son. I asked him about being a father and his commitment to being a successful provider. Danny paused and tears started coming. I respected Danny's tears and talked about them, but, more important, looked at what was it like for him to cry. Danny said that he was not used to crying. His father never cried. Then he told me that he does not spend enough time with his children. He admitted feeling anxious around his sons. He said he didn't always know how to talk to his wife about the boys or how to balance time on the road and at home. He was scared that his sons would have the same experience he had with his father.

Danny's father was a successful businessman, too. He was the head of the household and obsessive about order. The family spent weekends helping Danny's father clean and repair the house. Danny remembers spending hours one Sunday holding the ladder for his father to fix the roof. He was not allowed to complain or move and he hadn't. Danny had been afraid of his father. He felt judged and criticized by him. His father did not recognize his achievements or encourage him to explore his own interests. Like his father, Danny internalized anxiety and held a restricted view of how to be a father. It became obvious that Danny's anxiety, although intensified by his job, was rooted in his relationship with his father and messages he learned from him. Eventually, Danny saw its impact on his current fathering.

We started a process of exploring his anxiety in the context of his father. He considered how he wanted his relationship with his boys to be different. We looked at his strengths. How can you use what you are good at to balance your life? What are your strengths and passions that you can share with your kids? As our work progressed, Danny's anxiety decreased significantly and he became a more involved father and husband.

The questions I ask help me frame treatment. They also help fathers feel comfortable looking at their father experiences. Like with Danny, the questions helped us understand the root of his anxiety faster and on multiple levels.

Using Father-/Male-Friendly Language

Of all the suggestions for making therapy father-friendly, perhaps the most important tool has been using my father clients' language. Using words, phrases, analogies, and images that resonate and are part of daily language (work, sports, etc.) help establish rapport and demystify therapy. I've also found they help fathers "buy into" interventions.

A recent case, Ian, stands out. Ian, 49, is a father of six, with two kids from his first marriage. Ian reported that his wife had always wanted him to be more involved in her children's lives, especially her sons, and to be a role model for them. However, Ian avoids conflict and quickly disengages from his wife's sons when he feels disrespected and not listened to. He felt that he was losing control, along with his voice, in the family.

In my work, I used different interventions and analogies to help Ian gain confidence and engage with his family. The national hockey league playoff had been in full swing. Ian's favorite team, which had never peaked at the right time, surprised everyone and won the Stanley Cup. Ian went to all the home games and enthusiastically talked to me throughout the playoffs about the team's amazing run. Knowing hockey, I decided to use his language.

I compared Ian's family to his favorite team. Both for many years had lacked leadership skills, communication, respect, and teamwork (having each other's back—a common male phrase). This year was different. Everyone knew their roles and they had become a powerful system. I used many hockey terms like: line changes, power plays, momentum, taking a hit, etc. Ian was passionate and resonated with what became a complex analogy to his own family. He built on it and added more terms that described his ideas on how he could become a leader and champion as a father. He developed new goals along with a plan to improve his family. Ian has new energy and hope about creating change as an engaged father and stepfather.

As a therapist, pay attention to themes and listen closely to how a father expresses himself. Use his language to connect with him and deepen the work.

Help Fathers Identify Strengths

My father had strengths. But like a lot of kids, I saw the weaknesses. He was older than many of my friends' fathers. He was tired. He did not go out much. After his death and through my process of better understanding our relationship, I see that I missed the chance to recognize his strengths. My father was a hard worker and I could count on him. From his perspective he had sacrificed and married for me. He woke me up every morning so I would get to school on time. He made sure I had money in my pocket. Most mental health providers have been trained to diagnose the pathology, identify the issues that are not working. This approach reminds me of how I had seen my father.

As a clinician, I help fathers identify their strengths at work, sports, or in other areas of their lives. I try to show them how to bring these strengths to their roles as fathers. I use guided imagery focusing on what they do well or where they are competent. I ask questions that isolate and build on strengths, such as: What do you do well as a father? What do you do well at work? Are you a leader? A good listener? Fair? Patient? What activities do you excel in?

As an example, Damon, 50, is a married father of two teenage girls. He is a respected police officer. His children are important to him but he struggles with connecting. He explained that many times he does not go on family vacations, preferring to stay home, watch sports, and relax. When he first came to see me he rarely expressed emotion and reported headaches. Other than being a police officer, Damon had coached sports. I asked Damon what he does well as a police officer and what he respects about good coaches. He described his ability to communicate well with his men, with clear boundaries and respect. He gives his men the freedom to do their job, reinforcing what they do well and acting as a role model.

It was obvious what Damon needed to do to improve his home life. What his policemen needed and respected in him paralleled what his children needed. We explored communication skills, reinforcing his daughters' good behavior, keeping appropriate boundaries, and well into our therapy processed how to express his love and feelings for his daughters. Damon's relationship with his children changed. He reported feeling closer to and spending more time with them. He started to apply his new abilities as a father to his job and allowed himself to show more feelings. He was surprised that instead of being seen as weak, his men look up at him for knowing when to be strong, when to joke, and when to be caring and emotional.

Making Father Involvement Male Friendly

Father involvement is central to the discussion of fathers in political and social policy, within the media, and in the therapy room. Involved fathers are clearly good for children. Involved fathers help children learn to regulate emotions through active physical play, help them face challenges and be independent, model positive relationships with the mother/partner, etc.

My experience has also taught me that the word involvement is loaded and scary for some fathers. Fathers experience pressure to be involved or more involved in their children's lives. But many fathers are not sure what it means and how to do it in a way that makes sense. I educate fathers about the benefits of involvement for their children (which most fathers know about) but also for themselves (which many fathers have not thought about). Involved fathers take better care of themselves and engage in less risky behaviors. They are likely to be more physically and socially active and more satisfied with life.

While most fathers easily buy into the importance of being involved they frequently run into obstacles. Be sure to identify what the obstacles and challenges are. Some of the more common ones include balancing time between work and children (Fischer & Anderson, 2012; Reddick, Rochlen, Grasso, Reilly, & Spikes, 2012), fear of not knowing what to do or how to do it, not having nurturing role models, lack or perceived lack of support (Hawkins & Fagan, 2001; Isacco, Garfield, & Rogers, 2010), and not knowing how to ask for help. Based on the particular obstacle and feelings associated with it, I determine how to help my client. A common feeling that fathers experience is shame (Tremblay & L'Heureux, 2005).

Henry is a classic example. Henry, a young father in his 20s, was overwhelmed trying to juggle many responsibilities. He was a perfectionist who experienced shame when he failed to meet his unrealistic expectations. As a boy, Henry's father had been strict and critical of him and his shame led to a pattern of disengagement. When he forgot to attend a therapy session Henry withdrew and I did not hear from him. Atypically for me (I tend not to leave many messages as I believe clients need to be internally motivated to come to therapy), I left him a few messages recognizing his pattern and promising not to judge or criticize him.

When Henry did come back, he repeatedly expressed appreciation of my messages and being understood. We explored his pattern of withdrawing emotionally and sometimes physically from his wife and kids if he does something "wrong." We worked on better balancing his life by setting realistic expectations. Within time he learned to stay more engaged with his family.

I find that shame can also interfere with fathers seeking assistance and support. Fathers who feel supported are more involved and more confident in their parenting. However, many fathers acknowledge that they do not feel comfortable asking for help or support, especially when they do not know exactly what they need. Fathers may need support from different places including partner, friends, professionals, and community.

As therapists we are in a unique position to acknowledge fathers' difficulty asking for yet needing support and can educate and model for them how to do it. I practice role-plays and empty chair about what it would look like to ask for support from their partners or others. Explore their resistance and shame. Teach fathers how to ask to be respected when trying new things and how to ask their partners to recognize their efforts of being involved.

Johnny was a 17-year-old adolescent who came to counseling confused and in distress. His girlfriend had talked him into not wearing a condom (he admits that it did not take much to convince him) and she had become pregnant. His parents were concerned as his school performance had dropped and he had withdrawn, spending much time alone in his room. Johnny knew he was not ready to be a father but wanted to do the right thing. He was embarrassed to talk to his friends and did not feel supported by his parents. Many sessions focused on identifying the underlying issues that interfered with Johnny asking for help and communicating his needs. We role-played and did family therapy. He began to talk more with his parents and told his best friends about the pregnancy.

As the birth approached Johnny became increasingly anxious, confused, and guilty. He worried he would not know what to do when he saw the baby. He was afraid to hold him. How about if he cried? I decided to do imagery with him. I relaxed Johnny through meditation and then asked him to imagine himself entering the room and looking at his baby for the first time. When he opened his eyes he said: "WOW, that was interesting. I saw his face. It felt good. I patted his head and told him that I can't always be with him but we will be ok." He said that he felt a connection he had never known and wanted to meet his baby. Johnny told me he now knew what to do.

Nurturing, Feelings, and Involvement

I often hear complaints, especially when I do couples counseling, that are centered on the perception that the father is not nurturing or expressive enough. Fathers themselves usually hate hearing that they are "not really there." I understand that. I mean, it is not always comfortable to be vulnerable and express feelings. Many of the messages men heard growing up were about being strong, winning, and not crying. Many aspects of men's lives, such as work and sports, still encourage these norms. There can be a cost for being vulnerable and showing feelings.

I remember a poignant conversation I had with my friend, mentor, and group co-facilitator about helping fathers learn to be nurturing, a conversation that led to an American Psychological Association (APA) presentation (Stevens, 2009). I integrated his suggestions and interventions about nurturing into my work with fathers. First, explore clients' perception of nurturing, how they were nurtured, and how they see themselves nurturing and expressing feelings to their children and partners. Discuss their awareness of how their children would like to be nurtured and obstacles to being nurturing and expressive. I often find that unresolved feelings of anger and resentment, which are more acceptable for men and fathers to experience and express, can block nurturing potential.

It is usually a powerful and emotional exercise to help fathers identify what they would have liked hearing from their fathers and what they want to say to their children. I coach and do role-plays where fathers practice words of nurturance. I repeatedly explore the resistance and challenge of using words that increase vulnerability as they express nurturing. I help fathers recall stories of being nurturing while growing up as well as experiences of being taken care of by others. Many fathers report taking care of a pet, being a camp counselor, or being part of a team where they nurtured or felt nurtured. After recalling these experiences and through some bodywork (helping fathers remember and describe how it feels in their body), fathers learn ways to generalize and apply these nurturing experiences within their families.

Coaching and Guidance

A theme in my work with fathers is the use of coaching. I find that most fathers are open to feedback and welcome guidance. While there are many ways to coach, the way it is framed and introduced needs to be embedded in the context of the father. Make sure to ask for permission to give feedback and respect fathers who are resistant.

After the imagery, Johnny had expressed being ready to see his baby. It was a weekend evening when I got a text from him. It read, "Do you have a few minutes to talk". I called Johnny. He had been outside his girlfriend's house for the last 45 minutes too nervous to go in. We talked about his fears and I answered more questions about babies. Before we ended our call he asked if he could text again.

Initially I hesitated, but I remembered that Johnny never asks for help. There was too much shame and distrust to go to his parents. He had turned to me. My support and coaching could help him gain confidence in asking others for help as he learned to be a father. I decided that we could process this experience next session. He texted me a few more times during the following hour. When he came in for a session, Johnny thanked me many times. He said the texting helped him feel safe, mentored, not alone, and gave him confidence. I am not sure what Johnny and his son's future will bring. I do not know if and how involved Johnny will be in his son's life. But I learned more about myself as a clinician working with fathers and my growing certainty that fathers need more than traditional, deficit-based therapy.

Termination

I was able to say goodbye to my father before he passed away. I actually spent some quality time with him during the last six months of his life. I interviewed and videotaped him telling his life story. I was with him when he took his last breath. It was hard but helped me get closure.

Modeling for our clients how to have endings in relationships is important. Many clients don't know how to recognize the relationship and say goodbye. We can help fathers practice for the times in their lives when they will experience their own endings or their children's transitions like college, marriages, or deaths. I discuss our termination as a process and help clients summarize our relationship, their experience, and what they learned in general and as a father.

I like to end the termination session with a guided imagery exercise to help fathers remember where they have been and to see themselves as important to the next generation. I ask them how they want their children to see them today and in the future. How would you like your children to describe you as a father? What do you want them to learn from you? What are your hopes and dreams for them? What traditions from your father will you continue, which ones will you stop? What will your legacy be? After the exercise I explore their images, thoughts, and feelings and ask them to allow their imagery experience and answers to guide their continued daily interactions with children and family.

I find myself in a unique position to help fathers re-create their lives in a way that fits their vision and strengths. When father issues are addressed, men can grow as fathers. They can see their involvement differently and often realize that they are more capable than they had thought. Working with fathers continues to teach me about myself as a father and as a therapist. Now when I work with fathers I start by asking myself, "What are the strengths of the father who sits across from me? What does he do right? What is his story? How can I help him be the father he wants to be?" This chapter captured my journey and one way to work with fathers. I hope it can be a springboard for you to develop your own ways to use a strength-based counseling approach when you work with fathers.

REFERENCES

Duhig, A. M., Phares, V., & Birkeland, R. W. (2002). Involvement of fathers in therapy: A survey of clinicians. *Professional Psychology: Research and Practice, 33*(4), 389–395.

Fischer, J., & Anderson, V. N. (2012). Gender role attitudes and characteristics of stay-at-home and employed fathers. *Psychology of Men and Masculinity, 13*(1), 16–31.

Hawkins, A. J., & Dollahite, D. C. (1996). *Generative fathering: Beyond deficit perspectives.* Thousand Oaks, CA: Sage.

Hawkins, A. J., & Fagan, J. (2001). Clinical and educational interventions with fathers: A synthesis. In J. Fagan, & A. J. Hawkins (Eds.), *Clinical and educational interventions with fathers* (pp. 285–293). Binghamton, NY: Haworth.

Isacco, A., Garfield, C. F., & Rogers, T. E. (2010). Correlates of coparental support among married and nonmarried fathers. *Psychology of Men and Masculinity, 11*(4), 262–278.

Kiselica, M. S. (2003). Transforming psychotherapy in order to succeed with adolescent boys: Male-friendly practices. *Journal of Clinical Psychology, 59*(11), 1225–1236.

Lamb, M. E. (2010). *The role of the father in child development* (5th ed.). Hoboken, NJ: John Wiley & Sons.

Oren, C. Z., & Oren, D. C. (2010). *Counseling fathers.* New York: Routledge.

Pleck, J. H. (1997). Paternal involvement: Levels, sources, and consequences. In M. E. Lamb (Ed.), *The role of the father in child development* (3rd ed.) (pp. 61–103). New York: John Wiley.

Pleck, J. H. (2010). Paternal involvement: Revised conceptualization and theoretical linkage with child outcomes. In M. E. Lamb (Ed.), *The role of the father in child development* (5th ed.) (pp. 58–93). New York: John Wiley.

Reddick, R. J., Rochlen, A. B., Grasso, J., Reilly, E., & Spikes, D. D. (2012). Academic fathers pursuing tenure: A qualitative study of work-family conflict, coping strategies, and department culture. *Psychology of Men and Masculinity, 13*(1), 1–15.

Shappiro, J. L. (2001). Therapeutic interventions with fathers. In G. R. Brooks, & G. E. Good (Eds.), *The new handbook of psychotherapy and counseling with men: A comprehensive guide to settings, problems, and treatment approaches* (pp. 403–423). San Francisco, CA: Jossey Bass.

Stevens, M. A. (2009). Taping the potential of fathers: Stories of being nurtured or nurturing. In D. C. Oren, & C. Z. Oren (Chairs), *Counseling fathers: Gender sensitive interventions.* Symposium presented at the 117th Annual Convention of the American Psychological Association, Toronto, Canada.

Tremblay, G., & L'Heureux, P. (2005). Psychosocial interventions with men. *International Journal of Men's Health, 4*(1), 55–71.

United States Census Bureau. (2012). *Profile America: Facts for features.* Retrieved from http://www.census.gov/newsroom/releases/archives/facts_for_features_special_editions/cb12-ff11.html

Vann, N. (2007). Reflections on the development of fatherhood work. *Applied Developmental Science, 11*(4), 266–268.

CONCLUSION

Breaking Barriers

Expanding the Repertoire

Fredric E. Rabinowitz

MY JOURNEY TOWARD FREEDOM AS A MAN

The theme *Breaking Barriers* headlines our book because it resonates with many men's lives. My own is no exception. As the oldest of three brothers, I was raised in a traditional male environment. As a boy, I experienced both the best *and* the worst of growing up male. The camaraderie, competitiveness, and love from my dad, brothers, and male friends instilled a positive value on manhood. Yet, I was also negatively impacted by the arrogance, shaming, and bullying that boys and teens often engaged in, particularly on the school yard.

As a young boy, I loved to draw and paint. Unfortunately, by the time I hit adolescence, it was something I had to hide from my male peers. My internalized homophobia, represented by my fear of doing something "not so masculine" put a stop to these artistic yearnings. My dad, a successful attorney, lived and breathed sports. He was my coach, cheerleader, and validator of my manhood. As I wanted to please him so badly, I dropped the paintbrush and picked up every sport I could play. While not the biggest guy, I was a competitor known as "Freddy Hustle."

Somewhere along the way, I became an expert at noticing the rules of the *masculinity zone*. Even though I was emotionally sensitive (and still am), I did everything I could to not let anyone see my hurt or inner pain. I wore a poker face—far before I knew how to use this to my advantage on the poker table. The only time my emotions could genuinely surface, was when I was lost in the moment of playing or watching sports.

When I had trouble academically in junior high, my mom suggested I see a psychologist. I refused, thinking I was really not that messed up to have to see a shrink. Looking back now, I realized I was scared to expose potential cracks in my armor. I also feared being in a "one down" situation. Being a good student was part of my identity, but my poor performance in advanced math and science was where I was leaking oil. While locker room bullies made fun of my developing body, I was trying to figure out how to talk to the girls. In essence, I was deeply embroiled in the daily battle of being a boy navigating the tough zone of adolescent masculinity.

As the anti-war, civil rights, and women's liberation cultural revolution was taking over America, I made it to high school just in time. While I still played sports, I noticed a shift in those older boys enforcing the male code. I suspect that maybe they were smoking pot, and it took the edge off. Whatever it was, I felt less scrutinized. I decided to get back into drawing and found a voice in my literature and creative writing courses. I felt my imagination returning, my fears waning. While it was outside of my awareness, I was beginning to strip off the many complex layers that were dictating (often in negative ways) what kind of man I should be.

In college, I majored in psychology and art, definitely not masculine subjects. Fortunately, they ended up being the tools I needed to overcome the obstacles of having adhered to the masculine code that influenced so much of my early identity formation. The art let me find an outlet for my deep, passionate, and complex emotional self. Yet, I still struggled finding words to describe my experience. This is where the psychology came in handy. I started to build a vocabulary for my rich inner world. I believe this is a shared frustration for many men—and part of the need each of us have to find self-expression.

The rest is history. Since then, I have devoted much of my life to breaking the barriers of what it means to be a man. This passion has helped me personally and has been powerful for hundreds of my male clients. My calling as a psychologist has been to work with men who are struggling. I have walked the walk. I know restrictive masculinity from the inside, and I also know what it feels like to have a life without the internalized prohibitions. Countless hours of my own personal individual, group, couples, and body-oriented therapy, with years of being a therapist with men, has led me here.

I tell my story because I think it opened up my thinking about how to genuinely connect and intervene with men. The traditional models of masculinity do not really do justice to the potential lessons that each man has to learn on his journey. We are told to achieve, compete, win, and minimize our vulnerability for what? The implied promise is that we will be satisfied, content, and comfortable in our lives. In reality, each of us has to struggle to discover an identity, make friends, find meaningful work, explore creative outlets, connect deeply and emotionally with a partner, be a solid parent, and contribute to our communities. These powerful experiences don't come with a handbook. Most of us are left on our own without the tools to best frame our learning. Helping men navigate the experiences, often not easy, is why we wanted to write this book.

HELPING MEN BREAK BARRIERS

We chose authors for this book that best represent what we consider to be the next wave of creative and innovative practitioners. As described in the chapters via rich personal narratives, their approaches have allowed them to be successful with a wide spectrum of men—in need of help breaking their own barriers. Their work demonstrates how we can best draw out and interpersonally connect with these men. They understand the way men have been socialized and are proactive in finding ways to reach out to guys who are not necessarily comfortable with the traditional therapy model.

In his introduction, Rochlen emphasized a "lack of fit between men's socialization patterns and the counseling process…Counseling men needs to be more consistent with the way in which men relate, connect, and open up." These words and the client break-through story he shared, emphasize the speaking to our male clients' strengths before cracking defenses and exploring coping mechanisms. This key point is further illustrated by McKelley, who emphasizes that using metaphors is a key way to bridge the communication gap. By talking about objects, observations, and activities in his world, a male client can make analogies to his inner life.

Kilmartin reminded us that having a sense of humor really helps to dissolve male defensiveness. Getting a man to laugh and to tell his story without judgment goes a long way toward unfreezing his verbal expression. By displaying our humanness through relevant self-disclosure, Wexler showed how a clinician can strengthen the therapeutic alliance and allow a man to approach difficult, often shameful topics in counseling.

In line with the theme of going to where men are, Pittsinger and Liu described interventions that play off of men's life passions. Their work, utilizing surfing, reinforces the idea that there is wisdom, insight, and lessons to be learned from the activities we engage in. Men who used their surfing experience to find existential meaning and perspective showed gains in psychological resilience and internalized self-acceptance. Bhatia added to this element by sharing his passion with sports, and how it has served as a way to not only connect with his father when he was young, but also highlight the rules of masculinity: the good, the bad, and the ugly. Talking about sports figures and controversy can be another way to get men talking about their own issues.

Men are used to being in groups, whether it be school, teams, or work. By utilizing group activities, I have suggested that men have the opportunity to face many of their interpersonal fears about trust and vulnerability. Scheinfeld and Buser described how taking the group outside the office, into the wilderness, required the men to trust each other in order to survive and enhance their interpersonal relating. Englar-Carlson and Stevens also reinforced this notion that facilitating men's interaction outside of their everyday environment in a weekend retreat could produce unexpected camaraderie, openness, and personal growth.

Men have been the inventors and users of technology that has at times exaggerated the distance we keep from our emotions. McDermott, Smith, and Tsan reminded us that technology could also be used to enhance men getting in touch with themselves. Their chapter highlighted how our modern technology can be a productive starting spot for men, who might feel more comfortable with the privacy and control they feel with biofeedback equipment and the world of cyberspace.

By coming at men as a life coach, rather than a therapist, Benson suggested that there might be less resistance, and substantial benefit to this model. Sports teams and executives have coaches who are more directive and goal oriented. Many men find this less shaming and more in line with how they have been socialized.

Special groups of men, who have shared experiences or needs, may require more individualized and creative applications of male friendly interventions. Novack and Edwards used their experiences as soldiers to empathize and intervene with male clients in the military. Their understanding of the hazards and discrepancies between military and civilian life reinforce the notion that clinicians must listen, encourage, support, and utilize the strengths of their clients, and, most of all, be patient with the process.

Olver and Daniels highlighted that even those incarcerated men, who have committed horrific crimes, deserve our respect and understanding. Their work in a prison facility with sex offenders, who have limited cognitive skills, demonstrates how important it is to use non-verbal, creative, humorous, and non-judgmental interventions to help the men rehabilitate and learn from their actions.

Verhaagen's story about his therapy with an emotionally traumatized male teenager showed how important it was to transcend his fear of the young man's outward behavior to make a personal connection. Ultimately the trust and intimacy he developed was the key to counseling.

In their work with gay and bisexual clients of color, Nadal and Rivera emphasized that openly discussing race, gender, or sexuality, as well as microaggressions, led to more trust in the therapeutic relationship. They also made the important point that men can hold privilege in some areas of their lives and yet experience discrimination and biases in other domains.

Oren and Oren highlighted the fact that men have significant emotional intensity related to being fathers and in their relationships with their own fathers. Addressing the role a father plays with his children and exploring male nurturing is a powerful therapeutic line of inquiry that can lead to insight and growth.

FINAL WORDS

Working therapeutically with men requires that we know ourselves and our ethical and legal boundaries. Many of the innovative techniques and approaches described lie outside the traditional confines of counseling and psychotherapy. This means that we must be aware of potential ethical conflicts that could arise. For instance, it has been suggested that meeting a client outside the office, under the right conditions, might lead to more openness to the therapeutic process. This could be difficult in the setting in which you work. If you have doubts about an approach, discuss your ideas with a trusted colleague, supervisor, or legal counsel. We assume that you take into account the therapeutic context, the nature of the population with whom you are working, and the expectations of your individual client when implementing innovative interventions.

Finally, by challenging the barriers of our own gender role socialization, we can best help men do the same. We invite you to do your own personal therapeutic work to enhance your own openness, integration, and imagination. We encourage you to think creatively about each man with whom you work. For too long, the field has expected men to come to us. In order for us to reach them, we will have to go where they are. We hope that the insights and innovations described in this book are a starting place for a new perspective and an expanded repertoire in your work with men.

Index